From
Don
1983

THE PROPHET JONAH

THE PROPHET JONAH

BY THE REV. HUGH MARTIN, M.A.

BAKER BOOK HOUSE
Grand Rapids, Michigan

Reprinted February 1979 by
Baker Book House
from the edition issued in 1866
by Alexander Strahan, Publisher

ISBN: 0-8010-6072-9

PHOTOLITHOPRINTED BY CUSHING - MALLOY, INC.
ANN ARBOR, MICHIGAN, UNITED STATES OF AMERICA
1979

TO

THE CONGREGATIONS

OF THE

FREE CHURCH OF SCOTLAND

IN

PANBRIDE,

AND

GREYFRIARS', EDINBURGH,

This Volume

IS AFFECTIONATELY INSCRIBED.

PREFATORY NOTE

MY explicit acknowledgments of help in the composition of this volume, are due to Calvin; whose Commentaries on the Minor Prophets, as well as his other works, it would be presumption in me to praise. I have no doubt, also, that traces will appear of my having read Principal Fairbairn's book on Jonah. I have a distinct recollection of deriving much pleasure and profit from the perusal of it at the time of its publication. But as that is now about seventeen years ago, I am unable to specify my obligations.

Some of my readers may think that I have—to use the language of an intelligent friend—"taken Jonah's part too much." I can scarcely think that I have. It is a tacit tribute of honour that we pay to Prophets and Apostles, as still *living* powers in the Church, when we deny them the benefit of the maxim, *De mortuis nil nisi bonum.* But for that reason we ought to be all the more careful to do them no injustice. And when I think of his wonderful prayer in the depths,—of his perfect candour with the mariners,—of his magnanimity in prescribing his own death as the means of their deliverance,—and of his perfect candour with God also, in laying open to Him to the last even all that was wrong in his startling and most sinful state of mind, I cannot help thinking that the memory of Jonah deserves more of esteem and affectionate regard than has fallen to his lot. To the last we find his gracious Lord "not silent to him ;" so that we see the prophet not left to " become like them that go down into the pit." And though Jonah has closed the book of his prophecy without telling us what effect the Lord's gracious remonstrance had in respect of bringing him to a better frame of mind,—thus, in manifest humility, I think, consenting to disappear from our view as under a cloud,—Divine charity, " believing all things," will have little difficulty in believing that Jonah's silence, like that of Job, would have its meaning expressed by the pro- testation ;—" Once have I spoken ; but I will not answer : yea, twice ; but I will proceed no farther."

I wish my book had been greatly better than it is. For

one thing, it would have allowed me to say something on what I hold to be the yet unexhausted resources,—in respect of variety and versatility and literary construction,—of the kind of expository exercise of which this forms, in so far, a specimen. But I forbear. Such as it is, I desire to leave the volume with Him, who by His ministry within the veil can render it of sweet smelling savour unto God, and by His ministry of the Spirit in the heart, can render it a savour of life unto life to the reader.

H. M.

EDINBURGH, 1st *June* 1866

CONTENTS

INTRODUCTORY

I.—JONAH i. 1

II.—JONAH i. 1

PART FIRST
THE COMMISSION ISSUED—AND REFUSED

III.—JONAH i. 2

IX.—JONAH i. 6

PAGE

" He that formed the eye, shall he not see ? He that chastiseth the heathen, shall not he correct ? He that teacheth man knowledge, shall he not know ? "
" The Lord knoweth the thoughts of man, that they are vanity."—
Ps. xciv. 9–11.

X.—JONAH i. 7

*" The lot is cast into the lap ; but the whole disposing thereof is of the Lord."—*Prov. xvi. 33.

XI.—JONAH i. 8, 9

" And Joshua said unto Achan, My son, give, I pray thee, glory to the Lord God of Israel, and make confession unto him ; and tell me now what thou hast done; hide it not from me."
—Joshua vii. 19.

XII.—JONAH i. 9, 10

" Hast thou not procured this unto thyself, in that thou hast forsaken the Lord thy God, when he led thee by the way ?"—
Jer. ii. 17.

XIII.—JONAH i. 11–17

*" Thou answeredst them, O Lord our God ; thou wast a God that forgavest them. though thou tookest vengeance of their inventions."—*Ps. xcix. 8.
*" Righteousness and peace have kissed each other."—*Ps. lxxxv. 10.

PART SECOND

THE COMMISSION RE-ISSUED—AND FULFILLED

XVI.—JONAH iii. 1

I

JONAH'S MISSION; ITS PLACE IN HISTORICAL DEVELOPMENT

JONAH i. 1

"Now the word of the Lord came unto Jonah the son of Amittai, saying, Arise, go to Nineveh."

"A light to lighten the Gentiles, and the glory of his people Israel."—LUKE ii. 32.

SPEAKING generally, the prophet Jonah lived about midway between the revolt of the ten tribes under Jeroboam and their fatal and final captivity by Assyria. The commencement of his ministry—whether that ministry was more stated or more occasional we do not know—seems to have been contemporaneous with the close of Elisha's. And, like Elisha, Jonah prophesied in Israel—in the kingdom of Samaria.

The only prediction of his recorded is that mentioned in the 14th chapter of 2d Kings, which, indeed, is the only passage of Scripture in which our prophet is mentioned, except in the book which goes under his own name, and the allusions made to him by our Lord

in the days of His flesh.   In that chapter, at the 23d
verse, we read that, about 150 years after the disrup-
tion of the tribes, and about 825 years before Christ,
Jeroboam II., " the son of Joash king of Israel, began
to reign in Samaria, and reigned forty and one years.
And he did that which was evil in the sight of the
Lord: he departed not from all the sins of Jeroboam
the son of Nebat, who made Israel to sin.   He restored
the coast of Israel, from the entering of Hamath unto
the sea of the plain, according to the word of the Lord
God of Israel, which he spake by the hand of his servant Jonah, the son of Amittai, the prophet, which was
of Gath-hepher.   For the Lord saw the affliction of
Israel that it was very bitter: for there was not any
shut up, nor any left, nor any helper for Israel.   And
the Lord said not that he would blot out the name of
Israel, from under heaven: but he saved them by the
hand of Jeroboam the son of Joash."

It thus appears that, while Israel were in a very
wretched and oppressed condition, the Lord had employed His servant Jonah to predict an unmerited and
most gracious interposition of His power on their behalf,
to restore to them the territory of which their enemies
had deprived them.   It is very remarkable that living,
as the prophet did, in a time of abounding provocations,
when we might have expected his sole office in Israel
would have been to denounce judgment on the apostate
tribes and their ungodly rulers, the only one of his pre-
dictions on record is that of a most gracious and generous interposition on the part of Jehovah in defence

of His afflicted people; when "seeing their affliction that it was very bitter," He, as it were, forgot all their offensive neglect of His worship, and disobedience to His commands; and, unwilling to see their name blotted out—the name of Israel, the seed of Abraham, his friend, blotted out—from under heaven, He gave military strength and skill even to a wicked king, and "saved them by the hand of Jeroboam, the son of Joash." Abundant evidence thus, in his ministry among a rebellious people, has Jonah, of the Lord's singular long-suffering; so abundant, indeed, that, unable to vindicate, any more than to search, its greatness, he seems to have been at fault and at a loss concerning it; to have been difficulted in considering the character of God, and cast into great confusion of mind by his very knowledge of God's extraordinary patience. In fact, it is in this very difficulty that the explanation of Jonah's most singular conduct, both in first fleeing from the duty assigned him, and in afterwards being displeased with the salvation of Nineveh, must be sought. "But it displeased Jonah exceedingly, and he was very angry. And he prayed unto the Lord, and said, I pray thee, O Lord, was not this my saying when I was yet in my country? Therefore I fled before unto Tarshish: for I knew that thou art a gracious God, and merciful, slow to anger, and of great kindness, and repentest thee of the evil" (Jonah iv. 1, 2). However this may account for his amazing and almost unparalleled procedure, clear it is that it is this that does account for it. Jonah had unwontedly large and strong views of the Divine forbearance ; and, from some cause or other, losing his way or his reckoning in estimating the bearing of the Divine forbearance on the other attributes of the Divine character, and on the discharge of his own duty, his mind fell into a confusion of thoughts and principles, which issued in the marvellous adventures, experiences, and displays of character which this short but singular book of Holy Scripture narrates.　It is at least interesting to see thus early, in the one only brief allusion made to the history of his ministry in Israel, the rise of what alone can explain the astounding story of his mission and his manners in Nineveh.

Living, then, among the ten revolted tribes, and testifying alike against their iniquities, and for the riches of Jehovah's patience and the rectitude of Jehovah's ways, the prophet doubtless reckoned on spending the remainder of his days in his own land.　The very last thought, probably, that would have ever spontaneously entered his mind, would have been the idea of having to go forth from its sacred precincts, and exercise his holy office among the heathen.　For ages and for generations Jehovah had confined all His manifestations of Himself to the children of Jacob.　The ceremonial law, which at Sinai He had appointed to them, served, in its burdensome ritual and innumerable observances, as a middle wall of partition, excluding the Gentiles from their religious privileges.　Proselytes, indeed, were welcome.　And in the law of Moses itself, directions had been laid down for their admission into the commonwealth of Israel. But this had a bearing merely on individuals. The Gentiles, as a whole, as nations, were obviously given over in the meantime to the reign of spiritual death, cast out beyond the pale of that visible Church, within which alone salvation is ordinarily revealed. It is from this wretched and forlorn condition that Paul calls on the Ephesians to remember that they had been delivered :—" Wherefore remember, that ye being in time past Gentiles in the flesh, who are called Uncircumcision by that which is called the Circumcision in the flesh made by hands; that at that time ye were without the Messiah, being aliens from the commonwealth of Israel, and strangers from the covenants of promise, having no hope, and without God in the world " (Eph. ii. 11, 12). No doubt the peculiar people were separated from the Gentiles only for a time, and only for a purpose. They were separated from them for a time, for the very purpose of being the safe custodiers of that grace of which the Gentiles should in due time be fellow-heirs. They ought never to have forgotten that the covenant with Abraham, and Isaac, and Jacob embraced the Gentile world very specially in its gracious primeval provisions:—" In thy seed shall all the nations of the earth be blessed " (Gen. xxvi. 4). And they ought therefore to have known that, when the Messiah should come, He would be " a minister of the Circumcision for the truth of God, to confirm the promises made unto the fathers; and that the Gentiles might glorify God for his mercy ; as it is written, For this cause I will confess to thee among the Gentiles,

and sing unto thy name. And again he saith, Rejoice,
ye Gentiles, with his people. And again, Praise the
Lord, all ye Gentiles: and laud him, all ye people.
And again, Isaiah saith, There shall be a root of Jesse,
and he that shall rise to reign over the Gentiles: in
him shall the Gentiles trust " (Rom. xv. 8–12).

In the times of truest spiritual life, this was not forgotten
in Israel. The holy men who " obtained a good report
by faith " had large and world-wide views, and large
and world-wide hopes, as to the grace of God and the
reign of their Messiah. They expected Him to rule
over a kingdom co-extensive with the whole world.
They expected Him to dispense blessings sufficient for
every land. The more they appreciated their own sinfulness and the freeness and sovereignty of the grace of
God, the more did they clearly comprehend how the
Gentiles also might freely partake of the same free
mercy with themselves; and the more they felt the
vanity of all earthly good and the helplessness of their
whole earthly estate, and appreciated the promised kingdom and sovereign reign of their Christ as unworldly,
spiritual, heavenly, divine, and eternal, so much the
more did they clearly see how all nations, as they
needed, so they might be embraced by, this new,
heavenly kingdom of the Lord and His Anointed.
Hence, in the days of David, when true spiritual life
flourished, and un-Pharisaic knowledge of the grace of
God was comparatively widely diffused, the Gentiles
were looked on with no evil eye; their salvation was
felt to be clearly within the compass of the covenant of

Abraham; and their subjugation to the coming Messiah was regarded as one of the glorious events which should mark and grace His advent and manifestation. Hence such passages in the Psalms as these,—the first addressed by the Father to His Anointed, and the second by the Church to her covenant God :—" Ask of me, and I will give thee the heathen for thine inheritance, and the uttermost parts of the earth for thy possession;" "Have respect unto Thy covenant, for the dark places of the earth are full of the habitations of cruelty " (Ps. ii. 6; lxxiv. 20). And if any farther proof be needed that the Church, in the days of her true life and fidelity, looked for being enlarged with the believing brotherhood of the converted nations, we have it in that noble hymn of missionary prayer and hope, opening as it does with the well-remembered words, "God be merciful unto us, and bless us : and cause his face to shine upon us; that thy way may be known upon earth, thy saving health among all nations," and closing with the confession of free, unhampered, appropriating faith, " God shall bless us," and with the enlarged and unbounded expectation, " And all the ends of the earth shall fear him " (Ps. lxvii. 1–7). But in the days of Israel's degeneracy, when faith gave place to formalism, and contrite gratitude to cold and supercilious ceremony; when self-righteous pride, singularly enough keeping pace with increasing iniquity and worthlessness, arrogantly claimed right to the privileges of the covenant in very proportion as all the spirit of the covenant was violated; when the close and narrow spirit of legalism, resting its claims on carnal distinctions, and saying, " We have Abraham to our Father," superseded the true spirit of Israel, " I am not worthy of the least of all the goodness and the truth thou hast shown unto thy servant;" the idea of pure and sovereign grace being lost sight of—that grace whereby Jew and Gentile alike may be freely saved,—and the kingdom of the Messiah being conceived of as earthly and limited—set up, indeed, as a badge of distinction, to magnify the seed of Abraham according to the flesh; then the Gentile nations began to be looked upon as natural and irreconcilable enemies. The Jewish Church, in fact, in such a spirit, enacts exactly the part of the Pharisee of the parable, while the publican may represent the waste of heathendom; and the vain-glorious Church, claiming Heaven's favour on the ground of her carnal distinctions and pitiable tithings, thanks God that she is not as this poor publican!

For in every point of view, and on whatever scale, self-righteousness is exclusive and malignant, remorselessly consigning over others to a destruction which, on its own proud merit and pre-eminence, it counts itself entitled to escape. Perhaps, more properly indeed, it came to this, that the heathen nations, as to their moral and spiritual interests, were, among Israel, objects of simple contempt and neglect, and were dealt with as if Jehovah, the God of Israel, utterly neglected them also —as if, in short, they were beyond the pale of His government; or, in other words, as if Jehovah's government were not universal, but limited to their own nation alone. It is evident how, with such a view of their own God, their own adoring regards for Him must have been destroyed. Jehovah is the God of the spirits of all flesh, and ruleth over all the nations. Any other or more limited idea of His government, reduces Him, if not to the level, at least to the company, of the local, territorial, geographical gods of heathendom. And thus, by taking a wrong view of the relation of heathendom to the living and true God, the God of Israel, Israel virtually imbibed the very views of heathendom itself.

Indeed, nothing but true faith, contrition, adoring confidence, and loyalty to Jehovah, could prevent this painful perversion of the truth. It was, as Paul acknowledges, a great " mystery "—the introduction of the Gentiles into the Church of God. In writing to the Ephesians, he speaks of it as a mystery made known unto himself by special revelation. " By revelation He made known unto me the mystery; as I wrote afore in few words, whereby, when ye read, ye may understand my knowledge in the mystery of Christ, which in other ages was not made known unto the sons of men, as it is now revealed unto his holy apostles and prophets by the Spirit; that the Gentiles should be fellow-heirs, and of the same body, and partakers of his promise in Christ by the gospel " (Eph. iii. 3–6). It is in connexion with the blessed disclosure of this " mystery " that Paul utters the well-known thanksgiving for that grace of God which had assigned him a ministry, bearing so immediately on the extension of the Church of

God beyond the narrow pale of Judaism. For it was not merely as a preacher, but specially as a preacher to the Gentiles, that Paul magnified his office. "Unto me," the rejoicing and happy-spirited burst of holy glorying runs—"Unto me, who am less than the least of all saints, is this grace given, that I should preach *among the Gentiles* the unsearchable riches of Christ; and to make *all* men see what is the fellowship of the mystery, which from the beginning of the world hath been hid in God" (Eph. iii. 8, 9). In addressing the saints at Colosse, the Apostle uses similar terms. He speaks of "the mystery which hath been hid from ages and from generations, but now is made manifest to His saints; to whom God would make known what is the riches of the glory of this mystery among the Gentiles" (Col. i. 26, 27). Very singular and striking language! "The riches of the glory of this mystery"!

Israel of old had not this "mystery" revealed, explained, expounded, or opened up to them, as it is to us. They were in continual contact with a glorious, but veiled mystery. In such a case, there could be no intellectual and spiritual safety, except in a humble, contrite, adoring loyalty towards Israel's wonder-working, all-wise, and mighty King. That will keep a man safe, when fronting unrevealed mysteries. Nothing else will. Penitence—a sense of righteous exposure to the wrath of God, combined with a refuge from that wrath and the dread of it, in free and gratuitous forgiveness,—*that* would have kept the Israelites safe. A sympathy with the 32d Psalm, "Blessed is the man whose transgression is forgiven, whose sin is covered, to whom the Lord imputeth not iniquity, and in whose spirit there is no guile;" a firm hold on justification by faith alone, in a free and gratuitous forgiveness, in a free, and gratuitous, and borrowed, and imputed righteousness,—*that* would have kept them right as to the relation in which both their God and they themselves stood to the heathen world. Penetrated with that deep despair of their own righteousness, which leads a man to welcome with joy unspeakable a perfect righteousness freely offered, they would have humbly and clearly understood their own position in the sight of God; and, being deeply assured that on the very same terms also might the Gentiles, at God's mere pleasure, be adopted into their own gracious and firm standing in Heaven's free and undeserved favour, they might have borne the mystery without perverting the truth. And in this light it is very beautiful to notice here, that this is precisely one of Paul's most interesting inferences or conclusions from the doctrine of free justification by faith alone ; for having established the doctrine of justification solely in the righteousness or "redemption that is in Christ," and having shown that this excludes boasting, he adds that it opens the door of hope also to the Gentiles quite as widely as to the Jews : " We conclude, therefore, that a man is justified by faith without the deeds of the law. Is He the God of the Jews only? Is He not also of the Gentiles? Yes; of the Gentiles also, seeing it is one God which shall justify the Circumcision by faith and the Uncircumcision through faith" (Rom. iii. 28).

But, claiming the favour of Abraham's God, not at all on the free, gracious, and blessed terms—most comforting, but most humbling also—humbling, yet sweetly humbling—on which Abraham was content to rest his claim; resting theirs, not like their father Abraham, on the pure and simple grace of God, but on their own formal position and fancied pre-eminence, they inevitably fell into views of the state and destiny of the Gentile world utterly at variance with the character of God as the Moral Governor of mankind, and fitted exceedingly to nurse into increasing vigour their own proud, cold, stern, and malignant spirit of ecclesiastical self-righteousness and bigotry, and national intolerance and pride.

It is necessary to take these things into consideration, if we would appreciate the position which this most singular book of Jonah holds in the Sacred Scriptures; or, more exactly, if we would appreciate the mission on which Jonah was sent, and its place in historical development. He was sent to a Gentile city. He was sent to the most renowned city of heathendom then on the face of the earth. He alone of all God's prophets, had such a commission assigned him. His was a most extraordinary call. It was altogether an exceptional, a literally singular, case. It is impossible to understand or enter feelingly into the prophet's position on receiving this call—impossible to understand the circumstances acting upon him, and producing, though of course they do not justify, yet producing and explaining his most singular and anomalous conduct; and it is impossible to appreciate God's purpose and wisdom in introducing this very marvellous episode into Scriptural history, and into the original development, indeed, of God's plans, and of His revelation of Himself which Scripture records : all these things are impossible to us, and the book of Jonah degenerates into a mere perplexing puzzle, unless we give diligent heed at the very outset to the relation at this time subsisting between the seed of Abraham and the Gentile world, and to the bearing of God's special government over Israel on His keeping in store a glorious " salvation for all the ends of the earth—a light to lighten the Gentiles as well as a glory to His people Israel." It is when viewed on this high scale, and as bearing on the development of Jehovah's purpose to establish the throne of His Anointed One over all nations—a purpose yet only comparatively in the mere beginnings of its accomplishment—it is when viewed in this light that the book of Jonah rises in our estimation from the place that it has often held doubtless in many men's minds—from the place due merely to a strange marvel or miracle of adventure which they wonder why the glorious God of providence should have consented to work, or the Holy Ghost consented to afford His inspiration to record—to the lofty level of a splendid and worthy interposition of Divine power, and a glorious record of Divine wisdom, introducing a golden and indispensable link in the onward movement of that great redemption, the preliminary preparations for which were transacted among one peculiar people, but the issues of it designed to encompass all lands, and bind in one believing brotherhood of sonship to God, and of royal adoring priesthood, all nations of men from the rising of the sun to where he hath his going down. It was right, for the most part—so it seemed to Him who knoweth the end from the beginning—it was right that, for the most part, the Spirit of prophecy and the ordinances of worship should be confined to the sacred family and the special territory in which that family dwelt, till Messiah himself should come. But it was *not* right that Jehovah's moral government over all kingdoms should be misunderstood or forgotten. And above all, it was not right that Jehovah's gracious purpose towards all nations should be buried in oblivion. A very burst of light, therefore,—almost of lightning,—flashes out from Jehovah's throne on the dark Gentile world, and His connexion with it. Suddenly, when it seems as if He neither cared at present, nor would ever again show His care, for the aliens from the commonwealth of Israel, He has a sharp, an unmistakable, a terrifying message for the very chiefest of all their cities, the very citadel of heathen glory, monarchy, and worldly pride and power. He has a message for them, and He must find a messenger. A herald must cross the sacred precincts where the Spirit and word of prophecy hitherto had dwelt, and go out into the thick darkness, carrying with him the sound of Jehovah's voice, the torch of Jehovah's word. Marvellous beyond all parallel, yet with reasons replete with infinite wisdom, was that unheard-of proposal, that strait and imperative command, when "The word of the Lord came unto Jonah, the son of Amittai, saying, Arise, go to Nineveh."

These remarks may tend to exalt our conceptions of the mission of Jonah to the capital of the heathen world. That mission was a solitary, unparalleled, an isolated and unique transaction. In all the history of the prophetic Spirit and word in the Church, there had been nothing like unto it before, and there was nothing like unto it afterwards. The Lord did a new thing by His prophet Jonah,—a startling, marvellous, and new thing upon the earth. He caused the light of prophecy to overflow the channels in which for ages it had been confined. He violated all the current notions and all the settled expectations of the sacred commonwealth by manifesting His care and claims in regard to the heathen. Suddenly, when the pall of thick darkness and the shadow of death hangs over all nations, save the little central spot of Immanuel's land; when Jehovah would appear to have resigned all government of the world, save as in that one corner where His worship was established by special covenant, and yet was almost altogether overthrown; when the Most High is well nigh come to be regarded as a local and limited Deity, having no control and taking no oversight of other lands; when Israel, perverting His grace, has come self-righteously to think they can reckon by right on His favour, and may tamper with impunity with His law; when, looking on Him as a local God, Israel has learned to trifle with Him, as a local and limited

God may, of course, without much danger, be trifled with; suddenly, without note or warning, without preface, without explanation, assuming sovereign state as God Most High over all the earth, Jehovah, re-manifesting, if not reassuming His universal supremacy, conducts, on the scale of most amazing miracle, a movement of His ceaseless government as it extends over all nations; and, that it may not fail to compel the attention of all succeeding ages, He adorns that movement with the most marvellous and romantic incident, with one of the most striking, if not perplexing, developments of human character, especially as occurring in a man of God, and with the symbolic death and resurrection of the agent under whose hand that movement is conducted; a death and resurrection on the very type of Messiah's : " For Jonah was three days and three nights in the whale's belly, even as the Son of man was three days and three nights in the heart of the earth " (Matt. xii. 40).

By the aid of considerations like these, followed out perhaps somewhat more in detail, we may be able to gain a truer insight into the import and value of this portion of inspired history, than otherwise it would be possible to do. And above all, we will be prepared, by the Divine blessing, for taking a more accurate and a more edifying view of Jonah's character, as that of a man of God, placed in very singular circumstances and under very peculiar and spiritual temptation.

Meantime, it may be profitable to carry away with us this first lesson, viz., that Jehovah, the God of

Israel, is the God of all the earth. A very plain and easy lesson, some may be ready to think, and scarcely worthy to be specified. But it is the most worldly-minded who will think so; those not acquainted with the shallow, empty, narrow, and ever earthly impressions of the carnal mind. The man who walks with God in truth, who labours to realise the Divine presence and to be continually saying, "Thou God seest me," being reconciled to God and claiming Him as his God, yet feels the painful difficulty of retaining exalted conceptions of his Maker, and Redeemer, and Father in heaven, and will not think it any other than a blessed aid to his piety and spiritual joy, when called to remember that *his* God is in the heavens; that throughout all the nations of the earth He doeth whatsoever pleaseth Him; that the wars and rumours of wars in any land are all parts of the development of Jehovah's unsearchable but infinitely wise plan; that every event, however untoward it may appear, is but bearing onward the chariot of the King to that goal where His glory shall be seen advanced in every age and in every movement of history; that the rise, and overthrow, and replacing of nations are events that transpire under the eyes of Him under whose feet the ages move along in His own appointed order to the day of the consummation of all things; bringing forward the time when—the gospel having been preached for a testimony in all the earth and the believing meek ones gathered under His hand, the groans of creation being ended and the tabernacle of the Lord with men upon the earth—the song shall

rise from all the holy ones ;—"Great and marvellous
are thy works, Lord God Almighty; just and true
are thy ways, thou King of saints. Who shall not fear
thee, O Lord, and glorify thy name? for thou only art
holy: for ALL NATIONS shall come and worship before
thee; for thy judgments are made manifest" (Rev.
xv. 3, 4).

II

RELATIONS BETWEEN JEW AND GENTILE

JONAH i. 1

"Now the word of the Lord came unto Jonah the son of Amittai, saying, Arise, go to Nineveh."

> "*They have moved me to jealousy with that which is not God; they have provoked me to anger with their vanities: and I will move them to jealousy with those which are not a people; I will provoke them to anger with a foolish nation.*"—DEUT xxxii. 21.

THE whole subject of the relation between Jew and Gentile, in reference to God's historical development of the scheme of redemption—a subject to which the main purport of the book of Jonah inevitably draws attention—is a very singular one, affording striking and unmistakable illustration of the principles on which the God of grace deals with His disobedient subjects, the children of men. And what is of great value, it illustrates the action of these principles upon a large scale. Reference may be made at present to one of these principles. I allude to the manner in which—

when dealing with the Jews to convince them of their ingratitude, to bring them to reason, to recall them to loyalty and duty, and to put them if possible once more upon their honour—the Lord condescends, in the failure of His many methods through their continued perverseness, to have recourse, as a last alternative, to the plan of *casting up to them* His corresponding or contrâsted relations with the heathen, and thus reaching their sensibilities and awakening something like keen feeling at last, if they were not indeed utterly heartless and finally hardened. The Lord at a very early period intimated that He would freely betake Himself to this method of rebuking and rousing them, and that He would wield it unsparingly. It is of course a dangerous weapon in controversy of man with man. We look, however, for seeing it wielded by God in infinite honour, generousness, and wisdom.

When Moses had brought the children of Israel, after their long wanderings, to the borders of the promised land, and was about to go up to Mount Nebo and die there, he uttered a prophetic song in the ears of all the elders and the congregation of Israel, sketching the principles of Jehovah's righteous and gracious treatment of them, and their perverse and provoking dealings with Him. In that song, Moses, speaking in the name of God, or let us say, God speaking by the mouth of Moses, announces His determination—as one perplexed with a rebellious people, wearied with their iniquities, at a loss as it were to find any effectual method of touching their hearts or breaking in upon their torpor—His determination to fall back, as a last resort, on the law or plan of a holy retaliation; to pique their vain pride by reminding them how much less He had done for the heathen than for them, and showing them how much more the heathen would have done in the way of grateful return than they. The language in which He made this intimation is very emphatic: "They have moved me to jealousy with that which is not God; they have provoked me to anger with their vanities: and I will move them to jealousy with those which are not a people; I will provoke them to anger with a foolish nation " (Deut. xxxii. 21). They had insulted the true God, by preferring idols to Him. The terms of His covenant with them were: "I will be a God to you; ye shall be to me a people." The Gentiles were not a people. The idols were not God. They have moved me to jealousy by that which is not God; I will move them to jealousy with those which were not a people. The idols, which were not God, they have preferred to me. The Gentiles, which were not a people, I in like manner will prefer to them. With their vanities, their idols, which are sheer emptinesses,—for "we know," says Paul, "that an idol is nothing in the world "—with their vanities have they provoked me to anger. With a foolish nation I will provoke them to anger, saith the Lord. I will paint their black ingratitude in contrast with the ready obedience of a people little befriended by me compared with them. I will awaken, pique, rebuke, and confound them by exhibiting infinitely less than

their privileges bringing forth infinitely more fruit, and
cherished with infinitely more gratitude, by a people
whom I had long and righteously cast off, and whom
they had long unrighteously and self-righteously con-
temned.

It is to this principle or method of—what we desire
reverently to call—playing off the Gentiles against the
Jews that Paul alludes in the 10th chapter to the
Romans, when, quoting the first intimation of it from
the Song of Moses, and the commentary and confirmation of it by a later prophet, he says : " But I say, Did
not Israel know?" Had they not received most distinct intimation that God would send His word to the
Gentiles? Though it had been nothing else, were they
not assured of it in connexion with their own disobedience, as an act of the holy reprisals that God
would take upon them?

Let us mark the drift of the Apostle's argument.
At the 12th verse we have the general statement of the
suitableness and applicability of the free and glorious
gospel to Jews and Gentiles equally and alike: " For
there is no difference between the Jew and Greek: for
the same Lord over all is rich unto all that call upon
him. For whosoever shall call upon the name of the
Lord shall be saved." From this he infers the propriety and necessity of the message of Heaven's glad
news and great salvation being sent forth over all the
earth: " How then shall they call on Him in whom
they have not believed? and how shall they believe in
Him of whom they have not heard? and how shall they

hear without a preacher? And how shall they preach, except they be sent? As it is written, How beautiful are the feet of them that preach the gospel of peace, and bring glad tidings of good things!" Then, referring to the rejection of the gospel by the unbelieving Jews, he says, " But they have not all obeyed the gospel. For Isaiah saith, Lord, who hath believed our report?" —a proof that faith cometh by hearing a " report," and that report resting on the credit of God's " word "—" So then faith cometh by hearing, and hearing by the word of God." Referring now, on the other hand, to the reception of the gospel by the Gentiles, he says: " But I say, Have they not heard?" Is not " the word " by which "faith cometh" gone out through the *Gentile* world? " Have they not heard? Yes, verily, their sound went into *all* the earth, and their words unto the *ends of the world.*" And why should Israel take offence at this? Specially, why should they profess to take offence at this as an unexpected, unprepared-for, unannounced novelty? Why were they not prepared for it? How could they have kept themselves in ignorance of it? Did they not get most distinct warning to expect and look out precisely for such a movement or evolution in God's dealings? They can plead no ignorance—save the ignorance of blinded, blameworthy prejudice that positively refuses to see. For " I say, Did not Israel know? First Moses saith, I will provoke you to jealousy by them that are no people; and by a foolish nation I will anger you. But Isaiah is very bold, and saith, I was found of them that sought me not: I was made manifest unto them that asked not after me. But to Israel, he saith, All day long I have stretched forth my hands to a disobedient and a gainsaying people."

I say, Did not Israel know? Did they not know, were they not told, yea, told from the beginning, that God would give His vineyard to others? "First, Moses saith it." At the very beginning of their history, by the mouth of their earliest legislator and prophet, it was a principle definitely announced. *There* was the first of it. *First*, Moses saith, I will provoke you to jealousy by them that are no people. That was the first of it; but that was not the last of it, nor the least bold statement of it. It was not lost sight of—not suffered to be buried and lost sight of—with Moses. "Isaiah" took it up and handled it. He had no scruples in doing so. He took it up and handled it in a very unmistakable manner, in clear tones and a steady voice; with a "bold" confidence in the righteousness of this plan to which the God of Israel had recourse, —its righteousness, its necessity, its very necessity as bearing on Israel's own good, if anything whatever might yet be the means of recalling them to reason and repentance. Isaiah had no doubt, no scruple, no bated breath in showing how holily and righteously the Lord, to awaken, if possible, Israel to jealousy, to sorrow, to shame, to duty, played off against them the wretched Gentile nations, and His mercy towards them. "Isaiah is very bold, and saith, I was found of them that sought me not; I was made manifest unto them that asked not after me" (Rom. x. 12-21).

Painful, exquisitely trying and painful, as this would be felt to be on the part of any honourably sensitive Jewish mind when recalled and re-awakened to do justice to his God, the Holy One of Israel; yet just in proportion to that painfulness would be the true and holy and tender and sensitive feelings of contrition, and of returning loyalty, and gratitude, and lowliness, which the right exercise of heart under it was fitted to produce. And sweet and profound and joyful would be the emotions with which, in such a case, a reconciliation to his holy and glorious King would be brought round and sealed. We are indeed assured by the Spirit of prophecy, casting forward its light upon that most blessed event that still awaits the Church—namely, the return and restoration to her bosom of her first-born children, the house of Israel—that this very principle will be at work, nay, it shall be this very principle, pre-eminently, that shall be in operation, in bringing Israel to that better mind. It shall be this principle that shall secure their home-coming and salvation. Bitter and humbling, though in its very nature it may seem, it is nevertheless a principle of perfect rectitude in Jehovah's hand; wielded, also, for the most gracious purposes and intents: and the bringing of it into play is to prove ultimately the very salvation of Israel from extinction, their salvation from final apostasy and sure perdition. Were it not, in fact, for the sure operation of this principle, when "the time to favour Zion shall come" (Ps. cii. 13), it would seem as if there remained none other of sufficient piercing power and delicacy to reach the dormant heart of Israel. And but for *it*, they would seem to have stumbled to their utter destruction. "But I say, Have they stumbled that they should so fall? God forbid: but rather through their fall salvation is come unto the Gentiles, for to provoke them to jealousy" (Rom. xi. 11). Then, stung at last into spiritual sensitiveness, with fresh, keen, quick feelings, capable of hearing and responding to sentiments of holy generosity, there will tell, with overwhelming force upon them, this argument; "The men of Nineveh shall rise in judgment against you, and condemn you" if ye repent not: "for *they* repented at the preaching of Jonas; and behold, a greater than Jonas is here" (Mat. xii. 41).

Yes, the day is coming when the love of God to the Gentiles will tell with exquisite keenness on the Jewish heart, and kindle there a contrite longing for restoration to that favour which they had compelled Him to transfer to others. When "the fulness of the Gentiles" shall come in, "the blindness" that "hath happened to Israel," we are told, shall terminate. Simultaneously, the fulness of the Gentiles arrives, and the veil that is on the heart of Israel is removed. A Gentile church, complete in Christ, the very fulness of Him that filleth all in all, rivets the gaze of keen-eyed, sensitive Israel. And instantly Israel is jealous. What! the off-cast heathen! *these* the children of her that was called desolate? *these* a people that were not a people? Have they entered into our inheritance? And are they thus blessed and thus complete—complete in the Christ, in *our* Messiah ?   And is this the "riches" of grace and favour with the Father we have so long forsaken?   And has it been thus given to aliens and outcasts, while we, the children of the prophets and of the covenant, have had the alien's and the wanderer's wasting doom?   Alas for our provocations!   Alas for our idols that were no gods, our vanities that could not profit!   Thou art righteous, O Holy One of Israel. We provoked Thee by what was not God; Thou hast provoked us by those that were not a people.   But was it, O God, Thy gracious design to open our eyes to see our sin and loss?   Was this Thy scope and purpose in "provoking" us?   Was it with this gracious end in view?   Was Thy jealousy holy and gracious both?   Was it that Thou wouldst not give Thy glory to another; and also that Thou wouldst have us be partakers of Thy grace?   And shall not this be the very spirit of our jealousy now; even that we will not resign *our* glory to others, our covenant with Thee, our claim upon Thy love for our fathers and for us in them?   "Doubtless, Thou art our Father."   "Behold, we come unto Thee, for Thou art the Lord our God."   We cannot any more endure to see our place in Thy love occupied by others, while we wander in cold and dark estrangement.   O God of Abraham, and of Isaac, and of Jacob ! the children of Thy friend come unto Thee.   Be not a Father to strangers while they go fatherless and all unfriended.

But will Israel, therefore, be hard to reconcile to the continuance of the Gentiles in the love of God ? Rather, will they not, in the very spirit in which they come themselves to God in Christ, be swift to learn that " they who be of faith are blessed with faithful Abraham," that " they that are Christ's are Abraham's seed," and that the "light" as it " lightens the Gentiles" is for that reason all the greater " glory to His people Israel?"

And will the Gentiles fare the worse for the return of Israel?   It would darken the whole procedure of God as between Jew and Gentile if they did. God indeed had employed these Gentiles as a means of awakening the Jews to jealousy—a delicate procedure; the like of which in man's hand is almost certain to break down in unhandsomeness, craftiness, deceit.   But with God it is used in infinite holiness and honour and love.   He does not make a tool of the Gentile Church, when He brings her blessed fulness to bear on Israel to make the earlier people jealous.   He does not feign a deeper love to the Gentiles than He feels. He does not tamper with their affections, and play them off in heartless game upon their predecessors in His covenant and love.   How needless, it may seem, to vindicate thus the honour of Jehovah, Israel's God! But we may perhaps see here some reason for the beautiful truth that the return of the Jews shall be a time of great enlargement to the Gentiles.   The Lord will deal with the Gentiles in such richer and larger favour as shall prove that He had not sought their love for a purpose, and having gained it, is done with them or indifferent to them now.   He owns it, as one subsidiary end of His enriching them with blessing, that He thereby sought to pique the Jews to jealousy.   But, even as it is said, " He is not ashamed to be called our God because He hath prepared for us a city"—implying that He would be ashamed to stand in that relation to us without following out faithfully all that it could be held to import—so would He be ashamed to take the Gentiles into covenant and become their God, merely or chiefly to compass some secondary end. Nay, His love to the Gentiles and His blessing on them shall overflow the more abundantly because it has been successful in bringing Israel again to His covenant and His love. So that " if the fall of Israel be the riches of the world, and the diminishing of them the riches of the Gentiles, how much more their fulness? If the casting away of them be the reconciling of the world, what shall the receiving of them be but life from the dead? " The Gentiles shall fare the better, and flourish into larger prosperity when Israel is provoked to jealousy. The handsomeness and honour of Jehovah's procedure are implicated in His seeing that shall be so.

We have dwelt at some length on these considerations, because we recognise in the book of Jonah an instance of this relation between God's dealings with Israel and His dealings with the Gentile world. Besides His direct purpose of righteousness and mercy towards Nineveh, God had undoubtedly a design to rebuke Israel and provoke them to jealousy by sending His prophet to the capital of heathendom. He was giving them a preliminary warning of what their continued ingratitude would render inevitable — the re-

moval of the vineyard from them, and the giving of it
to a people who would bring forth the fruit thereof.
He was giving a specimen of His threatening, "Ye
have provoked me with that which is not God, and I
will provoke you with them that are not a people;" a
threatening, uttered in the youth of their sacred nation,
fulfilled in the calling of the Gentiles at Pentecost,
illustrated when Paul and Barnabas said to Jews
at Antioch, "Seeing ye put the word of God from
you, and count yourselves unworthy of eternal life, lo,
we turn to the Gentiles," and to be illustrated on the
grandest scale, as overruled and transformed also in its
action and issue into a gracious *promise* and a means
of Israel's conversion, when, successfully provoked to
a holy jealousy, they return as a nation and are received and reconciled; and "What shall the receiving
of them be to the Gentiles, but life from the dead?"

We can easily conceive that Rationalism, denying the
historic truth of Scripture narrative, and explaining all
by its devices of *myth*, *allegory*, *ideology*, and so forth,
should imagine it had found an admirable target for its
profane wit in lighting on the book of Jonah.   A man
three days in a whale, and disgorged again!   So utterly unhistorical, besides!   And such waste of miracle,
too, on what, even though true, has no bearing on real
history at all!   Thus the poor hit takes; and the well-
trimmed shaft is shot off with a laugh.   But does it
really hit?   Nay, the arrow shivers ere it reaches the
mark; and Rationalism is never so weak as when it
fancies itself strong.   Viewed in the light in which

other scriptures enable us to view it, Jonah's mission to Nineveh assumes an importance which, regarded as an isolated and merely romantic incident in sacred history, would by no means belong to it. It becomes one of the grandest events in the history of redemption, from the exodus of Israel to the advent of Messiah and the calling of the Gentiles; while we see in it, moreover, exactly midway in the history of the ten tribes as a separate kingdom, the bringing into play of a principle in God's administration announced in the earliest days of Israel's national existence, commented on afterwards by her greatest Prophets, illustrated in the earliest labours of Apostles, and yet again to be drawn upon and wielded, on a scale the most splendid and with issues the most glorious, in those "last days" when "the mountain of the Lord's house shall be exalted on the top of the mountains, and ALL NATIONS shall flow unto it" (Isaiah ii. 2).

III

JONAH'S COMMISSION : ITS SOVEREIGNTY AND
RIGHTEOUSNESS

JONAH i. 2

"Arise, go to Nineveh, that great city, and cry against it; for their
wickedness is come up before me."

> "*And he said unto me, Depart: for I
> will send thee far hence unto the
> Gentiles.*"—ACTS xxii. 21.

IT was partly, then, with the view of constructing, so to
speak, a handle against His professed and peculiar
people, and of "provoking them to jealousy," that Jehovah, the God of Israel, the God of all the earth, planned
and executed this memorable dispensation of His righteousness and forbearance towards Nineveh. And for
the prosecution of this purpose, and in selection of an
instrument, an agent suitable, a vessel meet, or to be
made meet, for the Master's use, the lot fell on Jonah.
"The word of the Lord came unto Jonah, the son of
Amittai, saying, Arise, go to Nineveh, that great city,
and cry against it : for their wickedness is come up
before me."

We may notice concerning this command as delivered to the prophet—(1) the sovereignty, and (2) the righteousness characterising it.

I. It is a Sovereign command. It is THE KING who speaks—"the King of kings," speaking in that character; a sovereign Lord, not giving account of His matters. His command is brief, imperative, laconic. There are no explanations accompanying it; no details given; no prediction of the issue ; no information offered, nor the hope of any. It is also a very sudden, abrupt summons to duty; no preparation going before—no vision paving the way, or throwing light on the purpose.

Usually, a prophet, ere thrown into a new and difficult position, might look for a new and special preparation. Thus, ere Isaiah was led to say, " Here am I: send me"—though it was on the very sad and sorrowful commission, " Go, and tell this people, Hear ye, indeed, but understand not : and see ye, indeed, but perceive not : make the heart of this people fat, and make their ears heavy ; and shut their eyes, lest they see with their eyes, and hear with their ears, and understand with their heart, and be converted and healed,"—his dutifulness and implicit loyalty to his Heavenly King were toned into fresh purity and power by his ever noble vision ;—" I saw also the Lord, sitting upon a throne, high and lifted up, and his train filled the temple." And when his " eyes had seen the King," and his soul was abased unspeakably ; and when his peace was made unspeakable through the fresh removal of his sin, the purging of his iniquity, sealed anew as it was by the sacramental pledge of the "live coal from off the altar;" in the joy of free and full forgiveness, in the charmed life of the acknowledged friend of God, in the reanimated adoration of one who had been admitted to the High Court-room, the audience and presence-chamber of the King, Isaiah is prepared for any message or mission, to any people, anywhere. His only care and question will be, Is this the message of my King and my God? Then, "Here am I : send me " (Isa. vi. 1–10). Thus did the Lord deal with Isaiah. But to Jonah there is given no vision— no special, predisposing, preparatory vision at all, such as might have disciplined his soul for stern and sorely-trying duty—duty altogether different from any he had ever had in hand before.

Jeremiah, also, besides his visions of "the rod of an almond tree," and "the seething-pot, with the face of it towards the north" (Jer. i. 11, 13), had another most blessed advantage. He was admitted to full and familiar conversation with the Lord concerning the commission assigned to him. Indeed, the Lord graciously so shaped His communication as, reverently speaking, to draw out the young prophet to a free statement of his feelings. Evidently, the word of the Lord, when it came to Jeremiah, seemed to court the prophet's full unburthening of all his mind. "Then the word of the Lord came unto me, saying, Before I formed thee in the belly, I knew thee; and before thou camest forth out of the womb, I sanctified

thee, and I ordained thee a prophet unto the nations."
Manifestly this was designed to be the introduction to
a free and unembarrassed conference. So Jeremiah accepted it. "Then said I, Ah, Lord God! behold, I
cannot speak; for I am a child." And to this the gracious Lord replied,—entering, shall we not say? most
feelingly and most fully into His servant's fears and
anxieties, accepting his confidence and honourable confessions concerning his infirmities, and graciously encouraging while arming him against them,—"But the
Lord said unto me, Say not I am a child : for thou shalt
go to all that I shall send thee, and whatsoever I command thee thou shalt speak. Be not afraid of their
faces : for I am with thee to deliver thee, saith the Lord.
Then the Lord put forth his hand, and touched my
mouth. And the Lord said unto me, Behold, I have
put my words in thy mouth" (Jer. i. 4–9). Most confirming to the inexperienced prophet-elect must this
most condescending interview with the Lord have been;
the Lord acting to him the part rather of his Father
than of his King.

Isaiah had a glorious view of the King; Jeremiah a
confidential conference with his Father. To Jonah
there is given no vision. To Jonah there is given no
conference. Simply and suddenly, the naked and imperative command comes forth, "Arise, go to Nineveh,
and cry against it." There is no illustrative, symbolical commentary as by vision; there is no explanation
proffered by word of mouth. In high and sovereign
state, as with the prompt and studied brevity of mili-

tary peremptoriness and precision—as when the general
on the field condescends on no explanation to his officers, but simply gives the word—so, when the Angel of
the covenant, the Head of the Church, Emmanuel, the
Captain of the Lord's host, the same that appeared to
Joshua with a drawn sword over against Jericho, has a
great evolution of his generalship to execute, and one
of his staff to send to Nineveh, the word is with all
brevity and haste, "Arise, go to Nineveh, that great
city, and cry against it."

Was this no trial to his poor servant? Assuredly
it was. Yet herein nothing happened to Jonah but
what is common to the faithful. There is much of the
military discipline in the discipline of the Christian
life. The Lord, as your Father, will uniformly admit you
to all familiarity of emotion and expression in your dealings with Him; but, in His dealings with you, He will
sometimes expect the implicit, immediate submission,
without inquiry, without explanation, and without delay, which an absolute sovereign may demand. Nay,
He may even painfully paint forth to you the difficulties of your duty—the greatness and soreness of your
trial. He may admit that the city against which He
sends you is great and wicked—"that great city, whose
wickedness is come up before me." The one only thing
which He may not conceal may be the danger of your
position. He may even touch the very core of your
most sensitive feelings—where the trenching on them
in the slightest measure must needs be very painful.
"Take now thy *son*, thine *only* son, *Isaac*, whom *thou*

lovest, and get thee into the land of Moriah, and offer him there for a burnt-offering, upon one of the mountains that I shall tell thee of" (Gen. xxii. 2). And what is your refuge, what is your strength, in such an hour? Is it not the character of Jehovah, which is "known in Judah—his name, which is great in Israel"? When the overstrained heart-strings are like to crack under some peremptory, inexplicable appointment from God, what shall restore their tone but a flight by faith and adoration to the rectitude of Jehovah; "Shall not the Judge of all the earth do right?" (Gen. xviii. 25): to the sure goodness of Jehovah; "Truly, God is good to Israel" (Psa. lxxiii. 1): to the unsearchable wisdom of Jehovah; "He telleth the number of the stars; he calleth them all by their names; great is our Lord, and of great power; his understanding is infinite" (Psa. cxlvii. 4, 5)? This God is your refuge. And all these His attributes, in their searchless glory, are committed to you in a covenant of promise—risking to you, therefore, ere you can be injured, the injury and ruin of Jehovah's faithfulness, and righteousness, and goodness, and wisdom: "Be not dismayed, for I am thy God."

To this refuge Abraham fled in the trial of his faith; and he was rewarded by receiving his son again from the dead in a figure, and being made to see—in the substituted ram for a sacrifice, and the symbolic resurrection of Isaac, when to his father he was already, by this mysterious command, "as good as dead"—a figure of the substitution, and death, and resurrection of the Lamb

of God, and of the salvation thereby of the children
of the promise; by " seeing," in short, in all this, " the
day of Christ afar off, and he was glad." To the same
refuge—in confidence of his Lord's righteousness, goodness, and wisdom—Jonah did *not* flee, till, having himself undergone, as the type of the same seed of Abraham, a symbolic death and resurrection of his own—
even as " the Son of man was three days and three nights
in the heart of the earth"—he returned to his allegiance,
chastened and subdued, ready to render implicit obedience to a Sovereign who giveth not account of any of
his matters—who " doeth whatsoever pleaseth Him in
heaven and in earth, in the seas, and all deep places "
(Psa. cxxxv. 6).

II. But this command to Jonah was also Righteous.
It was sovereign, but not in arbitrary sovereignty. It
had its foundation in perfect rectitude. And that
feature of His command the King condescends clearly
to state and establish: " Cry against that great city,
for their wickedness is come up before me."

Thus also in conferring with Abraham anent His
intended vengeance on Sodom, Jehovah seeks in great
condescension to justify His purpose to His friend; and,
speaking after the manner of men, " The Lord said,
Because the cry of Sodom and Gomorrah is great, and
because their sin is very grievous; I will go down
now, and see whether they have done altogether according
to the cry of it, which is come up to me " (Gen. xviii. 21).
Thus,—though knowing all things and needing not

to make investigation,—in order to express His rigid justice more emphatically, God clothes Himself, as it were, with the person of an earthly magistrate, who will pronounce no sentence on hearsay evidence, but will personally investigate the case and satisfy himself; and so He speaks of having " come down to see whether they have done altogether according to the cry that is come up unto me." It is formally judicial.

And so here. It is a case of judicial procedure. The judge is satisfied of the guilt. He is weary of keeping silence. He is at last "come, and will not keep silence, and the heavens shall declare His righteousness, for God is judge himself" (Ps. l. 2, 6). Nineveh has had a long day of grace, a long period of forbearance, an un-merited respite and reprieve, slighted also and utterly abused. The Lord sits down at last on His tribunal. The case is to be called and judged. And Jonah is sent forth as God's pursuivant to summon the culprit to the bar, to be the King's counsel also to plead against him.

In this light the trial of Jonah's faith and duty was not so intense as in the former. Unquestionably the trial is alleviated by this representation of the righteous-ness of what the Lord is about to do. And why may not Jonah, in the King's name, on the King's message, take the King's highway to his new sphere of duty, bidding calm defiance to all manner of evil, assured that in loyally prosecuting the quarrel, and maintaining the government and honour of his Lord, no evil can befall him? For " if God be for us, who can be against us?" What then though the city be " great," and the mission mysterious? The city is intolerably "wicked." The mission is in perfect righteousness. And Jehovah himself is Judge.

Jonah may not, indeed, be strong enough yet for thus prosecuting fearlessly the work given him to do. He may not yet set himself so simply, so fully, in the word and wisdom of the Lord as to silence and crucify the wisdom of his own carnal reason,—the light of the Lord not yet being allowed calmly and alone to shine upon his heart and indicate his path. He may need to be brought through a terrible experience of his own, before his faith be pure enough, before his shield and sword for such a warfare be wielded into sufficient tone and temper for securing him the victory. "Judgment may begin" first on himself, in the appalling affliction that his waywardness brings upon him. But shall the Lord's quarrel with Nineveh therefore not be pleaded? Nay; it shall be pleaded more emphatically by far on account of any such delay. Jonah shall come to them at last with all the unshrinking strenuousness and firm nerve of a man, who, fresh from terrific trial visible and invisible, feareth not the face of clay. The very presence of the man among them shall say, "If judgment begin upon the prophet of the Lord, what shall the end be of them that obey not His word? If the righteous scarcely be saved, where shall the wicked and the ungodly appear?" (1 Pet. iv. 17, 18). And when *then* he shall deliver Jehovah's word of judgment,— as if his own soul were standing in the gates of that eternal world from which he has been miraculously redeemed, and his eye filled with its tremendous revelations,—there shall be a tone of unflinching certainty and majestic terror in his voice, worthy of the redeemed herald of the King of kings, infixing amazement and conviction into the hearts of His foes.

And thinkest thou, O man, who hast learnt the melancholy work of persuading thy conscience to refuse the office of crying against thee, of hailing thee to judgment, of bringing thee before Jehovah till the controversy be pleaded out and closed—oh! thinkest thou that that messenger, though he flee from his work, never will return and resume it? Though that Jonah, that prosecutor, that disobeying prophetic conscience of thine, descend into the deep sea for secrecy, and tarry there for days or even years, the Lord shall command his re-appearance; and in re-invigorated, unearthly power at last shall he preach to thee the preaching that the Lord hath bidden him. " Hast thou found me, O mine enemy? " is the question which you are doomed to have on some future day to ask : " Hast thou found me, O mine enemy? " For, until " the conscience be purged in the blood of Christ from dead works to serve the living God," and so exercised as to be kept " void of offence towards God and towards man," you lie open at any time to a visitation of relentless and remorseless arrest, from which you shall find no open path of escape, no opportunity either for retreat or appeal.

Therefore, ere " thou goest with this adversary " still
an adversary, " to the judge, as thou art in the way,
give diligence that thou mayest be delivered from him ;
lest he hale thee to the judge, and the judge deliver
thee to the officer, and the officer cast thee into prison.
I tell thee, thou shalt not depart thence, till thou hast
paid the very last mite " (Luke xii. 58, 59).

IV

JONAH'S FLIGHT; ITS MEANING AND MOTIVE

JONAH i. 3

"But Jonah rose up to flee unto Tarshish from the presence of the
Lord, and went down to Joppa; and he found a ship going to
Tarshish : so he paid the fare thereof, and went down into it, to
go with them unto Tarshish from the presence of the Lord."

> "*Trust in the Lord with all thine heart ;
> and lean not unto thine own under-
> standing. In all thy ways acknow-
> ledge him, and he shall. direct thy
> paths.*"—PROV. iii. 5, 6.

WHEN it is said that "Jonah rose up to flee unto
Tarshish from the presence of the Lord," it cannot be supposed that he meant or expected to withdraw
himself from beyond the sight and absolute omnipotence
of Jehovah. It is altogether inconsistent with that "fear
of the Lord" with which the prophet was manifestly embued (Jonah i. 9), to suppose him capable of entertaining any such idea. The wicked, indeed, habitually act
as if God were not omnipresent. They feel it a relief,
a positive relief, to escape from the eye of some fellow-
creature whom they believe to be penetrated with a
profound hatred of their wicked purposes. And when

they can contrive to hide them from all such, to keep them from the knowledge of all save those who happen to be as tolerant of sin as themselves, or more so, they are at their ease. A most conclusive demonstration that they either altogether disbelieve the plain and fundamental Scriptural truth that 'God seeth all things,' or, that if they believe it, they have made up their minds to defy Him to His face! There are few more conclusive and continually operating proofs of the depravity and ungodliness of the carnal mind, than its strange, cool, unaccountable, and settled forgetfulness of the very existence and nature of God as an infinite and omnipresent Spirit. Well may it be said to the sinner, If there is anything to which you can give yourself on Sabbath or on week-day, which you could not bear to have some holy man acquainted with, or in which you could not bear to have some holy man your spectator and companion, what are you better than an atheist? Are you not practically denying a God altogether? for a Being not everywhere present, beholding the evil and the good, is no God but an idol. How can you profess to have in you even the very beginnings of religion, if you habitually and coolly set aside the foundation of all personal piety? You are not even begun to feel that Jehovah is the God with whom you have to do, unless you practically accept and labour to follow out that view of His glorious, all-inspecting omnipresence which David celebrates in the 139th Psalm, giving the very key-note of a pious man's integrity: "O Lord, thou hast searched me, and known

me. Thou knowest my down-sitting and mine up-
rising, thou understandest my thought afar off. Thou
compasseth my path and my lying down, thou art
acquaint with all my ways. For there is not a word in
my tongue, but lo, O Lord, thou knowest it altogether.
Thou hast beset me behind and before, and laid thine
hand upon me. Such knowledge is too wonderful for
me; it is high, I cannot attain unto it. Whither shall
I go from thy Spirit? or whither shall I flee from thy
presence? If I ascend up into heaven, thou art there.
If I make my bed in hell, behold, thou art there. If I
take the wings of the morning, and dwell in the uttermost parts of the sea; even there shall thy hand lead
me, and thy right hand shall hold me. If I say, Surely
the darkness shall cover me, even the night shall be
light about me. Yea, the darkness darkeneth not from
thee, but the night shineth as the day; the darkness
and the light are both alike to thee" (Ps. cxxxix. 1–12).

Yes! though Jonah should take the wings of the
morning and dwell in *the uttermost parts of the sea*, even
there should the Lord's hand lead him, and his right
hand hold him. And that the prophet knoweth right well.

Why, then, is it said that he rose up to flee from the
presence of the Lord? A comparison of one or two
passages of Scripture may indicate the meaning. We
read that, after the marvellous conversation that God
held with the first murderer, immediately after he had
killed his brother, " Cain went out *from the presence of
the Lord*, and dwelt in the land of Nod, in the east of
Eden " (Gen. iv. 16). That saying evidently implies

that for the primitive worship which immediately succeeded the fall, some special locality was consecrated as
the place where Jehovah's name was placed; where
His worshippers assembled ; to which they brought their
offerings, that they might call upon His name through
sacrifice, and receive tokens of their acceptance, and fresh
intimations, it may be, of the Lord's will. Most probably, in the days of the first family of our race, the
gate of the garden of Eden, where God placed the
cherubims and the flaming sword, constituted the seat
of sacred worship; occupying the place and serving the
purpose which in after generations were occupied and
served by the tabernacle in the wilderness and in Shi-
loh, and ultimately by the temple, on Mount Moriah.
Thither, to that gate from which they had been driven
forth—even a God reconciled to them through the
promised seed of the woman, " taking vengeance on
their inventions though forgiving their iniquity " (Ps.
xcix. 8),—thither would the humbled yet hopeful, the
contrite and comforted worshippers draw near ; and, as
they beheld " the flaming sword which turned every
way to keep the tree of life," would they feel the
terrible exclusion which avenged their iniquity; while,
feeling likewise the impossibility of making their own
way to eternal life, they would be constrained to consider by faith the memorials of redemption which the
cherubims presented, and to pray to a sovereignly
gracious God, infinitely, terrifically holy, yet reconciled, " dwelling between the cherubims."   Here,
therefore, was the face of the Lord—the presence of

the Lord. Here substantially were all the elements of the temple worship, and of that worship which now by faith we conduct, entering into the temple on high—entering by hope within the veil by a new and living way, by the blood of Jesus. Here was the " sword," fit emblem of the blood of death, of sacrifice ;—" Awake, O sword, against my shepherd, and against the man that is my fellow." Here also was the throne of love guarded by the sword—equivalent to the mercy-seat sprinkled by the blood,—the Lord dwelling between the cherubims, giving His gracious presence to all who came in faith of Him, " the woman's seed," who should " bruise the serpent's head."

Here, then, was Jehovah's presence, His presence-chamber, the place of His gracious manifestations of Himself, of the new revelations of His will, the announcements of His grace and truth. Here Cain refused that reconciliation which God offered to him, maintaining his wrath against his brother and his sullen dislike to his God, even in the face of the expostulations which the Lord condescended to press upon him, " Why art thou wroth ? and why is thy countenance fallen ? if thou doest well shalt thou not be accepted ? and if thou doest not well, sin lieth at the door : and unto thee shalt be his desire and thou shalt rule over him " (Gen. iv. 6, 7). Here, again, Cain presented himself after he had stained his hands with his brother's blood, and received that terrible sentence which rendered him a fugitive and vagabond for ever, though it authoritatively guaranteed his life, setting aside by Sovereign dispensa-

tion that law of nature which instinctively teaches that
" whoso sheddeth man's blood by man shall his blood be
shed." From the place, then, where Jehovah thus made
all His communications of His mind and will—from
the place of the Lord's special worship—the wretched
fugitive went forth, when, as the history records, " Cain
went forth from the *presence* of the Lord."

Or, to take an instance that will bring the matter
closer to the point in hand. In 2 Kings xiii. 22, we
read thus : " But Hazael king of Syria oppressed Israel
all the days of Jehoahaz. And the Lord was gracious
unto them, and had compassion on them, and had
respect unto them, because of his convenant with
Abraham, Isaac, and Jacob, and would not destroy
them, neither cast he them *from his presence* as yet."
Evidently by casting them from His presence,—a thing
which He would ultimately be provoked to do, though
not " as yet,"—the Lord alludes to their being carried
captive by Assyria. It is in fact equivalent to saying
He would not " as yet " cast them from the Holy Land.
There, His name and glory were placed. There,
especially, His presence was revealed. Hiding Himself
as yet from the heathen, and confining His name and
worship within the sacred territory, He speaks of that
territory as the locality of *His presence ;* and casting
them forth from the land is therefore called casting
them out of His presence. The same language is employed to predict the banishment and captivity of the
house of Judah, when they also, as well as the kingdom of Samaria, were in their turn, after more than a

century, carried captive to Babylon. The threatening was delivered from the Lord to them by Jeremiah: "Behold I, even I, will utterly forget you, and I will forsake you, and the city that I gave you and your fathers, and cast you *out of my presence*" (Jer. xxiii. 39). Thus, then, the holy place of God's acceptable worship and the Holy Land itself, are clearly designated in Scripture as "the presence," or place of "the presence of the Lord." To be banished from the holy place, or from the holy territory, is equivalent to, is described as, being banished from the presence of the Lord. It was in this sense, accordingly, that Jonah sought to flee from the presence of the Lord. Especially if there be any truth in a tradition that the Jews believed the spirit of prophecy to be confined to the sacred territory, we see the reason why, on the supposition of Jonah being resolved to resist the heavenly command, he should desire to escape from the land of Israel. Open continually, while there, to a return of the Spirit and Word of the Lord, he could not face the conflict with them of which his intended disobedience would give him the painful prospect. To escape that conflict, he was content to betake himself to exile. If passing over the sea, to the lands of the uncircumcised and the unclean, might only carry him where the terrible "voice of words" might not any more be heard,—for the disobedient, at the repetition of the disregarded command, must "exceedingly fear and quake,"—Jonah is prepared to forego all the comforts of home, to endure all the hardships of exile, of exile even among those with

whom he, a Hebrew, a fearer and a prophet of the God
of Israel, could have no sympathy, nothing whatsoever
in common. So terrible is a man's case when he is
involved in a conflict with God; "Shall the thing
formed strive with its Maker?" That he may no more
hear the broken, violated injunction,—that he may
escape the urgency of the prophetic Spirit—"Jonah
rose up to flee unto Tarshish from the presence of the
Lord."

But why was this commanded duty so painful, so
unacceptable to Jonah? so unacceptable that, rather
than render obedience, he consented to forego the land
of his nativity, and the place of the gracious presence
of the God of his salvation?

I. Shall we say that Jonah was alarmed at its
difficulties? It would not have been wonderful if he
had been. It was indeed a mission environed with
difficulties. And the difficulties are summed up in
the two, which the Lord himself depicted to Jonah in
giving him the commission.

1. The city was great: "that great city." God
himself being the judge, who in all things judgeth
accurately, this was true; for it is the statement of
God's own opinion that we have to go upon. It was
He who said, "Go to Nineveh, that great city." The
third chapter of this book confirms this fact, and states
it still more emphatically and minutely: "Now Nineveh
was an exceeding great city of three days' journey"
(Jonah iii. 3). In the last verse of the prophecy also,

a hundred and twenty thousand is stated as the proportion of infants in the population : " That great city, wherein are more than six score thousand persons, that cannot discern between their right hand and their left ; " a proportion such as to give an entire population of about two millions. Profane history reports it as a well fortified city ; " its walls were a hundred feet high, and so broad on the top that three chariots could run abreast, adorned with fifteen hundred towers, each two hundred feet high." In building this city it is said that no less than one hundred and forty myriads of men were employed for eight years. A myriad being ten thousand, the number must have been one million four hundred thousand. " Such a city none has ever built since," was the declaration of the historian, referring even to those early times when the tremendous despotisms of the East could command the labour of millions of slaves. " There is not probably on record an account of such a city. That it had large gardens and even fields within its walls, there can be no doubt."* Indeed, this last statement of history is confirmed by the last clause of the prophet's book, or rather by the Lord's own words there recorded—"that great city, wherein there is also much cattle" (Jonah iv. 11).

Now for a man to proceed, as the herald of one who to them was an unknown God, the God of another nation, and unsupported, single-handed and alone, to proclaim amidst the teeming multitudes that a day of

* See note by translator of Calvin on Jonah : *Calvin Translation Society; Minor Prophets*, vol. iii., p. 22.

destruction is at hand;—is it not as if absurdity could not be carried further? Is it not as if the man were mad? What response could he expect but ridicule at least—if not absolute violence? What! Nineveh destroyed in forty days? Where are the armies that shall break down its walls, storm its lofty towers, or waste with famine its rich and well-stored garrison? What likelihood of this pitiful and way-worn dreamer's dreams being fulfilled? "Come ye, let us eat, drink, and be merry—to-morrow shall be as this day and much more abundant." And as for this crazed enthusiast and fool, let him have out his say; and ere he tells his story, as he says he must, throughout and around our city, he will find, mayhap, that he has had enough of it!

Certainly Jonah could not but foresee that some such reception in "that great city" was about the most friendly he could anticipate. To be despised and simply laughed at, as a fanatic and fool, must have appeared to him inevitable, if indeed his fate should not be worse.

2. Besides, secondly, the city was "wicked:" pre-eminently, emphatically, intolerably wicked. The Prophet Nahum,—who about one hundred and fifty years afterwards denounced among the Jews that final destruction of Nineveh which their repentance in the days of Jonah postponed, but only postponed,—closes, actually closes up his prophecy, allows its animated and indignant strains to die away, with this terrible challenge and condemnation : " On whom hath not thy

wickedness come continually?" (Nahum iii. 19). And
the whole of that prophecy indicates the horrible
extent to which the pride of greatness, military pomp,
luxury, licentiousness, and violence prevailed. "Woe
to the bloody city! it is all full of lies and robbery;
the prey departeth not; the noise of a whip, and the
noise of the rattling of the wheels, and of the prancing
horses, and the chariot bounding! The horseman urg-
ing onward, and the flame of the sword, and the lighten-
ing of the spear; and the number of the slain, and the
mass of the carcasses. And there is no end to her dead
bodies; they stumble on their carcasses. Behold, I am
against thee, saith the Lord. And I will cast abominable filth upon thee, and make thee vile, and set thee
as a gazing-stock. I will make thy grave: for thou art
vile" (Nahum iii. 1–6).

Full truly did the Lord execute His vengeance on
Nineveh for her "wickedness;" and precisely in the
form of judgment threatened: He "made her grave."
And it has been reserved to the days of this present
generation, after more than two millenniums, to see that
grave discovered and opened, and Nineveh's graven
images cut off out of the house of her gods, as Nahum
prophesied—cut off, hoisted up in chains, exhibited as
" gazing-stocks" to the whole civilised world.*

In such a place of military hardness and haughtiness,
of luxurious contemptuousness and pride, of unbridled
licentiousness and violence, what could a poor preacher
of Jehovah's holiness and anger do? It was bad

* See Layard's Nineveh.

enough in Israel. Little comfort, little encouragement, could any faithful man find there. But a history, a covenant, a record also of God's marvellous deeds might be appealed to *there ;* and something like a national conscience survived. When ready to faint in his own land, and to say concerning his call and his commission perhaps substantially, what Jeremiah said so pathetically : " Ah, Lord God ! I cannot speak " (Jer. i. 6), or to say as Moses in the deep anguish of his spirit was tempted to say : " O my Lord, send, I pray thee, by the hand of him whom thou wilt send " (Exod. iv. 13),—the prophet had still *this* to call to remembrance as his comfort, that they were God's peculiar people ; that the memory of His mighty deeds had not been completely obliterated among them ; that all their provocations had not made void the covenant by which Jehovah chose them to be His people ; and that, even if the tree seemed stript of all its foliage, yea, all its leaves and branches, yea, swept utterly away from the face of the land, still its roots were safe though hidden, and " through the scent of water they would bud again " (Job xiv. 9). But when he looked towards Nineveh, the great and wicked city, well might his heart faint and die utterly away within him. Well might despondency and despair utterly unman him, and tempt him to act neither the man, nor the fearer, nor the prophet of the Lord.

Had these been the feelings that were gaining dominion over him, what would have been his proper course ? What would have been the remedy ? Inter-

course with God concerning them; a full statement in
secret to his Father who is in secret, and who would,
in that case, have rewarded him openly with a triumphant victory over the very evils of his own unbelieving
heart. He had only to appear at the feet of his Master;
to spread out there the fears, anxieties, and perplexities
which were unmanning him; to appear there, let us say,
not as a man, if he were unmanned, nor delay repairing
thither till he had regained his nerve, his manhood, and
his courage; but as a little helpless child, as a poor
orphan in the world, weak as a fainting woman, if such
were his great prostration; and waiting there on Him
who hath said, " Call upon me in the time of trouble,
I will deliver thee, and thou shalt glorify me," to give
up every wayward feeling and every traitorous and unbelieving fear, and, obtaining instead the fresh and
reassuring favour of the Lord, and the fresh and reinvigorating strength of the Lord, to readdress himself to
his difficulties, and in God's sight go quietly forward
to them and quietly through them. *That* was the
course that lay open to him, and that still lies open
continually to every child of Abraham. " I had fainted,
unless I had believed to see the goodness of the Lord
in the land of the living. Wait on the Lord: be of
good courage, and he shall strengthen thine heart:
wait, I say, on the Lord " (Ps. xxvii. 13, 14). And
though the believer have to wait, and wait long, ere his
deliverance come, certain it is at least that he has not any
time to wait for the promise. The promise waiteth already
for him : " My grace is sufficient for thee, my strength

is made perfect in weakness." And with that word, true faith, recovering its ground and action, rests content. "Therefore if the vision tarry, wait for it; because it will surely come, and will not tarry." And in the meantime and till it come, "Behold, his soul which is lifted up is not upright in him: *but* the just shall live by faith" (Habak. ii. 3, 4).

There is, however, not the slightest trace of any evidence to prove that Jonah was alarmed at the *difficulties* of the work.

II. Shall we say, then, that he was alarmed at its *dangers*—that he was afraid of his life?

Little wonder though he had. It was a most irritating message he was charged to deliver—to a most proud, headstrong, irritable people. Short work might they make of the poor prophet preaching death for their evil ways. Was it this that terrified the man of God? Was he very much afraid of death? Was he deeply in love with many days? A very deep misunderstanding of his character it must be that should lead any one to think so; and a very heartless, shallow insensibility and incapacity to sympathise with or comprehend this greatly tried child of God. There was little love of long life, little terror of death, in him who calmly did his duty in the storm, when "he said unto them, Take me up, and cast me forth into the sea; so shall the sea be calm unto you: for I know that for my sake this great tempest has come upon you" (chap. i. 12). And again, did he not say unto the Lord in the bitterness

of his soul—the bitterness of death being past—" Therefore, now, O Lord, take I beseech thee my life from me,
for it is better for me to die than to live " (chap. iv.
3) ? And again " he fainted, and wished in himself to
die, and said, It is better for me to die than to live "
(chap. iv. 8). Whatever may have to be said of the
sinful excesses of grief which characterised and dictated
these most passionate and mournful exclamations, they
abundantly enough bear out this, that it was not the
fear of being put to death that weighed with the prophet in forming his unhappy purpose to flee from the
presence of the Lord. An unholy man like Balaam
might indeed have acted from such a motive. The craven
fear and tell-tale conscious misgivings which dictated
in his mouth the desire, "Let me die the death of the
righteous, and let my latter end be like his " (Num.
xxiii. 10), comported well with the imbecility which
the prospect of death would have struck into such a
mind as Balaam's. But any loyal and leal-hearted prophet
in Israel must have been quite familiarised with the
expectation of being almost at any time called to lay
down this present perishable life and be gathered to his
fathers. A people of whom the Lord of glory, in the
days of His own commission among them, could say,
" Which of the prophets have not your fathers slain ? "
must have quite accustomed their prophets, and Jonah
among the rest, to reckon their life the most insecure of
all their possessions ; and if they had not made up
their minds to count it so, and be contented, their hearts
must have been discouraged, and their hands weakened

every day, and in all the work of God continually. The
boldness with which a prophet in Israel could rebuke
and reprove their wild rebellions against God, and their
gross violence among themselves, must have sprung in
all cases from a prior and conclusive triumph over the
fear of death. Let no one go forth from the schools of
the prophets in Israel, save the man that has learnt to
take his life in his hand—"counting not his life dear
unto him."

And, indeed, with regard to every true Christian, is
not this one of those things in which he will find his
character making progress, if indeed he be thriving in
spiritual prosperity at all, viz., deliverance from the
slavish fear of death? Will he not have growing reason
to feel that it is " better to depart and be with Christ "?
Reconciled in the blood of that sacrifice whose unspeakable
glory and unspeakably soul-refining power he can never
taste to the full extent he would desire ; and renewed by
that Spirit whose glorious love and power he cannot
cherish in his heart as he would ; living with God on the
terms of a covenant which has placed his eternal happiness on the security of an all-precious purchase, and of an
all-faithful promise ; and finding himself utterly incapable of entertaining the full and ever-glowing gratitude
which the placing of it on such a footing is worthy to
call forth ; he knows that he never will be at rest—
never will be at the goal and aim towards which his
deepest principles and feelings carry him, till, in the
unclouded serenity and glory of the world above, he
shall pour forth the whole energy of a perfected and

sinless nature in the song which in heaven alone can do justice to his feelings, when, with "the ten thousand times ten thousand and thousands of thousands," he too at last gets the long-desired opening of the mouth to sing, "Worthy is the Lamb that was slain, to receive power, and riches, and wisdom, and strength, and honour, and glory, and blessing;" when with every creature that is in heaven he unites in raising high again the echoing psalm of heaven's ceaseless family worship, choiring back evermore the rapturous refrain; "Blessing, and honour, and glory, and power be unto Him that sitteth on the throne and unto the Lamb for ever" (Rev. v. 12, 13).

In proportion as a believer's integrity, amidst life's many trials and the holy discipline of Providence and the growing enjoyment of ordinances, becomes to himself, through Divine grace, more and more manifest; and as he dutifully realises the attitude of one pressing toward the mark; the prize of his high calling brightens in its glory to his view: he is no longer afraid as he was when an unsettled controversy with God hung gloomily over him—no longer afraid to look at that prize, as if conscious that it is for others but not for him; the fascinating joy of real eternal life has broken on his weary heart; he turns with deepening intensity of interest and increasing self-jealousy to examine the foundations on which his hopes are reposing; and though not always confident, in reflex thought, as to his own state, he is growingly confident and satisfied in direct contemplation of Christ and the everlasting covenant;

the simple action of faith, whose chiefest glory and
very essence it is to be satisfied with Christ alone—
with Christ's sacrifice and covenant and word alone,
when no other grounds appear—the simple action of
faith becomes more and more intense, and the things
that are unseen and eternal consequently then unveil
and unfold themselves to his joyful encouragement.
Inevitably, in such a case, it is for the sake of others,
and not his own, that this man will care for living long
on the earth.   He will " have a desire to depart and be
with Christ, which is far better " (Phil. i. 23).   And
only if it be "more needful" for others, whether for
their temporal or spiritual advantage, will he be reconciled " to abide in the flesh," at a distance from that
full peace and full likeness to Christ which he has
learnt to count his only satisfaction ;—" As for me, I
shall see Thy face in righteousness ; I shall be *satisfied*
when I awake in Thy likeness " (Ps. xvii. 15).   The
physical pains of death are, after that, the only thing he
has to dread ; growing confidence in his Father's adorable wisdom—which may assign him protracted suffering, but *may* wrap him in translation's haste and glory
into the kingdom of the blest,—will enable him to trust
the ordering of his last hours to Him ; and thereafter,
save for others, the love of life here is gone ; " We are
confident always, and willing rather to be absent from
the body, and present with the Lord " (2 Cor. v. 8).

If to such considerations as these we add the fact
that this holy man of God had a very difficult office to
discharge among that portion of the tribes that soonest

and most deeply revolted from God and righteousness, and among whom, therefore, like all who had that lot assigned them, Jonah must have found himself almost continually uncomfortable, and altogether and continually destitute of sympathy, we have probably said more than enough in the way of showing that the dread of losing life was not the motive which prompted the inexcusable act of fleeing from the presence of the Lord.

III. Shall we say, then, thirdly, that astonishment and perplexity as to being sent to the *Gentiles* operated on his mind, and led him to refuse a mission to the heathen?

We have already spoken at length on the singular relations, in the development of the history of redemption, subsisting between Israel and the Gentile world. And in that subject it would not have been wonderful though the prophet's mind had found enough to fill him with darkness and confusion. Indeed, it must have been a severe trial to his confidence in God to be appointed a preacher to those whom all along he had understood to be in the meantime given over of the Lord. That seemed generally understood—yea, conclusively settled. It seemed a settled point that the heathen were, for the time being, abandoned; that on them the prophetic office had no bearing. Did not our Lord's own declaration point to this when He said, "I am not sent but unto the lost sheep of the house of Israel" (Matt. xv. 24)? Was it not a strange thing to a converted soul to be told, "Lo, I will send thee far hence to the Gentiles" (Acts xxii. 21)? And we remember how completely even such an one as Simon Peter, whom Jesus, even in the days of His flesh, had taught to call nothing outward " unclean," was puzzled and perplexed at the heavenly vision, and at the command connected with it, that he should go to the Gentile Cornelius and preach the gospel to him (Acts x. 15–28). And if Peter expostulated on this subject, even in the face of a vision illustrating the truth, and had his doubts, apparently, when sent for by an honourable man who had also been instructed by a heavenly vision and a visit of an angel from glory, how much more might Jonah have felt confounded at the sudden and unexplained command to go forth as God's prophet to the chiefest city of the Gentiles!

Yet there is not a trace of this as the explanation or the motive of his disobedience.

IV. It remains, therefore, that we now state—and we can at present do little more than state—the real cause. Jonah himself, in the utmost possible candour, has disclosed it and recorded it; and there is not the slightest reason to imagine the existence or operation of any other cause. When Nineveh was spared, "Jonah prayed unto the Lord, and said, I pray thee, O Lord, was not this my saying, when I was yet in my country? Therefore I fled before unto Tarshish: for I knew that thou wast a gracious God, and merciful, slow to anger, and of great kindness, and repented thee of the evil" (Jonah iv. 2).

Though we cannot at present open up very fully what is implied in this singular and artless confession, or the precise nature of the sin thus disclosed, we may not fancy that we have made little or no advance in considering the character of this most wonderful man. We see not a little into the marvellous power of Divine grace in him, when we see that the gigantic obstacles and difficulties of his mission did not, and never would have hindered him; that the fear of death was not a fear to which he was in any degree a slave; and that even the perplexities which, in so unspeakably more favourable circumstances, all but drove an enlightened apostle from his propriety and duty, even in the gospel age and in the fulness of Pentecostal times, had no weight to stagger the noble heart of this much misunderstood servant of God. To do *that*, it needed a deeper difficulty than ordinary minds need. It needed a more subtle and more spiritual temptation than the grosser cast of minds are even capable of feeling. Little credit as he may get, his God gave him credit for being moved to disobedience by no such commonplace motive as the dread of difficulties, the love of life, or the mystery of the relation of Jew and Gentile. He could appeal to God that another motive than any of these was at work in his sorely tried spirit. The Lord acknowledged the truth of Jonah's own representation; and so, surely, may we. The Lord exonerated him from the charge of everything mean, sordid, and of the kind that sways the worldly, and even oftentimes the more unrefined and low-toned Christian spirit. The Lord gave him credit for being influenced by a motive, no doubt mistaken, and leading him into sin, but still a motive which none but a highly honourable and keenly sensitive child of God, very loyal to his King, very tender to his Father's glory, could possibly have been influenced by, or able even to imagine, save from his own truthful consciousness of its influence.

We learn, therefore, these lessons from the subject.

1. " Judge not, that ye be not judged." Especially judge not hastily the motives of any whom you have reason to believe to be godly men. Godly men especially lie open to have misconstructions put, and wrong judgments passed, upon their conduct. If we heard their private prayers, we might get the true explanation of what otherwise may seem inexplicable. We *do* overhear a prayer of Jonah when his spirit was overwhelmed within him—when his soul was too agitated to speak anything but the bursting, burning truth. Were it not for that prayer and the explanation it affords, all manner of false motives might have been heaped upon the misjudged character of this most noble prophet. We learn from his communion with God— what the ever-blessed God did not for a moment cast doubt upon, for He is very gracious, and owneth all sincerity even where it may be sadly struggling to assert and keep its ground—we learn from his secret communion with God, as it is recorded by the Spirit of inspiration, that not even hindrances of the most painful, powerful, perplexing character, did, or would have, induced him to be disobedient to the heavenly command.

And it is just this little remnant of his prayers, saved
and put on record to all generations, which vindicates
him from the imputation of all manner of poor, pitiful,
and sordid, and commonplace motives, such as any rude,
gross mind, measuring the prophet's capacity by its own,
might have been pleased to cast upon him.

2. We learn how utterly worthless as a guide in duty
man's own wisdom must ever be, even though acting in
combination with the most exalted natural nobility, or
even gracious refinement, of spirit. We have said that
none but a soul of high-toned spiritual dutifulness
would have been open to the risk of being perplexed
by the idea that suggested itself to Jonah. Holy zeal
for the honour of God in a very singular crisis and
movement of His government; great fear lest, sparing Nineveh after the unmitigated threatening, God
might be regarded as a changeable God; fear, not at
all for himself, but fear lest his God should be misjudged; these things weighed with his anxious heart,
as on none but a regenerated heart could they practically have weighed at all. Yet even in these circumstances, and amidst gracious desires of the most self-
denying and self-forgetting kind, his own ideas ought to
have been all trampled under foot; and he ought simply
and immediately to have gone to " Nineveh, that great
city, and cried against it," believing that, without his
anxiety and without his aid, Jehovah could vindicate
His own character in His own way. Unquestioning
obedience to God is, therefore, most emphatically taught
in this passage. Leave all things to Him. Let His

word of command be enough for thy duty—His word
of promise enough for thy faith. Whatsoever more thou
shalt in any case seek shall turn out thy thorn and thy
trouble.   But " the word of the Lord is very pure :
therefore let his servants love it " (Ps. cxix. 140).

V

JONAH'S FLIGHT; ITS LESSONS

JONAH i. 3

"But Jonah rose up to flee unto Tarshish from the presence of the Lord, and went down to Joppa; and he found a ship going to Tarshish : so he paid the fare thereof, and went down into it, to go with them unto Tarshish from the presence of the Lord."

> "*Let no man say, when he is tempted, I am tempted of God : for God cannot be tempted with evil, neither tempteth he any man : but every man is tempted, when he is drawn away of his own lust, and enticed. Then, when lust hath conceived, it bringeth forth sin; and sin, when it is finished, bringeth forth death. Do not err, my beloved brethren. Every good gift and every perfect gift is from above, and cometh down from the Father of lights, with whom is no variableness, neither shadow of turning.*"—JAMES i. 13-17.

JONAH was afraid lest, the inhabitants of Nineveh repenting, and the Lord remitting the punishment threatened, the God of the Jews might be regarded as a changeable God. Inconsistency and inconstancy are

charges which a sensitive man can scarcely with equa-
nimity bear. When Paul did not arrive at Corinth so
soon as he intended, and when the enemies of the gospel,
ready to take any handle to disparage his character, represented this as "lightness" (2 Cor. i. 15-20)—levity,
fickleness, the characteristic of a man that did not know
his own mind—this gave the Apostle great distress.
"I was minded to come unto you before, that ye might
have a second benefit; and to pass by you into Macedonia, and to come again out of Macedonia unto you,
and of you to be brought on my way toward Judea.
When 'I therefore was thus minded, did I use lightness? or the things that I purpose, do I purpose according to the flesh, that with me there should be yea, yea,
and nay, nay? But as God is true, our word toward
you was not yea and nay:"—it was not equivocal, uncer-
tain, and inconstant; one thing to-day, and another
to-morrow; I meant what I said, with no reservation;
"as God is true," I did. But as an honourable
man repels such a charge as directed against himself,
how much more must a faithful servant of the Lord in-
dignantly repel such a charge against his King and his
God. For if such a thing can be said of God, there is
an eternal end of all constancy everywhere. Paul in
defending himself appeals, as the last prop and hold, to
God's own unchangeableness. Says he, "As God is true
our word toward you was not yea and nay." But if the
foundations be destroyed, what hath the righteous done?
If the very God to whom the last appeal must be taken
be not "without variableness or shadow of turning," who

then can prove, maintain, or assert his own truth? "Is God unrighteous? God forbid: for how then shall God judge the world?" So reasoned Paul concerning the Divine righteousness.* And, 'Is God capable of change? God forbid: for where then were any everlasting rock or stay?'—so, in imitation, we may reason concerning the Divine unchangeableness. It was an inconceivable grief to Jonah to utter any denunciation which he saw that, through infinite graciousness, the Lord might yet, through repentance on Nineveh's part, be, humanly speaking, prevailed upon to retract.

But why should he not allow the Lord to protect His own character in His own way? When he took counsel with flesh and blood, when he conferred with his own carnal wisdom, he forsook the first principle of piety, —subjection to the call and word and will of God. He did not need to be less concerned for the honour of God.

---

* How would a "Broad Church" Catechism run, in reference to these questions of the Apostle? In some such way as this:—

Question. "Is God unrighteous who taketh vengeance?"

Answer. He would be, if He did. Vengeance is in all cases unholy and devilish.

Question. How then do you account for Paul telling the Romans (chap. ii. 8, 9) that God will "render indignation and wrath, tribulation and anguish, to every soul of man that doeth evil"?

Answer. Paul had not sufficiently shaken himself clear of the vengeful and sanguinary spirit of the Old Testament.

Question. "Then how shall God judge the world?"

Answer. He won't do it. The "law of love" is working everything right of itself.

They should really try a Child's Catechism. HENRY ROGER has shown them the way very nicely, in an adjoining department:—See "Eclipse of Faith," pp. 89–91.

Therein he did well; therein his soul was far more upright within him than in the case of multitudes who think it quite an easy thing to discuss his character and pronounce upon his sin. Nobly did he exhibit, even in and by his error, the deep desire that glowed within him to see his God rightly understood and rightly honoured. But what he needed was a simpler Abrahamic faith, allowing this new disclosure of God's character to go forward at God's call, " not knowing whither" it "went;" but assured that God himself would bring it safely and in stainless glory, to the mark and goal which He had appointed.

Contrast for instance, as to the principle involved, the faith of Abraham in offering up Isaac, with the unbelief of Jonah in fleeing to Tarshish. Had Abraham so listed, besides the many temptations to disobedience arising from paternal affection and from the unspeakable darkness that seemed to arise when the child of promise, and thereby the future Saviour, the Seed, and in Him all the promises, were put in danger, there was another point to prove a temptation—another point in which Abraham was tried on this most renowned occasion, and in which his faith triumphed, exactly similar to that in which Jonah's faith was tried and failed. Abraham might well have reasoned thus:—'What will the Canaanites think—"for the Canaanite was still in the land"—when they learn that, at the command of my God, my hands have been imbrued in the blood of my child, offered a sacrifice upon His altar? How will they distinguish between this surrender which in unquestioning confidence and duty I make of my beloved one, and the bloody and accursed murders wherewith they stain the service and propitiate the favour of their unholy and abominable deities? Alas! ,alas! they will reckon my God,—my God, who is the Judge of all the earth,—and " shall not the Judge of all the earth do what is right?"—they will reckon my God altogether such an one as their own.' But no such imaginations were allowed to weigh with Abraham. If they arose and attempted to arrest his obedience, he warred against them with spiritual weapons. " The weapons of his warfare were not carnal, but mighty through God to the pulling down of strongholds ; casting down imaginations, and every high thing that exalteth itself against the knowledge of God, and bringing into captivity every thought to the obedience of Christ " (2 Cor. x. 4-5). Abraham brought " every thought into captivity " to the command of God. He cast down all his " reasonings." Every " imagination " of his mind he bound with cords to the chariot of God's Word, and made them follow as its humble captives. Against hope he believed in hope. He continued to believe that what God had promised He was able to perform—that He was able to raise up Isaac again from the dead, from which, indeed, he received him in a figure—and that He was able to justify His own character and procedure in the eyes of the Canaanites and of all the world, in His own time and in His own way. Casting down, therefore, all reasonings, all thoughts, all imaginations, and mastering them all in faith, Abraham calmly went to Mount

Moriah.   Jonah fell by unbelief under their power;
they mastered him, and ruled and drove him hard.
Jonah fled to Tarshish.

Blessed was Abraham's reward: terrible was Jonah's
chastisement.   In the upraising of Isaac from the altar
and in the substitution of the ram caught in the thicket;
in the trial of his own love also in surrendering his
beloved, Abraham " saw the day of Christ afar off," and
the eternal Father's inconceivable love to sinners in
giving His eternal Son to save them—and Abraham
" was glad."   Terrible was Jonah's punishment.   He
too may be said to have seen the day of Christ afar off—
but to have been exceedingly filled, not with gladness,
but with agony.   For the cross of Christ is God's work
of infinite love and God's work of infinite judgment too.
On the side of its love, Abraham saw it and was glad.
On the side of its judgment and terrors, Jonah doubtless
saw it and was overwhelmed with anguish, while for three
days and three nights his doom was as if entering into
the sufferings of Him who was " three days and three
nights in the heart of the earth."   So singularly suitable
in each case was the reward and the punishment.
" Great and marvellous are Thy works, Lord God,
Almighty; just and true are all Thy ways."

There are several principles of God's moral probation
of man brought out in this third verse, describing, as
it does, so graphically and rapidly Jonah's flight.

I. And in the first place, observe, that though Jonah
was not moved to disobey God originally by fear, alarm,

or cowardice; though it was under the force of a more subtle and spiritual motive than these—one having in it apparently more of holiness and godly zeal; yet no sooner is he, through his disobedience, in a false position, than fears and alarms get the mastery over him. He is evidently in the attitude of a man who has lost his self-possession. He betakes himself to flight. Though not a wicked man, yet engaged at present in a course of disobedience, he is doomed, for the time being, and in so far to feel the sore restlessness and alarms of the ungodly, according to the unchangeable and terrible oracle: "There is no peace, saith my God, to the wicked." It was not cowardice that tempted him to form his disobedient resolution. But he has no sooner formed it than the brave man is a coward immediately. He flees in terror. He is in haste to find a hiding-place.

And this teaches us that, though it may be from a comparatively higher and purer class of motives that we may be induced to disobey the Lord, no sooner are we committed to an act or course of disobedience, than motives far less high and far less pure, may immediately assert a most humiliating mastery over us. It matters not under what influence you take up the position of a rebel; you may have been omnipotent against your meaner enemies before; but you are weak as a child against them now. Once lay aside the spiritual weapons of implicit confidence in God's truth and wisdom, righteousness and grace—once take counsel with carnal reason and your own devices, distrusting and forsaking the light of God's Word and Spirit,—carnal wisdom and carnal weapons will not be found sufficient to protect you long from enemies that once would have been very lightly dealt with, very easily quelled and set aside. Principles of action too pitiful and paltry—nay, too mean and base—to have had any chance of securing your concurrence once, will present themselves now, in the hour of your revolt, claiming kindred with you, claiming control over you, with an insolence that may fill you with bitterness, but which it may now defy you to repress. The enemy at first may have needed to draw upon his more subtle devices, in order to waylay, deceive, delude, disarm you; but once you are disarmed, he can dispense with any peculiarly refined style of dealing. Coarser method now will suffice. Angels of light may have been required, as his messengers, to dazzle and mislead you from the narrow way into paths of disobedience; but once there, fiends or evils of ruder form may manage you; motives of impure and gross enough description may suffice to move you, now that you are at any rate within the meshes of his net. Cowardice may not have induced you; nay, such may have been the stuff of which your disposition, and especially as moulded anew by grace, is made, that cowardice never would have prevailed to cause you refuse the mission to Nineveh; motives far deeper and more subtle, much more akin to godliness and zeal, it may have been needful to ply upon you, ere you were induced to adopt the sinful determination; but once adopted—your God now clearly and consciously disobeyed, and your God therefore consciously and entirely distrusted, as distrust grows assuredly out of disobedience—you are at once the coward now. The " spirit of bondage again to fear " gets distressing dominion over you. You will flee now, even " when no man pursueth."

Ah! it is very necessary to ply this solemn consideration on believers battling the good battle of faith, too often feeling as if the tide of it were going against them, too often ready to despond and to despair when, after sustaining losses and wounds not a few, they seem ready to refuse to resume the fight. The time was when—in simple faith, in contrite humble-hearted gratitude, in loyal acknowledgment that you were a little child, and your Father's understanding alone fitted to guide you—you walked humbly with God, carefully keeping yourself unspotted from the world, rising nobly superior to the meaner forms in which the world's evil too glaringly appears. The liberties with God's pure and holy law which laxity of principle in worldly trade too often takes and pleads for, appeared to you then in their true character as bold offences against heaven's righteous King, earth's holy and omniscient Ruler. When offering their services to you, claiming your submission to them, in better than Hazael's spirit you might have said : " Am I a dog, that I should do this wickedness?" And loving God's Word, and throne, and Sabbath—and, in free and full reconciliation, walking with God—little success could the enemy expect in tempting you in these directions. The holy and sensitive spirit of a friend of God, enjoy-

ing actual experience, and living in present habits of
friendship with Him, recoiled directly from every such
suggestion or assault.   But did the enemy deal more
subtly with you?   Did he speak of your friendship
with God as now very steadfastly secured?   Did he
whisper that the constant, scrupulous, watchful, self-
denying self-jealousy, needed in the earlier stages of
your Christian walk, were not so necessary now?   Did
he insinuate that being one of God's friends and children you might warrantably enough take things into
your own hand more boldly, and tread in your daily
walk and life with less timid footsteps?   Did he speak
of the great difficulty of judging precisely and exactly
where the limits of worldliness terminate and those of
godliness begin?   Did he point out a sort of middle
land, as it seemed to be, between the Church and the
world—the children of God, and the children of the
wicked one—a sort of neutral ground on which, without resigning their special character, both alike might
meet and dwell, or at least mutually visit and compli-
ment each other, in something, if not more like unity,
at least less like bigotry and religious narrowness?
Your solemn views of the dreadful condition of worldly,
unconverted men, lying in the snare of the devil and
beneath the wrath of God, were gradually worn down.
Slowly at first, and step by step—perhaps under sem-
blance of wishing to commend religion to some whose
society you loved, whose souls you really cared for—
you went with them so far in their views and practices,

expecting thereby to bring them all the more easily round to yours. Ah! but, like Jonah, you were affecting to be wiser than God;—you were, under the cloak of spiritual zeal, really acting at the dictate of carnal wisdom. You were disobeying a clear command—" Be not conformed to the world,"—a command as clear as that peremptory word, " Arise, go to Nineveh." And, —having entered on a course of disobedience,—laxity of principle, worldliness of disposition, fear of man's opinion, and false shame keep you from promptly retiring to the ground you have forsaken, and a thousand other very commonplace and coarse principles and motives, to which you would once have nobly and easily risen superior, have you in their power now; and it may be only through some sore crash of affliction, as in the case of Jonah, or at least through deep repentance, as in the case of Peter, that at last you return, softened and subdued, to trust the wisdom of God more than your own, and to walk with Him, not in sparks of your own kindling, but rather in the light of the Lord.

Let this then be our first lesson. We may disobey God from subtle and spiritual and holy-like motives; but we no sooner yield than the coarsest may too sadly overmaster us. The angel of light may be needed to betray us into sin. But our armour, our simplicity, our singleness, our strength, being then gone; the ruder evils and meaner kinds of sin, starting from their concealments and surrounding us, claiming us now as their own, saying, " Persecute and take him, for God hath forsaken him" (Ps. lxxi. 11), may assert over us a power which in days of our integrity and good conscience we found it comparatively easy to refuse and resist.

No alarms prevailed with Jonah to disobey his King. But disobedient Jonah is easily alarmed. He flees in haste and terror.

II. There is a second and very solemn lesson in the words, "he found a ship going to Tarshish." Committed to a course of disobedience, "he found" the means of holding on in it; his heart set on fleeing to Tarshish, a ship chartered for Tarshish without difficulty he "finds." As evil luck would have it, as some speak; as his malignant stars appeared to rule, to use language equally heathenish; as God's holy providence arranged, to speak as godliness and right reason dictate—Jonah finds events conspiring, as it were, to aid him in carrying out his evil purpose. Being in the way of disobedience, helps to disobedience meet him. A very terrible consideration! One that is always solemn and always seasonable.

Beyond all question, if you are on the paths of sin, on the broad road, which, if you be not turned aside from it, lands you ultimately in everlasting ruin—beyond all question, in that path, in that road, you will find means and opportunities, help and facilities to sin. Ah! how often the angry boy, on the playground, has found the ready stone with which to prosecute his quarrel and vent his wrath, creating long-lasting matter of pain to another and grief to himself! How often the man of unbridled temper and murderous envy, jealousy or rage, in the heat and fit of overboiling hatred of his brother, " breathing out threatening and slaughter," has found as at his very hand, so opportune, so fatal, the deadly weapon by which the murder in the heart and feeling embodied itself beyond recall in the murder of the hand and of fact !—as if the very fiend of malice placed the ready javelin in Saul's hand, wherewith, save for special providence, the youthful Psalmist of Israel, their future king, had been pinned to the wall in instant death.

Yes; it is a terrible truth that the sinner will usually find provided, as it were, to his hand, the implements and opportunities which a heart set to do evil will easily transform into helps to sin. Doubtless this must be so in a state of probation such as that under which in this world we are placed. Omnipotence, indeed, might work so as that, when passion sways and rules the transgressor, every help to evil should, as it were, retire before his footsteps and elude his grasp. Miracle might snatch the weapon of murder beyond the reach of the hand of revenge. Miracle might draw a cloud of obscuration between the eye of lust and the object on which it feeds its secret and unhallowed fire. Miracle might make fire refuse to burn when applied by the incendiary's hand. Miracle might make the atmosphere refuse to carry the sound of words when the hoary blasphemer essays to innoculate youth with his profanity. Miracle might so arrange as that Jonah, seeking to flee to Tarshish, shall find no ship bound for Tarshish. Nay, it is conceivable that God might institute a kind of government and providence among men, in which these things should form not miraculous and astonishing exceptions, but the very style and staple of the system. But it would be a wholly new system, proceeding on new principles, making void and setting aside altogether our present probationary condition. To a state of probation—a state in which God suspends the immediately deserved retribution, delays the instant and exact measuring out of justice till a day when the great drama shall be wound up and all outstanding cases settled—to such a state in which the sinner gets space or scope, time and opportunity, to prove his rebellion or repentance, time and opportunity to return and be reconciled, or to disclose thoroughly of what manner of spirit he is, so that justice in the ultimate judgment may be easily and clearly vindicated; to such a state it seems essential that the sinner should find, if he seek, the means of prolonging his rebellion to its aim of embodying the spirit of rebellion in its actions. To snatch away from him, as God no doubt could do if He chose, the incentive to his lust, the weapon of his wrath, the vehicle of his flight, were for God to cease dealing with him as one under probation. But God will not thus interfere to make completion of a sinful purpose impossible. And can you complain of this? Can you *reasonably* complain? If your "heart is set in you to do evil," and the ready means of evil most temptingly present themselves and lie ready to your hand; if you love worldly talk on Sabbath, and a worldly companion waylay you at the very door of the sanctuary, and you refuse not his

converse till every sacred impression of the word and
house and Spirit of God are worn off; if, in short, you are
under a state of trial, and God actually arrange events
to try you, can you complain ? Would you wish this
probation to end ? Would you wish swift and sudden
wrath to fall, as in every case where probation unimproved terminates, the wrath then swiftly falls at last ?
Would you wish it to fall immediately ? Do you wish
your probation ended ? Will you quarrel with God
for so ruling in His providence that what is *essential* to
a state of probation—essential, therefore, to your deriving the benefit of a state of probation—falls to your lot ?
Will you say when " tempted, that you are tempted of
God"? * Nay: if the benefit of probation is assigned
you; if your eternal estate is held in suspense, and you
are now dealt with so that that eternal state shall depend
on how you decide and act now; if God thus patiently
deals with you on His part; then all that is essential to
a probationary state must be submitted to on your part,
and this among the rest—namely, that if, in rebellion
and revolt against the clearly revealed will of God, you
continue in the way of transgressors, you shall find the
means and incentives and facilities for sin surrounding
you on all sides, and multiplying as you go along;
you shall find this as one of those continual facts and
features which go to make that road " the broad road,"

---

* See MACLAURIN's Sermon, "The Sins of Men not Chargeable on
God," and Principal CANDLISH's Sermon, "The Alleged Necessity of
Sinning" (' *Scripture Characters* '); the one the more profound and
exhaustive as a philosophical discussion; the other the more powerful
and encouraging as a personal expostulation and appeal.

even as the gate of it is the wide gate, whereat, alas! the many enter in.

The righteousness of this arrangement on God's part might be more clearly demonstrated were we to set forth the converse view of it, the corresponding fact, namely, that if your heart be fixed and thoroughly set in you to do the will of God, you will find just as readily, and just as abundantly, the means and incentives and facilities for doing good. This is hinted at partly in that lovely declaration, "The Lord meeteth him that rejoiceth and worketh righteousness." Providences—the God of providence Himself even, and oftentimes very obviously His providences—come forth in friendly forms and helpful action to aid the devoted and joyful "worker of righteousness." The Lord maketh straight His people's way before their face. Those very ways of the Lord in which "transgressors fall" are all "upright," and "the just shall walk in them" (Hosea xiv. 9). He will keep *them* from the evil that is in the world; and the very events which the wickedness of the wicked transform into helps to sin, the righteous shall find the Lord disposing into hindrances. Ah! how often the humble believer, in the morning seeking increase of grace and usefulness throughout the day, has seen the means and occasions of usefulness come round about him to his hand as the day wore through; and in noticing his Father's hand in so arranging them, with what heart of joy has he seized and improved them! Thus Abraham's godly servant, having gone to his master's kindred to take a wife unto Isaac, and having committed the matter to the Lord in prayer, with what lowly gratitude and adoration does he recognise and acknowledge the interposition of the Lord to aid and prosper him! In the path of his duty the facilities for success are found beautifully placed around him. "And the man bowed down his head, and worshipped the Lord. And he said, Blessed be the Lord God of my master Abraham, who hath not left destitute my master ·of his mercy and his truth : *I being in the way*, the Lord led me to the house of my master's brethren " (Gen. xxiv. 26, 27).

Thus twofold, or double-edged, is the providence of God—even as the Word of God also is;—as the gospel is, a savour of death unto death to some, of life unto life to others;—as the person of Christ also is, a foundation to them that believe, a stone of stumbling and rock of offence to the disobedient; even as aged Simeon prophesied, "Behold, this child is set for the *fall* ,and *rising again* of many in Israel; and for a sign that shall be spoken against; that the thoughts of many hearts may be revealed " (Luke ii. 34, 35).

Consider, then, your position in the world. You walk, while here, in the midst of means, temptations, facilities to evil, innumerable. A heart at enmity to God will certainly, in one form or another, close with and accept these inducements to sin. It is by these means that the god of this world blinds, snares, and rules the ungodly. In the opposition of their hearts to God's holy law and honourable rule, they are right-eously tried, judged, and punished, by being left to fall under the degrading rule and tyrannising sway of the god of this world, plying upon them, as he does in his malice, that singular state of things which God in His holiness has established for rebels to whom He is patient and whom He places under probation. Ah! there is no security save in returning, surrendering, and being reconciled to God. Owning our unreasonable rebellion, our most heartless alienation from our Father in heaven; confessing and abjuring our suspicions, prejudices, and perverse misunderstandings of His glorious nature and gracious desires to us-ward; accepting the sure peace which His Son's blood has made, and tasting the free and full reconciliation which His sacrifice has established; embracing also, by free and firm faith, the regenerating Spirit of adoption to dwell in us and keep our hearts in the love of God and righteousness; dwelling then in the secret of the Lord, and claiming, as His children and servants, the protection of the King amidst the dangers of an enemy's country, and the perils of our probationary state; we shall find that the Lord keeps us from temptation or opens up a way of escape, and, delivering us as our "shield" from evil, He will be our " glory " also, and " the lifter up of our head " (Ps. iii. 3). Then, even amidst many dangers, amidst facilities to evil-doing through which the wicked plunge onward in accelerating speed to ruin, we " shall walk at liberty, having respect to all God's commandments " (Ps. xix. 45).

III. This verse reads a solemn lesson as to the intense determination with which the evil heart of unbelief will, when scope is given to its reasonings, depart from the living God.

It is hardly possible to conceive of a firmer, a more dogged, determined, resolved purpose of transgression than is indicated in the words which describe the flight of Jonah. Step after step the disobedient prophet takes in consummation of his purpose—and each following fast on the back of its predecessor, without repentance and, as it would almost seem, without reflection. (1.) He "rose up to flee." (2.) He "went to Joppa." (3.) He "found a ship." (4.) He "paid the fare." (5.) He "went down into it." And all "to go with them unto Tarshish from the presence of the Lord." There is something awful and ominous in the very sound of the words. Read them continuously : " But Jonah rose up to flee unto Tarshish from the presence of the Lord: and went down to Joppa : and he found a ship; and he paid the fare thereof ; and he went down into it,—to go with them unto Tarshish from the presence of the Lord."

These words are like relentless, consecutive, fast-falling blows, under which his whole character as an obedient man of God is beaten to death and trampled under foot of Satan. If Jonah's past life of piety were likened to a field, and his character as a child of God were the harvest ripening on it, these successive clauses, telling the story of his wild rebelliousness, are, in our ears, as if the rasping swing of death's scythe time after time passed through with mighty sweep and levelled all that waving harvest with the ground—no good angel nigh to gather, but the storm looming down which is to scatter it to the four winds of heaven! Or, if Jonah's future destiny might be conceived to be told off upon "the great bell of the universe,"* these same remorse-less sentences, that utter forth his disobedience, are as if there fell fast and gloomily upon the ear stroke after stroke of the hammer of doom, pausing only with still more fearful omen when the criminal has gone down into the ship, the convict down into the hulk,—gone down into the cell of his condemnation!

Ah! beware of disobediences like these, stroke upon stroke. You may think you gain your end; but the Lord has you in His hand, and never more so than precisely when you think you have succeeded. You may resolve to disobey; you may rise up and flee; you may find your way to Joppa; you may find the ship ready there; you may find the mariners make no objection to your company, and are ready to receive the fare. You may crown all, and think the day is gained, when you go down into the ship. How successful has your scheme been! Not a single step in it has mis-given. The whole project thrives. Jonah is "gone down into the sides of the ship;" and after the weary conflict in his spirit, and the weary flight to Joppa, he is quiet at last, and "fast asleep." You think it is all right now, and your plan is safe and your project sure. The last move has been all that you could wish it to be.

Yes; but that last move is your move into the very prison in which God holds you now under lock and key, and will hold you, till He either cast you out for execution, or bring you to repentance.

* John Foster.

VI

THE STORM

JONAH i. 4

"But the Lord sent out a great wind into the sea, and there was a
mighty tempest in the sea, so that the ship was like to be broken."

"Stormy wind fulfilling his word."—
Ps. cxlviii. 8.

THE Lord now begins to deal with Jonah with the
view of bringing him to repentance and obedience.
He has permitted him to carry out his project of fleeing
from the shores of the sacred land. He has quietly left
him to succeed so far, that he thinks his plan is now
safely on foot. He has not interfered to baffle any one
of the successive steps he has had to take in putting his design into execution. Jonah has been
allowed thoroughly to show all his desire, and
thoroughly to prosecute all his design. And now,
when the utmost success he could have wished has
crowned his efforts, immediately the Lord interposes
to show their futility.

For the Lord can afford to wait. You may trespass

against Him, and pass on apparently unpunished, the Lord apparently uncognizant. But the path along which you pass has the punishment lining both sides of it, and looming dark at some surely fixed point farther on. In combination with your envious brothers you may succeed in quietly selling Joseph into the hands of Ishmaelites, and there may be no word of him and your offence against him for many days. But a day full surely comes, when, in combination with the same brothers, ranged in full number, rank and file, and face to face, you have to cry out, "We are verily guilty concerning our brother, in that we saw the anguish of his soul when he besought us, and we would not hear; therefore is this distress come upon us" (Gen. xlii. 21). God has many an agent whom He may commission in pursuit. He may therefore make no haste in putting any of them under commission; and you may have enormously the start of your pursuer. But the fire, or the tempest, or the water, or the pestilence, when once under the command of the Most High, calmly and surely hunt down the fugitive, and bring him resistlessly to the bar. There is no art that can elude or baffle the messengers of Him who is the Judge of the quick and the dead. There is no blinding them; there is no bribing them. There is no loophole of escape. "Be sure your sin will find you out." "With what measure you mete out to others, it *shall* be measured to you again." "They have sown the wind, and they shall reap the whirlwind." "Though they dig into hell, thence shall mine hand take them; though they climb up to heaven, thence will I take them down; though they hide themselves in the top of Carmel, I will search and take them out thence; and though they be hid from my sight in the bottom of the sea, thence will I command the serpent, and he shall bite them " (Amos ix. 2, 3).

Surely if there be "no divination against Israel," still less can there be against Israel's God. All things are naked and open unto the eyes of Him with whom we have to do; and all the powers and elements of nature are in His hand, to prosecute His controversies and to serve His purposes. Flight from Him is futile, useless, and in vain.

Oh, what praise is due to that blessed Mediator, through whom flight *to* God is possible, yea, blessed! Seek no hiding-place *from* God. Let God himself be your hiding-place. " Deliver me, O Lord, from mine enemies : I flee unto thee to cover me " (Ps. cxliii. 9). " For this shall every one that is godly pray unto thee in a time when thou mayest be found : surely in the floods of great waters they shall not come nigh unto him. Thou art my hiding-place; thou shalt preserve me from trouble; thou shalt compass me about with songs of deliverance " (Ps. xxxii. 6, 7). Ultimately Jonah also learnt to adopt this more excellent way; but not till he had been taught by the discipline of sore and stern experience.

Accordingly "the Lord sent out a great wind into the sea, and there was a mighty tempest in the sea, so that the ship was like to be broken." A " great wind ; " a " mighty tempest ; " and " the ship like to be broken,"

—as when the Lord sends forth " the east wind that breaketh the ships of Tarshish."

I. Now let us observe here that it is not said there *arose* a great wind; but, " The Lord sent out a great wind." The Lord's hand is recognised. The storm is attributed not to the elements of nature, but to the God of nature; to Him who is over all and " above all." He has established laws in nature; but they cannot administer themselves. The Lawgiver administers them. He has arranged a series of causes and elements, and placed them in various adaptations towards one another. But He supports, maintains, controls, and moves them at His own pleasure. " Praise ye Him, sun and moon : praise Him, all ye stars of light. Praise Him, ye heavens of heavens, and ye waters that be above the heavens. Let them praise the name of the Lord : for He commanded, and they were created. He hath also stablished them for ever and ever : He hath made a decree which shall not pass. Praise the Lord from the earth, ye dragons, and all deeps : fire and hail; snow and vapour ; stormy wind fulfilling his word " (Ps. cxlviii. 3–8). " They continue this day according to thine ordinances, for they all are thy servants " (Ps. cxix. 91). Such is the doctrine of Scripture concerning the elements and laws of nature. They are distinguished, indeed, by permanence of properties and constáncy of operation. Their regularity is unbroken, save when miracle has occasionally intervened. Their movements are calculable, or at least fit subject for calculation. The movements of the planets

have actually been calculated by human wisdom; and
the motions of every mote of dust and drop of water
are capable of being as accurately predicted, were man's
powers of calculation as great as we can conceive them
to be. But while perfect regularity pervades all nature,
and thus man can reckon on a steady order of progres-
sion, in respect of "day and night, summer and winter,
seed-time and harvest," surely this is not to exclude
the superior and supreme action of a living and personal God superintending and directing all. The order
and regularity with which events fall out, surely does
not go to invalidate the truth, that it is by Divine super-
intendence, appointment, and control that they do so.
It only shows in addition that the Being who arranges
and guides all, is a God not of confusion but of order.
That very regularity which scoffers found upon as a
proof that the laws of nature may account for all without introducing the idea of a Supreme Ruler, will be regarded by right reason, as well as by spiritual faith, as
not only proving that there is an almighty personal
Governor sitting above all, and guiding all continually,
but that He is characterised by no fitful, arbitrary,
capricious changeableness; that He is a " God of order,"
" the Father of lights, with whom is no variableness,
neither shadow of turning."

The Scriptures, in speaking of natural events, are remarkable for the unfaltering and continual ascription of
them to God. " There *arose* a great wind," the vast
majority of men would say. Holy Scripture uses this
style; " The Lord sent out a great wind into the sea."

Hence, according to the same style, those who go down into the sea are said not merely to see great works and wonders, but the works and wonders of the Lord; as in that magnificent—that unrivalled description of a storm —" They that go down to the sea in ships, that do business in great waters; these see the works *of the Lord*, and *his* wonders in the deep. For *he commandeth, and raiseth* the stormy wind, which lifteth up the waves thereof. They mount up to the heaven; they go down again to the depths : their soul is melted because of trouble. They reel to and fro, and stagger like a drunken man, and are at their wit's end. Then they *cry unto the Lord* in their trouble, and he bringeth them out of their distresses. He maketh the storm a calm, so that the waves thereof are still. Then are they glad because they be quiet; so he bringeth them unto their desired haven. Oh that men would praise the Lord for his goodness, and for his wonderful works to the children of men!" (Ps. cvii. 23–31.)

Throughout that splendid ode, the hand of the Lord in sending forth and recalling the winds, and conducting the whole terrific drama of the storm from first to last, is sedulously and sustainedly acknowledged.

This is a peculiarity distinguishing the Scriptures. In them, justice is ever done to the Supreme Being; and, in a measure, by all those, and by none else than those, who have drunk into the spirit of the Scriptures. Believers must be conscious of this, as forming part of the great change which they have undergone in being turned from darkness to light. Formerly they had no

pleasure in retaining God in their remembrance; they
had no disposition to observe His hand and work in
creation and providence. They took no delight in
generously doing Him the justice of attributing the
stores of plenty wherewith the world is replenished to
His bounteous liberality; nor in reverentially owning
His voice in the tempest and the thunder, or His hand
in the bolts of lightning, or the stormy wind fulfilling
His command. Their thoughts of God, indeed, may at
one time have been little better than as of some ab-
stract, impersonal, infinite terror, hanging like a pall
of death on their spirits. A living God, capable of
entering into fellowship with them, and striving to
bring them into fellowship with Him, may not have
been in all their thoughts. But when they underwent
a change that may be described by saying that the
principles of their nature were brought into harmony
with the principles of Scripture, so that the language
of Scripture became the language of their heart,—in
other words, the language and mind of God's Spirit
became the language and mind of their spirit also;—
then, just as Scripture witnesses unfalteringly for the
supremacy and sovereignty of God—of our God, who is
in the heavens, and doeth whatsoever pleaseth Him;
yea, doeth all things, and doeth all things well—so
also did their thoughts and tendencies turn towards
the acknowledgment of their God, the living and the
true, the One and the only God; and nature became
to them an open volume, in which they have ever since
been reading "the invisible things of God, even His

eternal power and Godhead," understanding and seeing them in the mirror of "the things that He hath made," and the events which He causeth to fall out.

There are few surer signs of a change of heart and feelings towards God than a strong disposition to trace with delight the working of His hand and the evidence of His presence in the works of creation and providence. The renewed soul longs after God—the living God: "When shall I come and appear before God?" It hath a feeling many times as if it would "break" (Ps. cxix. 20) in its yearning to get near unto God. There is at such times a deep feeling almost of impatience at the present necessity of walking by faith—of having to be content with fellowship conducted only by faith. But in this trying life of faith it is delightful to read in the heavens, stretched out with their glittering hosts of mighty mansions; or in the urgent ascending journey of the morning sun, scattering with his glory the shades of darkness; or in the mighty roll of the billows, when they rise to assert their utmost majesty, as if each in turn were king of the ocean realm; or in the voice of thunder, that breaketh the cedars of Lebanon; or in the lightning flash, seeming to create out of darkness, and bury with utmost speed again, the scenery on which, from heaven above, it glanceth forth its rapid glory :—in all these it is delightful to a child of God to read the working and the hand of the Father who hath promised to bless and to protect him. And though nature's estate carries in it, in the meantime, many a ground of sorrow, and many a remembrancer of

sin,—as when the low monitory wail of tempest prophe-
sies the storm that shall put many a life in jeopardy ; and
the sullen underswell and moan of the waves, outliving
that storm, is too often but the requiem of victims that
failed in their weakness to outride it,—it is a relief to the
believing heart to know that these sore evidences of de-
rangement and misrule shall not always last ; and that
even already they are the "groanings" of creation,
"travailing" in pain to be emancipated from the bondage of corruption, "waiting for the manifestation of
the sons of God," and longing to be delivered, as at
last creation shall, "into the glorious liberty of the children of God" (Rom. viii. 19–22). At such times the
believer learns to glory in this hope ;—"Nevertheless
we, according to His promise, look for new heavens and a
new earth, wherein dwelleth righteousness." Nor is he
backward to remember the solemn admonition ;—"Seeing then that all these present things shall be dissolved,
what manner of persons ought ye to be in all manner
of holy conversation and godliness?" (2 Pet. iii.
11, 13).

II. Another very interesting and important point is
raised in reading this verse. We see God's controversy with one individual involving many others in
danger. The storm is sent forth to pursue, arrest, and
punish Jonah, but it implicates in his punishment
multitudes, doubtless—multitudes who had neither
share nor knowledge of his guilt. Certainly it
implicates all that sail with him ; and many other

vessels, in all probability, were exposed to the same tempest.

Now, God can easily vindicate His righteousness in involving many in the chastisement of Jonah; but Jonah cannot escape the responsibility and guilt of having been the occasion of injury to others.

1. The righteousness of God is easily vindicated. No doubt the storm was primarily designed to prosecute His quarrel with Jonah. It was appointed for *him,*—for him so specially and expressly, as that, *save* for him, we have no reason to believe it would have been sent out at all. And as a pursuer to arrest the flight of a disobedient subject, the commission given to it is manifestly and wholly righteous. With regard to the other sufferers from the storm, let us bear in remembrance God's great long-suffering and forbearance. Let us not forget that ' every sin deserveth God's wrath and curse, both in this life and in that which is to come.' If this solemn statement be true, everything less, in the case of unconverted sinners, than the execution of the sentence on the barren fig-tree, " Cut it down; why cumbereth it the ground?"—instead of being difficult to reconcile with Divine justice, must rather be attributed to the Divine forbearance. And hence, though not conspirators with Jonah in his particular sin, these mariners, with the multitude of their own sins, and with these very idolatries of theirs which they insult the living God with on this occasion itself (Jonah i. 5)— were sufficiently obnoxious to be overtaken and involved in this tempest, as well as the guilty prophet.

No doubt the one leading aim—the immediate Divine design—of this particular storm was to arrest and chastise a particular offender. But all were offenders. And while pursuing one special end, God might combine with it various subsidiary purposes, and in connexion with His leading one, He might gain them also. The iniquities of the sailors were not unduly punished by this affliction coming upon them, though, so far as appears, it would not have come upon them save for Jonah. Great and marvellous is the scheme of God's moral government. Ten thousand purposes is the Lord daily prosecuting by the measures of His providence. One purpose, for the time, may rise into a position of prominence and importance that seems to us to cast all others into the shade. Yet while that one alone, from its palpable and forcible prominence in our view, may concentrate and engross all our attention, it neither engrosses the Divine attention, nor deranges the Divine designs. The subsidiary and subordinate ends are advancing under the Divine control with a regularity never interfered with, and with a wisdom past searching out. The Lord's controversies on this occasion with these mariners may have been very indistinctly pointed out, and are very partially explained to us, compared with the flood of light that is thrown on His controversy with Jonah. Yet while His punishment of Jonah has all this light thrown upon its perfect equity and righteousness, equally righteous is God's dealing with the rest, though its righteousness is not equally, or rather so broadly, exhibited.

2. But this consideration, while it vindicates the justice of God, affords no relief for the compunctions of Jonah. Jonah cannot vindicate himself from the charge of being the guilty means of involving others in the Divine displeasure, and bringing down upon them a most afflictive dispensation. For while God—continually meting out to sinners, while they are on earth, more or less largely from a free fund of patience, which, though ever righteously administered, is at the disposal of His mere mercy and forbearance—can easily justify Himself, if at any time He diminish the measure which He deals forth from that fund, always finding sufficient reason in the offences against Himself which He thus calls into reckoning; yet Jonah, when he stands in between these mariners and the amount of Divine patience which, save for him, they would have enjoyed, can never justify himself herein, inasmuch he cannot plead their offences against him as God can,—for they had never injured Jonah,—and even though they had, *he* is not to be acknowledged as the judge by whom providential dispensations and punishments are to be meted out to them. He, therefore, remains as blameworthy as if the righteousness of these men's sufferings could not be vindicated at all. They, indeed, have no right to lay the blame on him, as if they were innocent. But Jonah himself must take all the blame because he is guilty. They are not innocent; God in thus dealing with them is righteous. God is righteous in visiting upon them transgressions of their own, and in punishing them in this particular way, namely, by sending among them a

man whose very presence and company involve a storm, and exposure to death by means of it. But Jonah is not innocent of the distress entailed on the mariners, because he carries about with him a disobedience which God is righteously avenging upon him in a way that must inevitably involve multitudes besides himself.

Thus may a calamity fall righteously upon a whole family for the sake of one guilty member; and in the grief of none of them is God unrighteous, while yet, in a sense, the whole guilt lies on one. The father of a household may so offend the Lord, as that the adequate punishment of his provocation shall not alight solely on his person, but may involve all his house. "Is God unrighteous" in chastising them? "God forbid: for how then should God judge the world?" But does this exempt the guilty man from the blame, the compunction, the remorse, springing from his being the responsible agent in bringing down on those around him the complicated distress in which he and they alike are sharers? Assuredly not. And when the king of Israel disobeyed the Lord and numbered the people, and was punished by a pestilence on his land which slew threescore and ten thousand—innocent in this particular crime—it was not as one arraigning the justice of God, but in the bitterest and most mournful compunction for having been himself the guilty cause of suffering and death to others, that he exclaimed, "Lo, I have sinned, and I have done wickedly; but these sheep, what have they done? let thine hand, I pray thee, be against me, and against my father's house" (2 Sam. xxiv. 17).

There is a very solemn lesson in this.

In our different families, we may without taking heed to it, be the guilty instruments of deeply injuring those we are bound, and may be anxious, to benefit. For, our individual provocations may be provoking the Lord to limit the temporal prosperity, and still more the spiritual blessing, which otherwise He might bestow upon them. His righteousness in so dealing with them He can easily demonstrate. But our guilt in leading Him so to deal with them He can demonstrate as easily. He can prove that He is just. But how can we avoid the blame of temporally and spiritually injuring those to whom we ought rather to be the instruments and channels of good? The benefit of God's vindication of His own procedure can never be arrogated by us—can never pass over to us for our vindication. He vindicates Himself on grounds which cannot be pleaded ·by us, for they do not pertain to us. He vindicates Himself on the ground, that the pains and penalties from His hand, brought through us on others, are the righteous punishment of their own offences against Him, or are the beneficial chastisements through means of which He designs ultimately to crown them with benefits which in no other way could He have conferred, or in no other way so well. We, on the other hand, have had no righteous quarrel to prosecute, and have been seeking to confer no ultimate good. With us lies the naked evil—the unalleviated guilt; and if there be aught of generous feeling remaining, it will, when we awake to face the facts, sting us to the quick with deep compunction and remorse. Let it not

be forgotten that in this way a single individual may be
a source of calamity to multitudes; and that this may
result the more surely and extensively as that individual
is more closely connected with the cause and kingdom of
the Lord. Because of a single private member of a
congregation, God, in visiting his provocations with the
punishment deserved, chastising his sensuality, or pride,
or covetousness, or passion, may involve in much spiritual
leanness and unprofitableness all his fellow-worshippers.
For one single Achan, altogether unnoticeable and insig-
nificant, save for his sin, the whole camp of Israel may
be troubled; and victory may never return and tarry on
their standards, till "judgment return unto righteousness,
and all the upright follow after it." But how much
more if the guilty individual be no private and unnoticeable Achan, but a prophet such as Jonah! In that case,
may not the "wind sent out into the sea" be expected
to be "a great wind,"—"a mighty tempest in the sea,
so that the ship is like to be broken"?

If, therefore, the question be raised by members of
families, Why is there not more of God's blessing on
our households? or by members of congregations, Why
is there not more spiritual life in our assemblies?—
surely it is for each individual to examine himself, and
prayerfully to inquire, "Lord, is it I?" The same
truth and generosity of spirit which would revolt
from inflicting injury upon another, and which would
say with the greatly agitated king,—"Lo, *I* have
sinned, and *I* have done wickedly; but these sheep,
what have *they* done? let thy hand, I pray thee, be

against me, and against my father's house,"—will be
incapable of resting under the mere possibility of standing in the way of good, or proving a channel of evil, to
another. The bare possibility will give pain: the bare
possibility will suggest inquiry; "Lord, is it I?" And
when the risk, the danger, the possibility of being an
actual source of disadvantage, whether temporal or
spiritual, does not tenderly touch the soul with sorrow
and induce examination, there is reason to fear that the
clearest demonstration of this being not only a possibility, but the actual fact, would be met with a heart-
lessness which neither Achan nor Jonah exhibited, and
which would go far to destroy the sympathy and pity
with which, in the one case, we listen to Joshua advising
the culprit to " give glory to the Lord God of Israel,
and make confession unto Him " (Joshua vii. 19) ; and
with which, in the other case, we look on while they
" take up Jonah and cast him forth into the sea, and
the sea ceases from her raging " (Jonah i. 15).

To be instruments of good or evil to each other is
what, in the present state of God's government over
us, we cannot possibly avoid. " None of us liveth to
himself, and no man dieth to himself" (Rom. xiv. 7).
Society is constituted by Divine ordination into a body
politic; and the Church, by eternal covenant, and by
every fundamental principle of its nature and estate, is
a body spiritual. It is one body. No member can
isolate himself. If he could, he would thereby destroy
himself. " But God hath tempered the body together,
so that there should be no schism in the body; but

that the members should have the same care one of another. And whether one member suffer, all the members suffer with it; or one member be honoured, all the
members rejoice with it. Now ye are the body of
Christ, and members in particular. But God hath set
some in the Church—first, apostles; secondarily, prophets; thirdly, teachers; after that, miracles; then
gifts of healing, helps, governments, diversities of
tongues. Are all apostles? are all prophets? are all
teachers? are all workers of miracles? Have all the
gifts of healing? do all speak with tongues? do all in-
terpret? But covet earnestly the best gifts. For
though I speak with the tongues of men and angels,
and have not charity, I am become as sounding brass
and a tinkling cymbal. And though I have the gift
of prophecy, and understand all mysteries, and all
knowledge; and though I have all faith, so that I
could remove mountains, and have not charity, I am
nothing. And though I bestow all my goods to feed
the poor, and though I give my body to be burned,
and have not charity, it profiteth me nothing. Charity
suffereth long, and is kind; charity envieth not; charity
vaunteth not itself, is not puffed up, doth not behave
itself unseemly, seeketh not her own, is not easily provoked, thinketh no evil; rejoiceth not in iniquity, but
rejoiceth in the truth; beareth all things, believeth all
things, hopeth all things, endureth all things. Charity
never faileth " (1 Cor. xii. 24-31, xiii. 1-8).

VII

THE PRAYER OF TERROR, AND THE SLEEP OF SORROW, IN THE STORM

JONAH i. 5

" Then the mariners were afraid, and cried every man unto his god, and cast forth the wares that were in the ship into the sea, to lighten it of them: but Jonah was gone down into the sides of the ship; and he lay, and was fast asleep."

> "*Lord, in trouble have they visited thee ; they poured out a prayer when thy chastening was upon them.*"—ISAIAH xxvi. 16.
> "*And when He was come to His disciples, He found them sleeping for sorrow.*"—LUKE xxii. 45.

IN last chapter we were engaged in considering the prophet, not only as overtaken with punishment himself, but as a source of calamity to others. We saw in this that God was righteous, and Jonah guilty ; —that God was righteous, not merely in pursuing Jonah, but in involving others in the calamity which was sent forth immediately for Jonah's punishment, while Jonah was guilty in entailing distress upon those who sailed with him. Let us watch against carrying about with us a cloud of God's anger, that may break upon ourselves and all round about us. The Lord our God in such a case can easily clear Himself, but He will not hold us guiltless. If the man is reprobated who, knowingly bearing in his body a most virulent and infectious disease, ultroneously mingles with society on all hands, and extends the plague to multitudes, why is it that in moral and spiritual things the same sharp and righteous judgment is not pronounced? "One sinner destroyeth much good" (Eccles. ix. 18). But one backsliding saint may destroy even more good, and originate even more evil. For, on the one hand, God pursues with much sharpness and severity His erring people. He can let His enemies alone; but He must, in very love, chastise and correct His sons,—even at the risk of judgment that may swiftly involve many around them, and it may be, terminate to many their day of grace and probation. He must chastise His children: "You only have I known of all the families of the earth: therefore will I punish you for all your iniquities" (Amos iii. 2). A sinner, therefore, in your home or household, may not so swiftly nor sorely be dealt with as a backsliding and rebellious son. And on the other hand, as God's righteous chastenings in this case are more immediate and severe, so also are Satan's malignity and malice: for, an unconverted sinner he has always in his power, and when he will he can blind him and soothe him into deeper insensibility than ever. But when he has advantage over a saint ensnared in sin, he knoweth that "his time is short," his opportunity precarious, and his work by no means easy; therefore is he strung to the utmost pitch of subtlety and power, "having great wrath," and drawing forth on such a case his uttermost resources. Hence, whether from Satan's devouring malice, or God's correcting chastisements, a saint in rebellion is, in some respects, a more dangerous inmate of a house, or congregation, or community, than a sinner—more likely to prove a centre of danger, a source of calamity to many.

What a thought is this! How impressively ought it to tell upon the hearts of believers! And with what watchfulness and jealousy ought it to inspire them! For, what can be more painful than to see the godly, through indwelling sin and indulged corruption, acting on the surrounding world, not as the lights thereof, not as the preserving salt thereof, the centres and sources of providential blessings and prolonged forbearance, prevailing to ameliorate the condition, and prolong the probation, and delay the condemnation of the ungodly,—but as swift provocatives to wrath; no more binding up the hands of God from " His strange work " of indignation, but loosening the avalanche of judgment, and entailing on many a swift destruction? Oh, how unutterably more desirable the position of Paul in the selfsame seas, and overtaken by the same " strong wind which breaketh the ships of Tarshish "! How different with Paul, in the prosecution of *his* ministry, from Jonah in fleeing from his!—not entailing danger, but deliverance: " And now I exhort you to be of good cheer: for there shall be no loss of any man's life among you, but

of the ship; for there stood by me this night the angel
of God, whose I am, and *whom I serve*, saying, Fear
not, Paul; thou must be brought before Cæsar: and lo,
God *hath given thee all them that sail with thee*" (Acts
xxvii. 22-24).

Believer! are you, in this respect, as Jonah; or as
Paul? Are you, to others, a source of deliverance, or a
source of danger? Is your company and neighbourhood
dangerous, because you are provoking the forth-flash of
the bolt of anger? Or is it truly to be desired?—
according to what, while you are faithful to God, shall
evermore be God's faithfully fulfilled promise to you,
"I will bless thee, and *make thee a blessing*."

Let us proceed with the narrative. In the verse
now before us, the fifth verse, the immediate conduct of
the mariners is described—and the immediate conduct
of Jonah,—under the storm.

I. The effect of the storm on the mariners.

They "were afraid, and cried every man unto his
god, and cast forth the wares that were in the ship into
the sea, to lighten it of them."

1. We read first, that "the mariners were afraid."
From this we learn that the storm was singularly violent
and the danger imminently great. Sailors are not speedily
alarmed. They are proverbially brave and bold. But
when even the crew themselves on this occasion were
alarmed, we gather that the tempest was unusually
terrific. God, indeed, employed no miracle in raising

this storm ; but having a special purpose to serve by it, He stamped upon it a special terror, that His power and will might be the more readily recognised as engaged in it.   When we provoke a controversy with God, and constrain Him to send after us a prosecutor or pursuer, He can easily confer on His agent some mark of majesty or terror,—some insignia of special power,—some resist-less tone or token, whereby we may be baffled in attempting to hide from ourselves the source of his commission.   The Lord, the great Judge and Lawgiver, can clothe His officers with somewhat of His own dele-gated attributes, and compel us to recognise them as sent by *Him*.

2. The mariners "cried every man unto his god." Their heathenism here displayed itself in their worship of many gods, every man praying to his own god : while the amount of religion natural to the human mind comes to light in these poor heathen men.   For there is in the bosom of every man by nature the conviction that there is a God ; that there are at least superior beings, if not One Supreme.   There is wrought into the inmost frame of our minds a conviction that we are dependent creatures ; not our own masters, not gods unto ourselves.   The consciousness of sin—and sin is just an attempt to be gods unto ourselves—is itself sufficient to testify to us of a God.   Were our effort to be independent a calm, simple, strengthening thing, the proof might fail.   But no man can consider his own feelings without being con-vinced that the attempt to be his own lord and master, to do just as he pleases, to be in subjection to no lord

over his inmost will, to walk in the light of his own
eyes—the attempt, in short, to be his own ruler, or his
own god, is really a revolt against the deepest convictions
in his soul; that it carries with it anything but rest, calmness, strength, and satisfaction; that, on the contrary,
it has in it all the marks of a struggle, of an unsuccessful
struggle; that he remains still restless, unsatisfied,
struggling—struggling still in vain.   The stronger his
will is, the more is he doomed to feel that he cannot
assert its supremacy; and circumstances outwardly
conspire to aid the inward conviction.   There is a
power controlling all things, and not to be controlled
by us.   The will of man *must* break or bend; it cannot
possibly reign supreme.   The very restlessness—the
very impatience of restraint or contradiction—which
men so often exhibit against the allotments of providence, is a confession that they feel themselves in the
grasp of a power mightier than their own.   Whether
we bend in submission, meek and patient, or resist and
defy, we are alike owning a superior power.   We are
constituted so as that we cannot help doing so.   A
knowledge, a feeling, an intuitive belief in a God, is one
of the deepest principles created in our nature, and never
extinguished.

Nor is it merely a superior power that we are by
nature so profoundly convinced of, but a living and
personal Being; and this profound conviction manifests
itself in calling upon Him, as one who can exercise
His power voluntarily, or refrain from exercising it.
This knowledge of a God may be unattended to by

multitudes, whether of heathens or of nominal Christians. For the most part, it lies buried under worldly security. Sensual indulgence seems to drive it farther and farther back into a region of concealment and slumber. The prosecution of worldly interests as the chief good tends more and more to impair its testimony. But it is never dislodged. Men may "not like to retain God in their knowledge;" but the knowledge of a God abides within them still. Seasons of danger and terror call it forth to view; and the sudden prayer of alarm is the proof that even the most profane and profligate carry in their bosom the evidence of their righteous condemnation; when, not liking to retain God in their knowledge, they are "given over to a reprobate mind" for being unfaithful to the knowledge conferred upon them from the first (Rom. i. 28).

We learn, then, from the conduct of these heathens, how deeply rooted in human nature is the conviction of a God. But we learn also the great worthlessness of prayers wrung out under terror. There is inlaid in human nature a central assurance or conviction of a God. In the case of the ungodly it is allowed, for the most part, to lie utterly dormant and concealed. If imminent and appalling danger force out some alarmed manifestation of it in some excited cry to God for mercy or protection, there is really as little evidence of grace or virtue in such a prayer, as when the war-horse, in the instinct of self-preservation, rears in terror as the gleaming sword flashes round his head. The prayer that is acceptable to God is the prayer of faith, of calm confidence and reliance on the word and love and wisdom and power of a gracious and a reconciled Father. Very different from this is the prayer extorted amidst the terrors of a storm from those with whom otherwise prayer is unknown. Such prayers have in them as little holiness or grace as the crash of the elements amidst which they mingle, on the instincts of animal life. They are prayers which a heathen may offer up— which these heathen mariners on this occasion offered. Alas! how much trust is often placed—and how groundlessly—on prayers presented where the terrors of providence, acting on the mere instincts of nature, have forced out something like the appearance of religion! It is said of the children of Israel that, when the Lord "slew them, then they sought Him; they returned and inquired early after God. And they remembered that God was their rock, and the high God their Redeemer." Under the constraint of afflictive dispensations and retributive judgments, they could not avoid calling God to their remembrance; and with much appearance of sorrow for their offence, and promise of better things, they seemed to return to their allegiance to the Lord, the King of Israel. They remembered their obligations to Him as their Redeemer and Deliverer—their high tower and their rock. Better feelings seemed for the time to gain the ascendancy; and, judged of by their conduct under these punishments and trials, they would seem to have been turned from the error of their ways to the living and the true God. But it is added by the Spirit, through whom holy men wrote as they were moved to put on record the melancholy narrative : "Nevertheless, they did flatter Him with their mouth, and they lied unto Him with their tongues. For their heart was not right with Him, neither were they steadfast in His covenant" (Ps. lxxviii. 34-37). And what are the enormous majority of prayers extorted by the smart blow of affliction, or the sudden apparition of danger or of death? What are they but a "flattering" of God, and a telling of "lies" unto Him? In the near view of eternal woe, the sinner may make promises of any kind or to any amount; and no wonder though he should. To escape immediate and eternal ruin, no wonder though the most abject, submissive, servile resolutions should be formed. The alarmed wretch cringes at the feet of Omnipotence, and promises whatever conscience may demand or superstition may suggest, careless utterly for the time whether he have the power or prospect of fulfilling his promises or not. But does such a style of religion or religious exercise honour God? Or is it honourable to man? The God who is so addressed is not honoured as a holy, righteous, good and gracious Father; He is flattered, fawned upon as a tyrant, and cozened as a fool; while the worshipper himself, clutching at false arguments and coining false promises, if by any means he may avoid destruction, is clothing himself more abundantly with disgrace, and sinking his moral nature into deeper degradation. By such worship God is robbed of His glory, and man of his manhood. Oh! there is no "glory to God," no "peace on earth," except through the great Advocate and Intercessor, and through the prayer of faith presented in His name. Through Him, and His infinitely perfect sacrifice, how manifestly does our God appear to us, as no terrific tyrant under whom we must cringe in abject servility; as no flexible fool whom we may flatter into a change of purpose to suit our convenience, or secure our impunity in sin. No: He is the God of infinite Love, giving up His Son to die for sinners. He is the God of infinite, inflexible Justice, subjecting His Son to death for sinners. It is an unspeakably righteous thing to pray to Him. It is to be in calm, deliberate, perfect resting in His right-eousness and love in Jesus:—no fit of momentary fervour: no sentimental flash of feeling, drawn forth as by the loveliness and beauty of the heavens above; and no instinctive spasm of soul created as by the terror of the scene when all is changed, and storm and death seem to fly around:—but the passing over unto God, on the terms of an infinitely righteous and gracious covenant, of the whole inner man, to take up its rest in God, as a Father and a Friend—the Lord and King of the con-science, the Governor of heart and life. Ah! there is often an impetuous blasphemy in the prayers of the ungodly, when sudden danger or death first forces them to pray. Nothing then of the spirit of godliness, adoring the majesty of the Most High;—nothing of tender, mourn-ful sorrow for sin, owning the righteousness of every punishment however great, of every threatened blow however terrible;—nothing of the meek submission that says, or essays to say, "Not my will, but Thine be done;"—nothing of the filial, unbounded trust which believes that in any case all shall be well, and says, "Though my house be not so with God, yet hath He made with me an everlasting covenant, ordered in all things and sure." Oh, if these are some of the elements of true prayer, how offensive unto God must be many of those howlings amidst danger, when the wild cry of terror dictates impetuously to God what He shall do! And in how many cases does the danger serve only to bring to light that original and instinctive knowledge of God which the wicked so wickedly suppress till by such means it is forced into the light, and its existence discovered only to become the means of discovering also the righteous ground of their final condemnation! How solemnly do such considerations teach us, that the time of health and quiet is the time for prayer; and that if we leave prayer to the time of danger or the approach of death, there may be wrung from us, in that case, some instinctive cry to God, that may serve merely the purposes of condemnation, and be only our own sealing of our own death-warrant for ever! "Behold, now is the accepted time: behold, now is the day of salvation."

It is not meant to say that every believer, at the approach of appalling danger, will be able to pray with holy calmness, with undismayed and holy courage. He may, on the contrary, be overwhelmed by the thought of having speedily to appear before God in judgment. And every believer must know how insufficient he is in himself for maintaining the honour of God, and the honour of his own profession, in such a crisis. But it will be his earnest prayer that, in such circumstances and scenes, in which the raging selfishness and evil conscience of the ungodly are often so frightfully displayed, he may receive grace to manifest the superiority of the Christian's character—to maintain the calmness of the Christian's hope. It cannot be that, in such a case, holy trust can rise superior to terror without a conflict, a good fight of faith—the calm courage and believing confidence of the spirit surmounting and suppressing the unbelieving terror and distracted cowardice of the flesh. Every manifestation of Christian character is indeed a triumph; a triumph over precisely the very principles which rule supreme in the sinner. And hence, amidst scenes of sudden terror, a man's Christianity may not be denied, though he cannot at once and immediately confront danger with a hero's calmness. Nevertheless, Christianity inspires a calmness and a courage in the hour of danger, which nothing else can inspire. And every Christian ought to pray, that in the hour of danger his Christianity may triumph. We do not know through what scenes of unspeakable danger or distress it may yet be our lot to pass. We may have to witness—we may have to share—the overwhelming dangers of the tempest and the shipwreck. We may have to pass through that most searching of all ordeals, discovering, perhaps more intensely and correctly than almost any other, whether the conscience is still guilty, or the heart established in grace. It is for each of us to inquire whether there be a well-founded probability of our passing through such a scene, with anything like true peace to ourselves, and credit to the profession which as Christians we make. Soon may some such trial overtake us. With what lowly humility does it become us to think of it—to seek the grace that is sufficient!

3. But we read further concerning these mariners, that "they cast forth the wares that were in the ship into the sea, to lighten it of them." Yes: "skin for skin; all that a man hath will he give for his life."

Thus the infinite littleness and triflingness of all earthly possessions is revealed. In such an hour, the heir of a hundred estates is on a level with the humblest peasant: the richest and the poorest meet together: the riches of the one must be tossed overboard: for the life of either is more—infinitely more than them all.

Why is not this habitually remembered? Why should it need storms, and tempest, and shipwreck, and threatened death, to remind reasonable beings that their souls are infinitely more precious than all earthly things? Why should men not notice this and act upon it, until God compels them, as in this case, to see it? He forces, in such circumstances,—He *forces* a sight of the uselessness of all worldly good. "Thou fool," that lovest these things more than God, more than thy soul; if "this night thy soul shall be required of thee," "whose shall these things be?" Were it not better to prefer thy life to them now, and sit loose to them ever henceforth? "The life is more than meat, and the body more than raiment." "Wherefore spend ye your money for that which is not bread, and your labour for that which profiteth not "—which must be thrown overboard —which must be parted with at last? Oh, rather "eat ye that which is good, and let your soul delight itself in fatness." Feed it not on husks. Prefer not perishing idols.

What will they do for thee in a dying hour? The cry to the physicians has been heard from the dying lips of the rich, 'All my fortune for another day of life.' And, 'We could not prolong your life for another hour, though you gave us the wealth of worlds,' was the answer. Blessed they who have the pearl of great price! "Though I walk through the valley of the shadow of death, I will fear no evil, for Thou art with me."

II. But having considered the manner in which the mariners were affected by the mighty tempest which the Lord sent out: let us inquire after the unhappy prophet who was the guilty occasion of this alarming calamity. While terror reigned on the decks, and the very mariners themselves were unmanned, strange to say, he formed a singular exception. "Jonah was gone down into the sides of the ship, and he lay, and was fast asleep."

It has been customary with commentators to deal out very hard measure to Jonah; and it is an easy task. Nothing can be easier than to denounce his disobedience in fleeing from the presence of the Lord, and refusing His commission to Nineveh. And this has been done abundantly by many who have shown little real knowledge of Jonah's actual position, and still less insight into his character. And in particular, he has been much abused for being asleep during the storm ; and his sleep has been spoken of as if it were the very acme or model of insensate spiritual stupidity and godless security and apathy. Alas! how little do such persons understand this singular man of God! We venture to say that had Jonah been distinguished for less sensibility, he would have been more likely to be awake than asleep. It was not insensate, secure, and slumberous apathy that lulled the prophet into this singular, and so curiously timed, and so very deep sleep. It was not because the things of God, and the will of God, and his relation to God, were topics of negligent or slight consideration with Jonah—but precisely the reverse.

Ah, how deeply agitated has this poor prophet—this frightened fugitive—been! Has it been costing him little care, think you, that he is on the footing of a disobedient servant, a self-banished son, with God? Have his thoughts been few, and slow, and calm, and easily arranged, and fully mastered? And has he been quite quiet in mind, and altogether self-possessed? Oh, very far from it. A thousand anxieties cut and harass his weary heart. The sore sense of all being wrong between him and his God ;—the sad consciousness of being the victim of his own rebellion, and yet choosing to continue in it, a voluntary slave, disobedient knowingly ;—the resignation of his ministry, a ministry so honourable, though difficult ;—the loss of his native land, and such a land, Emmanuel's land!—the dark future wrapt in gloom, having nothing to promise, and

everything to threaten ;—the countless fears and fightings
with which, "in the multitude of his thoughts within
him," he must have been exercised, while in the multitude of these thoughts no "comforts of the Lord delighted" or relieved "his soul : "—these things must
have cost him an amount of anxiety and of mental excitement, that, working on a temperament like Jonah's,
naturally nervous, and sensitive to the very excess of irri-
tation, must have worn him out both in body and in mind,
till at last, as he ended his weary flight, and laid down
his weary head in the hold of the ship, excited and now
exhausted nature locked him fast in sleep. *Discrimination* is needed in judging of Scripture characters. And
discrimination is needed—and charity—in judging one
another among ourselves. *Sorrow*, not insensibility,
shall account to a gracious Lord for His disciples sleeping at Gethsemane's gate. " He found them sleeping *for
sorrow* " (Luke xxii. 45). May He not graciously accept
the same explanation of Jonah's deep sleep, while tempest and terror reigned around?

But while a more charitable account may thus be
given of the prophet's deep sleep, it does not hinder
that we should see in it the deplorable effects of being
overtaken in a state of disobedience to God. Jonah
sleeping in the storm reminds us that the officers of
God's justice may be on the track of the fugitive, and
hemming him in on every side; and he ignorant that
they are let loose against him. *He*, in fact, may be
the very last to suspect that they are already in pursuit.
O sinner! the bolt may be almost on the wing that is

to pierce your heart. The tempest may be at its very height which is to ingulf you. The pestilence may be gathering up its chiefest virulence to discharge into your body, and reduce it to a putrid mass of corruption: and in your prayerless and ungodly estate, you may be locked in deep sleep of spirit. How can you tell, but substantially this may be your very case now, if you have never yet entered into peace and fellowship with God? To be verging into the imbecility of second childhood, or to be nearing the grave, without knowing it, is a melancholy picture. "Strangers have devoured his strength, and he knoweth it not; yea, gray hairs are here and there upon him, yet he knoweth it not." But, for God to be gathering around you the fuel and flame by which to burn down your self-complacency and your refuges of lies, and to be setting fire to them, and still you not knowing it,—this is indeed alarming. Such a thing is, however, but too possible in the case of those who are still neglecting the question of their peace with God. "Who gave Jacob for a spoil, and Israel to the robbers? did not the Lord, he against whom we have sinned? for they would not walk in his ways, neither were they obedient unto his law. Therefore he hath poured upon him the fury of his anger, and the strength of battle: and it hath set him on fire round about, yet he knew not; and it burned him, yet he laid it not to heart" (Isa. xlii. 24, 25).

Even so. The rage of the tempest alarms others, while he for whom it ravins is asleep.

VIII

THE WORLD REBUKING THE CHURCH

JONAH i. 6

" So the shipmaster came to him, and said unto him, What meanest
  thou, O sleeper? arise, call upon thy God, if so be that God will
  think upon us, that we perish not."

> "*If the salt hath lost its savour, where*
> *with shall it be salted?*"—MATT. v. 13.

HERE we may profitably consider, in the first place,
the rebuke administered to Jonah by the pilot;
and, thereafter, the proposal made to him. The shipmaster has a proposal to make to him: "Arise, call
upon thy God, if so be that God will think upon us,
that we perish not." But first he rebukes him sharply:
"What meanest thou, O sleeper?"

It is a melancholy scene: a scene for a friend of
God to sorrow over; for His enemies to rejoice in.
A prophet of the Lord rebuked by a heathen pilot!
The Church reproved by the world! And not in

mere insolence and enmity; not as the fruit of an ingenious and malicious search for something to hold up to scorn; but in a matter that needed not the keen scent of malice to hunt out—a matter that could not possibly be overlooked.

Ah! there is an enmity in the carnal heart towards God, that shows itself in malignant dislike of those that are His—of those that bear in any measure of distinctness His image, and that maintain with any degree of decision His cause. How often do worldly men maliciously search out the faults of the godly, applying to them an altogether different measure from what they mete out to their own worldly companions! The godliness of the godly provokes them. Conscience attests the superiority of the truly religious man, and that attestation rises in their souls whether they will or not. On that point, however, as on many more, they are at war with conscience, and labouring to suppress its dictates and decisions. They have a kind of perverse interest in making out the godly, with all their professions, to be no better than themselves. They would fain minister to their own ease, and suppress their own misgivings, by concluding that, after all, there is no reality—no permanent, effective, substantial reality—in the piety of those that shun their ways and testify against their wickedness. And in prosecution of this desire, how readily will they bring out to view, and harp upon, failings, infirmities, inconsistencies, such as, occurring in their earthly-minded companions, would never for a moment be mentioned! Eagerly they will seek out the evidence, long will they keep up the memory of such inconsistencies, such unworthinesses, on the Christian's part. They will watch for your halting; and when they find it, they will hail it with joy, and perpetuate its remembrance with delight.

But if they watch for your halting, and search out diligently your infirmity, what shall be said, if, without the need of their search at all, you put your infirmity in its worst form under their very eye? What if, in the very eye of the world, you sleep as do others— yea, sleep more soundly than others can? What if Jonah falls asleep, when even heathen pilots are awake?

What is to be expected then? Why should you look for anything but rebuke—for being put ignominiously to shame—for being covered with confusion? In such a case, you cannot attribute that rebuke to pure malice, to special enmity, to an over-searching inquiry into evidence, or an over-stern verdict on your sin. In no case, indeed, are you entitled to palliate your infirmity or abate your remorse and grief in bringing dishonour on your high name, on the ground that the world has dealt with you in keen and stern severity. Their motive in blaming will never attenuate your blameworthiness. And even when clear malice can be proved against them, confounding your mere infirmity with sheer hypocrisy and wickedness, your grounds of sorrow still remain. But how unspeakably more poignant and piercing must your grief and contrition be, if you have so fallen, so sinned, so shown yourself indifferent to the will of God, as that, even in friendliness itself, the worldling could not help expostulating with you on your fall!

It was thus with Jonah, the servant and prophet of the Lord. It needed no malice, and it argued no enmity in the pilot to rebuke him. He could not, indeed, have done otherwise. The pilot spoke sharply, but he spoke well—better than he himself knew. The rebuke was more fully deserved than the pilot himself understood. "What meanest thou, O sleeper?"

1. For, in the first place, and speaking merely negatively, Jonah deserved rebuke for what he did *not* do.

He was not bearing testimony for his God at this moment. He was not exhibiting the power of trust in God. He had a splendid opportunity of doing so,—and lost it. He lost a very remarkable opportunity of bearing a noble and timely testimony to the living and true God, "which hath made the sea and the dry land" (chap. i. 9), and who sitteth above the floods, and keepeth His people's souls in peace. Amidst the crashing storm and the terror that reigned in the ship, Jonah, had he been in the way of duty instead of fleeing from it, and in the exercise of faith instead of worn out and worn down in a conflict with his own conscience, might have stood forth, as Paul on a similar occasion, fearless for himself—a sort of bulwark, a rock of strength to others also. In the way of his duty to a reconciled God, and in fresh and immediate confidence in Him, he might have been free from the exhaustion caused by a long spiritual conflict; awake; vigilant; in perfect peace, in holy calm; bold as a lion while others trembled; waxing stronger and stronger as the strength of others waned. Ah, the question might have been asked him then, "What meanest thou?"—but it would have had another import. How canst thou thus look on in peace, while heaven and earth seem dashed together and commingled? And he might have answered from the Psalm,—for he well knew the Psalms, as his prayer in the depths reveals,—he might have answered for himself and for all believing Hebrews, "God is our refuge and our strength, a very present help in trouble: Therefore will not we fear, though the earth be removed, and though the mountains be carried into the midst of the sea; though the waters thereof roar and be troubled; though the mountains shake with the swelling thereof" (Ps. xlvi. 1–3). *That* would have glorified his God in the eyes of the heathen mariners. That would have been a testimony to the living power of the true God to support and strengthen His waiting ones in all circumstances. And doubtless such a testimony could not have been borne without making its own impression on all who saw it, evoking in substance the question put by the king to Daniel, "O Daniel, servant of the living God, is thy God, whom thou servest continually, able to deliver thee from the lions?" (Dan. vi. 20.) O Jonah, servant of the living God, is thy God, whom thou servest continually, able to give thee peace like this? Yes; "Thou wilt keep him in perfect peace, whose

mind is stayed on thee, because he trusteth in thee"
(Isa. xxvi. 3).

This noble opportunity of witness-bearing for his God,
however, Jonah allowed to pass unimproved. And do
not we often allow many a precious opportunity to
pass without taking advantage of it? Are you careful,
believing brethren—ye who serve the living God—ye
whose consciences have been purged by the blood of
Jesus from dead works to serve the living God,—are you
careful, in time of trial, adversity, poverty, anxiety, or
bereavement, to show the world how the grace of God,
how the faith of Jesus, how the fellowship of the Spirit,
can suffice to keep your soul in perfect peace and perfect patience? Do you loyally feel the duty lying
upon you to your King, to prove to those who know
Him not, and see not the light of His countenance,
and receive not His supplies of strength, that the
strength He gives is nevertheless very real, and that
the light of His countenance sweetens the afflicted
heart, and sustains the anxious, waiting, longing desire, which being delayed would make the worldling's
heart altogether sick while yours is strong? Do you
feel the holy obligation, not merely of avoiding palpable and plain matter of offence, but of—over and
above a certain style of innocence or inoffensiveness—
positively causing your light to shine, so that others,
seeing your good works, may glorify your Father
which is in heaven? Deliberately think now. What is
it you do, what is it you design or attempt, in the way
of positively commending the excellence, the acceptable-

ness, the beauty of true Christian character, the value, the strength, the sweetness, the cordiality, the true cheerfulness of having trust and confidence in a reconciled God? Would the world be led to feel from you, and from what they see in you, that living piety, the piety of faith and fellowship with God, of God's society and God's service, is really excellent and precious—promotive of strength and purity of character, promotive of peace and power of mind, promotive of beneficial issues to yourself and beneficent dispositions to your fellow-men—promotive alike of your comfort and usefulness here, as well as of your high hopes and prospects for hereafter? And when the dark night of trial and forebodings descends, and others lose all their comfort and all their courage; when, in the sight of death and eternal destinies, the hearts of others fail them; do you make it plain that in the faith of a crucified and risen Saviour there is a power which no adverse power can baffle, and a peace which no storm can break, and a hidden life—a life hid with Christ in God, in the secret of His presence, in the covert of His peaceful pavilion? Ah, then you are indeed among the children of light, not sleeping as do others, not sleeping as did Jonah; children of light—lights in the darkness; your light so shining that men shall glorify your Father in heaven.

But do you really watch thus to shine? Do you not often forget your duty thus to shine? And yet, why hast thou seen the light? Why hath the Lord thy God shone upon thee, and His glory risen upon

thee? Why hath He given thee the light of salvation
—the light of the knowledge of the glory of God in
the face of Jesus Christ? Is it not that thou mayest
reflect that light? If thou art not reflecting it, must
thou not conclude that thou art receiving it in less
measure than thou oughtest? What meanest thou, O
believer?—shining little; showing others little of the
light, little of Christ; doing little to tell of thy Saviour,
to shine upon thy brother as thy Saviour, thine Elder
Brother, has shone on thee? Arise; "what meanest
thou?" Ay, what meanest thou? and what meaneth
Jesus? Meanest thou other than He means? Breakest
thou thy fellowship with Him in this matter? Jesus
meaneth some light to others as well as to thee;
He meaneth to show them some light by means of
thee. To this end, wouldst thou but rise and reflect
the light, He would shine on thee more sweetly, more
brightly, than hitherto He hath ever done. Come, and
in the faith that Jesus shines upon thee, and will
shine upon thee more and more unto the perfect day,
arise thou and shine on others. "Arise, shine; for
thy light hath come, and the glory of the Lord hath
arisen upon thee" (Isa. lx. 1).

Negatively, then, or in consideration of what he did
not do, of what he omitted, of what he lost the opportunity of doing, Jonah merited the heathen man's
rebuke.

2. But secondly. Jonah not only deserved this
rebuke on negative grounds, but also because he was a
positive scandal or stumblingblock in the circum-

stances. And from the picture, as it appeared, of shameful supineness, stupidity, and insensibility, which the prophet presented, the pilot was surely most justifiable in somewhat sharply, or even roughly, reproving him. No doubt the prophet's sleep had a very different origin and cause from any that the pilot could have dreamt of or understood. Weary and worn with spiritual conflict, and anxiety, and sorrow, the exhausted fugitive sunk to sleep, very much as the sorrowful Apostles at the gate of Gethsemane,—not from utter and shameful lack of feeling, but from wrongly governed strength of feeling. And it is, indeed, indicative of very poor powers of appreciation or sympathy with the spiritual mind to treat the prophet's slumber as if it were quite parallel with the levity or lust-drugged apathy of the senseless or sensual sinner. With us, to whom the whole facts are revealed, it would be inexcusable to class the sleeping fugitive with worldly sleepers—with those that are at ease in Zion. But the astonished mariner had not the means of judging that we have. He knew not the explanatory circumstances that we know. The plain fact was before him, of the prophet's slumber at such a time; his being fast asleep, while the storm had brought death to gaze upon them and to claim them.

And so, O believer, it may be on an occasion with you. The evil in you that meets the world's eye may be connected with your spiritual experience, with your knowledge and service of the living God, much more closely than the world can be expected to understand. Instead of arguing your utter hypocrisy—as the shallow

130 THE WORLD REBUKING THE CHURCH

world, with its short and easy method, its quick and off-
hand receipts, is ever ready to argue—your infirmity
may be such as could not exist, or at least not in you,
in its particular form, save for your being, in the main,
godly. For instance, you may be ill at ease in conscience concerning some duty omitted, or some offence
given to your God. The iniquity may be such as the
world would smile at thinking fitted to give any sane
man trouble. It may be merely,—ah! you would not
say *merely*, though they would,—it may be *merely* your
want of realising positive and happy fellowship with
Christ. You may have been growing strange towards
your best Friend. Your enjoyment of His word and
ordinances may have been growing tame and dull, your
joyful and cordial communion with Him desultory; your
alacrity and happiness in His service may have greatly
diminished, and your work for Him who loved you
been hanging heavy on your hands. You are ill at
ease; and no wonder. Your conscience upbraids you.
You are uncomfortable. You are almost irritable. You
become unsocial, ungenial, uncongenial, sour, fretted,
an unhappy and unpleasant companion. The very
worldling can afford to point to you as far inferior, in
real frankness, and freeness, and cordiality of feeling,
to many who make nothing like your professions of
piety to God and charity to man. True, the worldling
cannot appreciate, and will not make allowance for,
those elements of Christian integrity with which your
temporary peevishness and fretfulness, your present
want of social kindliness and geniality of temperament,

are connected. And, in one sense, it is very easy for him to cast a stone at you. It is very easy for him, on his smooth sea, and with his shining sky, and coasting gaily along in his tiny shallop, to blame on your part the anxious face, and knitted brow, and hard compressed lips, and abstracted air, and unsocial bearing, while all the waves and billows of inward anxiety are passing over you. It is very easy for him to blame you; and it is very hard that such as you should be blamed by such as he. Still the question is, What can the world take you for, but what you appear to be? And if inevitably they must form a judgment that will not take all the trials of your conflict into account, are you not the more bound to see that in that conflict you so fight by faith, and, having done all, so stand, that the cheerfulness of true Christian peace shall, if not uniformly, yet usually be seen shining upon you, while the joy of the Lord shall be your strength?

The worldling's conscience has not the tenderness of the Christian's conscience, and therefore is not so readily pained. The worldling's peace has not the purity of the Christian's peace, and therefore is not so readily marred. It is easy for the one to take things coolly; to be quite gay and cheerful, frank, and free-hearted, and joyous in his way; while the soul shaken with eternal verities, and watching to walk with a holy and eternal God, may oftentimes be deeply tried, and liable to be greatly fretted. And it is easy for the shallow, earthly-minded man, who has let alone Christ, and whom now in judgment Christ is well-nigh letting alone; it is easy for him, knowing nothing of the trials, the terrors of sin finding him out, of God mercifully *not* letting him alone, but proving, chastising, disciplining him lest Satan should gain dominion over him; it is easy for him to make a mock of a sensitive, scrupulous, conscientious soul, under the hiding of God's countenance for sin, and backsliding, and unbelief. But still the question returns, What right have you to be bringing up an ill report on the religion of the Son of God, as if they who profess it lose much in the way of cheerfulness, joyousness, sweetness of temper, geniality of disposition, frankness of heart and manner, which those who profess it not may retain? Bring no such scandal on the brotherhood—on those that are within. Be no such stumbling-block to those that are without. Let there be nothing which the world can point to and say concerning it, We are more distinguished for this excellence than you, —we, who make no profession, than you, whose profession is great. Hast thou no inward peace to sit enthroned on an open placid brow? Hast thou no joy within to break into a peaceful, placid smile, the smile of frank and loving joy, that would tempt the very child to flee to thee as, in its innocence, its very choice and chief companion? Hast thou too much inward anguish with sin,—with great and weary thoughts of life, and death, and everlasting things? And, as on a very sea of trouble, with the wind boisterous, art thou so filled with anxiety and fear, as that tender Christian peace and the lovely garniture of attractive Christian graces have little chance to be seen in thee? Behold, O brother, a mild majestic form walking on those very waters, wending His way towards thee! Dost thou not recognise Him? "It is the Lord." Canst thou not say, "Lord, bid me that I come unto thee;" or, 'Come thou, good Lord, into the ship, and dwell with me'? And as you go to meet Him, even walking on the waters, or, as you welcome Him into the ship,—and behold! there is a great calm,—O learn, while now peacefully sharing His dominion over all waves and winds, His victory over all tempests and trials—learn in His society to cultivate all those graces which shone in Him; the mildness, the meekness, the genial lowliness and kindliness that made even the face of "the Man of sorrows" shine joyfully on little children, and made His bosom the refuge where they might so securely reckon on a place of nestling and of love.

Why should the Church allow the world to bear away the palm in reference to any one element of excellence whatsoever—candour, courtesy, charity, kindliness, large-mindedness, liberality, self-denial,—any virtue whatsoever? Why should there be one single department of what is good—good in any sphere, moral, physical, social, scientific—concerning which the world can with any show of fairness profess to school the Church, or say, Stand aside, for we are more at home here than you? Nay: "Whatsoever things are true, whatsoever things are venerable, whatsoever things are just; whatsoever things are pure, whatsoever things are lovely, whatsoever things are of good report; if there be any virtue, if there be any praise, think on these things." The pilot rebuking the prophet! The world rebuking the Church! These things ought not so to be.

A Hebrew rebuked by a heathen! a Hebrew prophet by a heathen mariner! Yes; but there is more in it than that. It is a Hebrew prophet fleeing from a commission to reprove a heathen city, himself reproved by a heathen! Surely it is punishing his sin in kind. It is graving his libel on the rod that punishes his offence. Verily it is his sin finding him out.

How exact are God's retributions! How strong, how exact, how minute! In their great leading features— also in their manifold, minute details—the actings of His moral government bear evidence of One who is the all-searching God, to whom the darkness and the light are both alike. You cannot blind Him. You cannot baffle Him. You cannot evade His notice. Also, you cannot engage His attention so as to distract His memory. In ten thousand ways He can, without a moment's warning, show you forgotten sin, in mirrors from which you cannot turn aside. He can adapt His punishments, so that it shall be mere affectation for you to doubt what the sin is He punishes for. He may keep it secret between Himself and you, if the ends of righteousness do not demand its exposure. But between Himself and you there shall be no shadow of doubt left. A heathen shall reprove the man who would not carry God's reproof to the heathen,—so that a man shall say, "Verily there is a God that judgeth on the earth."

Young man, do you know that Almighty God has a

moral government? Do you know that He keepeth count and reckoning? Do you know that the pages of His reckoning never fade? Do you know that He sometimes copies out a page upon the memory and conscience of him whom it doth concern, painfully, startlingly, alarmingly; and he whom it doth concern, though he shrink, though he scream, cannot break loose from the hand, graving into his soul as with the point of a diamond, writing on it as in lines of burning fire? Ah! young man, companion of fools! thou knowest not the mysteries of God's government—the mysterious capacities of conscience. Above all, thou knowest not the relations between thy conscience and the all-searching, all-reckoning government of thy God. "Rejoice, O young man, in thy youth, and let thy heart cheer thee in the days of thy youth, and walk in the ways of thine heart, and in the sight of thine eyes: but know thou, that for all these things the Lord will call thee into judgment" (Eccles. xi. 9).

But what! wilt thou wait till then? Wilt thou not rather take the judgment into thine own hand and judge thyself? "If thou wilt judge thyself, thou shalt not be judged" (1 Cor. xi. 31). But at what judgment-seat shalt thou judge thyself; and to what penalty shalt thou condemn thyself? Every sin of thine deserveth God's wrath. In every sin of thine thou hast forged another chain binding thee over a prisoner to the day of His wrath. Oh, these countless chains! "O wretched man that I am! who shall deliver me from them?" I am loaded as with irons. Who shall deliver me? Who shall break them and set me free? Brother, there is but one only means of breaking these irons and giving thee thy freedom again. They shall yield to fire, and fire alone. The furnace of Jehovah's wrath, His righteous wrath, will melt them, dissipate them, abolish them, if it blaze in its undivided fierceness. It does so blaze. It blazes in all its fierceness on Calvary. Yon cross is the furnace of wrath, and He who suffered there comes and takes thee by the hand. ' Brother,' He says, ' guilty, weary, wretched, yet brother still, partaker of flesh and blood as I am, wilt thou go with me through yon devouring fire? Every sacrifice shall be salted by fire. Every chain of sin shall be abolished by fire— by fire only. Wilt thou go with me? On me alone shall the heat kindle—on me, and on thy chains, thy sins, which the Lord hath laid on me. One in the furnace with thee, such as I am, the Son of God, thou shalt suffer no evil; the fire shall have no power over thee; not an hair of thy head shall perish, nor the smell of fire pass on thy garments. I shall be made sin for thee, that thou mayest be made the righteousness of God in me (2 Cor. v. 21). Only, it must be *in me*. Brother, it is essential that I pass through the fires with thee,—I in thee, and thou in me.'

Oh, most amazing proposal! Oh, most gracious offer! Wilt thou not embrace it? Wilt thou not go with Jesus? He is the sacrifice for sin. The flame kindles on Him, exhausts itself on Him; kindles on Him alone—on Him wearing thy chains, that He may abolish them. He alone is the burnt-offering. *In Him,* " It is finished." When thou goest with Him, the flame kindles not at all on thee. And now, proving by faith this glorious relief; going by faith with Jesus through all the anguish of His death and cross; purified by His blood; living by His sacrifice; emerging from the fire with Jesus—emerging into new life, as at that empty grave where the angel of light shineth, showing you "the path of life;" standing there now with thy risen Lord, thou art free as He is, unfettered, unhampered, emancipated from all chains of darkness, bonds of condemnation, cords of death. Thou art free as Christ is. Thy chains are gone. Thy sins are punished, avenged, abolished. Thy conscience is purged and clean; thy heart at ease—broken, contrite, weeping, mourning for Him whom thou hadst pierced, for Him on whom the fire kindled instead of thee—yet still joyful, grateful; grieving gladly, glad though grieving; pure, affectionate, holy, childlike, free;—free to love thy wonderful Redeemer, free to serve thy risen Lord; free to say " Lord, what wilt thou have me to do?" and free to say unto Him, "Here am I; send me" (Acts ix. 6. Isa. vi. 8). Stand fast, therefore, in the liberty wherewith Christ hath made thee free. Sin no more, lest a worse thing befall thee. Thy sins are forgiven thee; go in peace : go and sin no more.

And as thou goest, holy, sinning no more,—be cheerful, be joyful, be strong. The dark night—the dread wrath—the furnace of fire, are all behind thee. In the fresh morning of thy new life, an elastic, bounding sense of freedom throbs within thee. " The path of life," with the glory yonder, stretches in shining light before thee. And now, "forgetting the things that are behind, press on towards those that are before,"—forward, upward, heavenward,—straight "to the mark for the prize of the high calling of God in Christ Jesus" (Phil. iii. 13, 14).

IX

NATURAL RELIGION : ITS STRENGTH AND WEAKNESS.

JONAH i. 6

" Arise, call upon thy God, if so be that God will think upon us, that
we perish not."

> " He that formed the eye, shall he not
> see ? He that chastiseth the heathen,
> shall not he correct ? He that teacheth
> man knowledge, shall he not know ?
> " The Lord knoweth the thoughts of man,
> that they are vanity."—Ps. xciv.
> 9–11.

THE pilot not only rebuked the prophet; he had a
proposal to make to him,—a call to address to him
—a call to prayer: " Arise, call upon thy God." And
he backs his proposal by a reason, a motive, an expectation of benefit: " If so be that God will think upon
us, that we perish not."

All this, as coming from a heathen, is peculiarly
instructive. And the two great truths it conveys
are these:—First, That in man's inmost nature, originally and radically, there are certain principles of reli-

gion most strong and inerradicable; and, *Second*, That these, without the guidance of revelation and faith, are altogether insufficient as guides in his real relation to God. Man's natural helplessness, as he stands related to the material world, liable continually to become the victim of powers and elements far mightier than he; and his natural conscience, as he stands related to the moral world, liable continually to be the victim of a sentence and a condemnation which he is constantly passing on himself, and constantly feels that a living Being far mightier than he is passing;—these two facts and conditions of his existence on the earth necessarily imply a capacity for religion and a certain religiousness, appertaining, of necessity, to human nature, and developed in peculiar strength even in heathen worship. In fact, the strength of these natural principles of religion in the heathen reads a very solemn and alarming rebuke to multitudes in civilised and Christian lands. In the progress of modern civilisation, man may emancipate himself from the solemn awe with which the heathen contemplate the powers of nature; but if he rise not to a holy veneration of the one Supreme Author of nature, as a revealed and reconciled God, it is very questionable whether he does not become in some respects a more shallow and trifling being than the worshipper of idols. And the weakening of this element—the sense of his littleness as in the grasp and at the disposal of power higher than his own,—weakens also the other element—his sense of the gravity of his moral relations. Between these two, there is a strange interplay and interchange of action. The one—his relation to the material world,—when rightly realised, tends to impress him with a deep sense of his extreme insignificance—of his perfect helplessness and littleness. A rotting worm in the ship, or a raging wind in the heavens, may sink him; a flash from the thunder-cloud, the pestilence that walketh in darkness, the arrow that flieth by noonday, may lay him low. Any one of a thousand accidents may remove him from this passing scene of things. He is extremely unimportant, it would seem; and when nature gathers up her energies, and, as in the storm before us, puts forth her mighty powers, the pride and self-sufficiency of man are swept away in a moment, and he feels his littleness. Strange to say, he thereby feels also his greatness—his true significance as a moral, responsible, immortal being. Is there a judge? Is there a great court of the universe—a final tribunal for all creatures—an ultimate throne, occupied by a King of kings? Before that throne he feels that it is his high prerogative to stand; before that throne he is under call to compear. He feels *that* most of all, when, in the great excitement and alarms of nature's threatening and uncontrolable powers, he is led most of all to feel his littleness. The very hour when, in relation to the material world, and partly by the display of its gigantic elements, man learns to read his helplessness, is the hour when, in relation to the moral world, he learns to feel the high significance of his being.

Now, weaken the first of these, as in a highly artificial state of society, where man seems to bend the elements to his pleasure, making the very lightnings pass safely where he pleases, or constraining them to bear his messages; and let there be no corresponding improvement in his knowledge of the true God: feeling less his real littleness, he becomes more blind than ever to his true greatness, and (apart from grace) becomes more dependent upon some alarming providence, such as now threatened the ship and all on board with destruction, for being wakened up to feel his true position as a moral, responsible being, under law to the great Ruler of the universe, and bound to compear and stand at His bar.

It is on grounds like these that we might very easily maintain and prove the assertion, that godless men, in the days and in the state of society in which we live, are more thoroughly irreligious than the heathen are; that covetousness, which is idolatry—the rage for money-making, which supremely governs multitudes, and is adopted by them as man's chief end—is more contemptible than the worship of stocks and stones; and that under its sway human nature becomes even more perverted, and, as to every element of natural excellence, suffers a more complete break-down than in the case of the poor savage who roams the forest trembling at the thunder's voice and bowing the knee to the glories of the setting sun.

But we cannot prosecute this line of thought. It would lead us too far from our present purpose. Be it simply remembered, without attempting to trace their mutual relations and mutual actions on each other, that, apart from revelation, prior to it and pre-supposed by it, as what revelation itself appeals to, there are these two facts conspiring to make man naturally and necessarily a religious being, namely—*first*, his observation of the powers of nature, and, *secondly*, his experience of the powers of conscience.

Let us now, in the first place, estimate the strength of these principles; and then their weakness: both of these as exhibited in the proposal of the heathen pilot. Let us consider, in a word, how far natural religion can go, and where it fails. We have before us a fair opportunity of settling this question. In this hour of nature's terrors, where man's littleness comes into clearest light, and where, in the prospect of death, man's greatness also comes out in its fullest proportions; when the speaker, moreover, is no nervous and excited timid female, but a self-possessed mariner, habituated to the dangers of the deep, and not unduly alarmed; in such a man, at such a time,—when not overdriven by alarm, yet stimulated to the highest pitch of earnestness,—we seem to have a very embodiment, an impersonation of natural religion in the very crisis of its power, acting to the utmost of its capacity, and pausing only where its capacity ends. Hence, in the proposal of the pilot, we may read—*First*, the power; and, *secondly*, the weakness of natural religion. And then we may see that, whether among heathens or merely nominal Christians, natural religion is substantially the same; in other words, that without converting and enlightening and renewing grace, without the evangelism and spirituality of the gospel, without the blood and Spirit of Christ, man's religion, anywhere and everywhere, is essentially heathen.

I. What is it that reason, unenlightened by the word and Spirit of God, can do towards furnishing man with a religion? What can natural religion do for us?

1. First of all, then, it may tell us that there is a God, and that that God is One. The existence and the unity of God may be proved by reason. These heathen mariners had many gods. "They cried every man unto his god." And the pilot would have Jonah to call on *his* God: "Arise, call on thy God." Jonah, he took for granted, would have a God too. There were "gods many," according to the mariner's views. And yet under this multiplicity there lurked the idea of a unity also. For while the pilot speaks as if he had the idea of many—"Call on thy God;" see, we are all calling each to his god; call on thine too;—yet he closes with a remark that seems to indicate that this system of multiplication was rather, after all, a system of division, and that out of the many they re-constructed and rose to the idea of a single, Supreme Being. For he adds, "if so be that God will think upon us, that we perish not,"—"if so be that *God*,"—*the* God, the *One* God, the Supreme.

And unquestionably the whole herd of inferior deities whom the heathen worshipped, were only so many sectional representatives of a portion of the powers believed to reside in a God, to whom might fairly be given, even by reason, the lofty designation, " God over all."

And in point of fact, it is easily shown that, however it may have been usually in the history of the world, it is quite within the competency of reason to demonstrate the unity of God. Man's connexion with the natural world,—his observation of nature,—suggests a designing mind ; a being possessing wisdom, and power, and purpose : it never suggests more than one. The wisdom, power, and goodness, which it sees to be requisite for creating, preserving, and controlling the visible universe, are felt to be unbounded, infinite. One such infinite Being is felt to be necessary to account for things as they are. But not more than one is felt to be necessary. Rather, more than one such infinite Being, possessing all knowledge and power, is felt to be impossible. The same result follows from our connexion with the moral world. Conscience tells of a Ruler and Judge, but only of one. Its whole dictates would be misread, misinterpreted, and reversed, by the introduction of two rival Gods claiming co-ordinate shares of its veneration. The most distinct and sharp intimation which conscience gives is that of One higher, one supreme Ruler claiming undivided allegiance. The good conscience—tender and true and confessing—owns this :—"Against Thee, Thee only, have I sinned." The bad conscience, whether in man or lost angels, if examined aright, is seen to take this for granted, to have this graven on itself as by a pen of iron, to have this as the foundation of its terrors :—" Thou believest that there is ONE God ; thou doest well : the devils also believe, and tremble." The trembling, the terror, the fearful looking-for of vengeance, is all in one direction, —all concentrated in one.

2. But further; reason, fairly interpreted, assures us that this God is a being capable of intercourse with His creatures. Reason, indeed, cannot tell on what terms God will conduct intercourse with His creatures; or whether He will actually do so at all. But reason can tell that God is a being capable, if He pleases, of conversing with His intelligent, reasonable, responsible creatures. And this it deduces from the general principle, that God, the Creator, cannot confer powers or privileges on His creatures, higher than He himself possesses. It is one of the plainest arguments that can be framed, " He that planted the ear, shall he not hear ? he that formed the eye, shall he not see ? he that giveth man knowledge, doth he not know ? " (Ps. xciv. 9, 10.) The very purpose or desire on God's part to create man capable of seeing, proves that seeing—vision —is familiar to God himself. The creating of an intelligent being, is surely the work of a Being who Himself is intelligent. And so the bestowal on man of a capacity of holding intercourse and converse with another, implies, on God's part, the possession of the same capacity, and that in the highest degree. For if I, God's creature, can reveal my mind and thoughts to you, and am capable of receiving the revelation of your thoughts, and wants, and wishes, which in turn you

make to me; assuredly God, who made us both, must much more be capable of disclosing His mind to both of us, and hearing us when we go to disclose our mind to Him.

Hence reason itself demonstrates the possibility of a revelation from God; and the possibility of prayer, and of the efficacy of prayer.

This the heathen pilot, you will observe, proceeds upon, when he summons Jonah to " arise and call upon God."

These are the two great truths that reason is competent to establish : *first,* that God exists ; and *second,* that prayer is possible, reasonable. The superior power observed in nature, in the material world; and the supreme authority felt by conscience, in the moral world ; these two great general facts testify of a God. And then the danger to which man is exposed in the material world at the hands of nature and its elements ; and the distress which man suffers in the moral world at the hands of conscience ; these two great general experiences, prompt intuitively to deprecate God's anger, "that we perish not," and prompt to seek His favour, "if so be that God will think upon us," or shine upon us, be propitious, or favourable to us; prompt, in short, naturally and necessarily, to prayer. A God; and a God to whom prayer may be offered : these are the dictates of reason. In establishing these two truths, reason is within its own sphere, thoroughly within its competency ; and in establishing them irrefragably, reason exhibits its excellence and power.

II. But now observe reason's limit, and reason's weakness. The God whom reason knows to exist, that God reason does not personally know at all; and the prayer which reason teaches to be possible and reasonable, reason cannot conduct. Here, therefore, is the twofold need for revelation from God on His part, and for faith in that revelation on ours.

1. Reason knows that God exists; but reason does not know God. Reason tells that there is a God; but we need revelation to make us acquainted with Him. To know His existence is one thing; to know Himself is another.

I go into a gallery of paintings. My reason at once infers a painter. These pictures did not spring into existence by chance. They are the products of a designing mind, an agent, an artist. The existence of such an agent is at once proved by the existence of the paintings. Further, I examine them one by one; I find them all connected with each other. They are a closely concatenated series. The same style is visible in them all. The same ultimate idea is kept in view by them all. They present, let us say, a single individual in childhood, youth, manhood, old age. They exhibit the great leading incidents of his life. From this order and design, this purpose and idea, and from the manner in which the painter has carried it out, I am gathering information about him, about his style, his abilities, and powers in his art. Nay, more, from the hearty manner in which I may see he has brought forth all his finest powers to depict some scene, we shall say, of home enjoyment, I may gain an insight into more than his artistic and professional abilities. I may read not a little of his personal predilections, his moral tendencies and tastes.

All this, however, I may learn, and much more. All that in this way, at the very best, any man could learn, I may be supposed to reach; and yet the painter himself I may never have seen—him as yet I know not. "I have neither seen his shape, nor heard his voice," nor understood his character, and mind, and heart. Clear it is that wholly another style of knowledge of him is possible; yea, that another style of knowledge, not higher in degree merely, but especially *different in kind* is needed, before I can be said to know himself.

But let him enter his own gallery of paintings, and meet me face to face.* Let him come into converse with me. Let him tell me the idea which he meant, by this series of pictures, to convey and impress; let him carry me from one to another in regular order, from first to last, and tell me all his purpose and design. Clearly I am beginning to know him after another fashion now; and he casts more light now on the scope of the paintings, than the paintings formerly threw upon the skill of the painter.

Still, however, if all that passes between him and me refers exclusively to these works of his hands, I may have got a high intellectual treat; I may have

---

* This is but the reproduction, in another form, of a fine thought of Dr Candlish's in "Contributions towards an Exposition of the Book of Genesis," vol. i., pp. 3-5.

got great light on the finest themes of the finest of the fine arts; his intellect, and skill, and art, and science, may have been all made to pass before me, and here and there a gleam of deeper principles and feelings may incidentally have flashed forth: yet still I cannot yet be said, in any real sense, to know the painter himself. For aught that has passed between him and me, we may part, never to meet again, never to feel the slightest interest in each other's fate and character. It may live in my memory as a familiar recollection and a gratifying incident that I had this rencontre with him; but personal knowledge of him I have not gained: and in an hour of sadness, and of sorrow, I could no more proceed to cast myself on his sympathy and aid, than on any stranger whom I had never even seen in the flesh.

And the reason is, that you never become acquainted with, you never really know, any person, merely by discovering his intellectual or scientific abilities. You never do know a neighbour, save by knowing his moral character and his heart. It is when you have evidence of his unbending rectitude, and get an experimental insight into his unbounded beneficence; when you know that your friend can do you no wrong, and know that he is disposed, to the limits of his power, to do you all good; it is then you know himself. When you know his righteousness and goodness; when you have experimentally ascertained that in these two qualities he is all that you can ever need to draw, or depend upon him for; that in these respects you can thoroughly lean upon and trust him : then you have formed a true acquaintance, not with the man's abilities, but with himself. Till you reach and arrive at this knowledge, you must feel that you have not the pleasure of his real acquaintance. If you have sought in vain to get this knowledge, you must confess that you do not know him,—perhaps that you do not know what to make of him.

And the same principles hold good as to your acquiring a knowledge—a true knowledge of God; your essaying to obey the command, "Acquaint thyself with God." You may know *about* God from the works of creation; but in this way you never rise to a true and *personal* knowledge of *God* himself. It is one thing to *know about* God : another to *know* Him. Nature and conscience may tell about Him ; but revelation alone discloses *Him*. Reason may discover much truth concerning His intellectual powers, so to speak—His natural attributes ; but His moral character and His heart it remains for Himself to reveal. Is He so inflexibly just that rather than allow the least unrighteousness to prevail—that is to say, to be unpunished ; for where unrighteousness is not annihilated or married to its eternal punishment, there it does prevail—is He, I say, so inflexibly just that rather than allow the least unrighteousness to prevail, He would suffer all heaven and earth to become one everlasting hell ?—and my conscience can get no rest and no satisfaction in estimating His character for righteousness till this be admitted. But if this be admitted, what hope can there be for me, a sinner? Is it possible that at the same time He can be, towards me a sinner, a God of grace, one infinite, boundless ocean of free, forgiving, saving love? Is this possible? I cannot trust in God unless He be infinitely, inflexibly, eternally righteous. If He could do the least wrong,—or, which is the same thing, wink at the least wrong,—even for the purpose of saving me, I cannot respect Him; I cannot trust Him. But if He cannot do on His own part, nor tolerate on my part, the least unrighteousness, oh, how can I trust in Him, or draw near to Him in peace? He is to me, more and more, an infinite mystery. As a living person, with whom I have to do—my Maker and my Judge—the more I think of Him, and the more I scan all that reason teaches and conscience tells, so much the more do I find that, in proportion as I thus *know about* Him, the less do I seem to *know* Himself. Himself, in fact, I cannot know, till He reveal Himself to me as in the holy Scripture, shining forth there as in a mirror infinitely more bright than creation, infinitely more serene than conscience. There I see His glory, when I look to Christ. There I see the light of the knowledge of the glory of God in the face of Jesus Christ. In Him, dying the death of agonising wrath for sin—thirsting, mourning, bleeding, outcast, condemned, and dying—I see that God, not only rather than tolerate the least unrighteousness, would suffer all created beings to become as hell, but bringeth hell into the very soul of His beloved Son; while rather than suffer me, the hell-deserving one, to become as hell, His love to me is so inconceivable that for me He giveth His eternal and beloved Son, a sacrifice for me. If the Holy Ghost open my heart to receive this revelation, I know my God now. I know Him personally. I know Himself. I know Him far better than I know any other person. My truest brother, my dearest friend, cannot so reveal and make known himself to me as my God can and does. By the Spirit and word of the Lord, the Lord God in Christ Jesus becomes truly and surely known to me.

Thus while reason may tell that there is a God, and tell about God, it is by revelation—by faith—that you know God himself.

2. In like manner, secondly, as reason tells that prayer is possible, yea, reasonable, revelation alone puts us in possession of the terms on which God actually hears prayer—puts us in a condition actually to pray.

And, here, to speak solely of the essential point, reason tells that, prior to obtaining aid and blessing, it is essential that the Divine anger should be removed. "If so be that God will think upon us;"—literally, If the Lord will shine upon us, if the Lord will be propitious to us—"that we perish not." So spake the pilot: and he spake the language of universal reason and conscience. If God be propitious; if God be favourable; if God turn away His anger, and turn to us in kindness—then, only then, "we perish not." This, therefore, becomes the hinge of all the inquiry: How shall God be propitious? How shall man be just with God? How shall God be favourable to man?

Take away my Bible from me; obliterate from my

mind the knowledge which, from holy Scripture, I have derived; or, in the hour of my storm of terror in conscience, or alarm in the approach of death, let me be incapable of spiritually realising, believing, using and improving the information which holy Scripture conveys on this point; let it still be to me a question, 'How shall God become favourable?' and I am incapable of true prayer; my prayer is simply heathen. I cry to a Supreme Being, perhaps—it may be in a very agony of earnestness; but mark the tremendous error of my prayer. I pray in order to make God favourable. And that is a work too great for me. That is a work in which I can have no success. That is the aim and object of all the sacrifices, penances, and prayers of Popish and heathen worship. They are designed, if possible, to make God favourable. With this intent —with this end in view—a heathen pilot prays, and calls the prophet to prayer. And with this same end, every awakened, startled, unconverted, unbelieving man prays, whether nominally a heathen or a Christian.

It is the reverse with the converted—the believer. He prays, not because he imagines God to be unfavourable and tries to propitiate Him, but because God in Christ *is* favourable, and he believes in Him as a propitious, pardoning, gracious God. He does not pray in doubt, like the heathen pilot—" if so be God may be propitious;" but because God is propitious. A doubt on that point quells all his power to pray. So greatly does he fear the Holy One of Israel, that a doubt as to

whether He be propitious strikes him dumb, and he dare
not pray on such a supposition. The prayer of faith,
which alone is truly prayer, takes hold with tenacious
grasp on the declaration, "There is forgiveness with
Thee that Thou mayest be feared." And maintaining
this glorious ground—resting on this sure foundation—
knowing the terms of infinitely free and sure grace, and
the gift of perfect and imputed righteousness, which, in
Christ Jesus, is the basis of holy, trustful, true, and
pure-hearted prayer, the believer casts away all such
"perchance," and "perhaps," and "if," and "if so be;"
all such hesitations and uncertainties as spring from the
unbelief of heathenism and the heathenism of unbelief;
and relying on the truth of the Father's gracious revelation, and the freeness and perfection of the Son's
righteousness, and the secret security of the Spirit's light
and grace; in one word, taking God at His word, and
taking God's proposal as good and true; feeling more
and more deeply his tremendous weight of sin, but looking more and more intensely to the perfect sacrifice, and
realising it as an all-worthy object of immediate faith, and
an all-worthy theme of immediate gratitude and praise, the
believing worshipper, with a true heart, and in the full
assurance of faith, may be heard exclaiming;—"Praise
waiteth for thee, O God, in Zion: and unto thee shall
the vow be performed. O thou that hearest prayer, unto
thee shall all flesh come. Iniquities prevail against me:
as for our transgressions, thou shalt purge them away.
Blessed is the man whom thou choosest, and causest to
approach unto thee, that he may dwell in thy courts: we

shall be satisfied with the goodness of thy house, even of thy holy temple " (Ps. lxv. 1–4).

Thus we have seen both the power and the weakness of reason in reference to religion. Reason is powerful enough to tell, *first*, that there is a God; and, *secondly*, that He is a Being capable of holding intercourse with us if He pleases. But reason is so weak that, in the *first place*, this God, whose existence it teaches, it does not enable us to know; and, in the *second place*, this exercise of prayer whose possibility and reasonableness it teaches, it cannot enable us to conduct.

Reason, therefore, without revelation, is sure fatally to err; and whether in ancient Paganism, or in modern rationalisms, which are heathenisms, or in Popery, or in nominal, formal Christianity, the error at bottom is identically one and the same. If you would avoid being at heart altogether as the heathen, there is no course for you but one. Awake to a sense of sin, and of your tremendous yet glorious responsibility to God; and come in truth of heart to the cross of Christ's humiliation, agony, and shame—His vicarious sufferings and death. There you must by faith unite your responsibility with Christ's, or take His for yours. Your guilt—your righteous liability to wrath, you must terminate and quench in His blood; your Judge by that blood appeased, your Father by that blood reconciled. And in the unlimited brokenness and gratitude of heart which will thus be inspired; in the perfect trust in God and adoring admiration of Him; in the fervour of thanks which you render at the remembrance of His holiness, and the reverence of filial joy with which you contemplate and share His love; you will feel a new life begun, a life of prayer, the prayer, not of probability, of doubt, of hesitation, of timid, shrinking, creeping fear and bondage; the prayer, not of abject flattery, of craven cringing, of labouring to propitiate, or persuading to cease from wrath; but of faith, of the full assurance of faith, of access with boldness and confidence through the faith of Christ; for " this is the confidence that we have in Him, that, if we ask anything according to His will, He heareth us: and if we know that He hear us, whatsoever we ask, we know that we have the petitions that we desired of Him " (1 John v. 14, 15). This is Christian prayer; less—less in essence or principle—is heathenism.

There is one other remark to be made on this verse before closing, and it is this;—that a heathen pilot may here be accepted as teaching us the reasonableness and propriety of united prayer. Nature itself teaches that there is something in united supplication more calculated to secure an answer. And what nature suggests, the Scriptures confirm. We are told by our Lord that " if two of us shall agree on earth as touching anything that we shall ask, it shall be done unto us of our Father which is in heaven " (Matt. xviii. 19). Do we then bring the concert and union of our prayers into Christ's family with us, if, indeed, we have entered that family? If we have made common cause with the kingdom of Christ—if we have embarked in this ship—

can we really be indifferent to its general interest and safety, to the comfort, and interest, and safety of our fellow-passengers for eternity? If we can—if we can sleep at our ease while the vessel is in danger, are we not marked out thereby as the very souls for whose sake the danger has come upon the vessel? And what a call does this thought address to us, as in the very language of a heathen rebuking us; while—making allowance for the heathenism—we may well on that account also be all the more ashamed by the peremptory earnestness of a heathen man's demand:—"What meanest thou, O sleeper? Arise, call upon thy God: if so be that God will think upon us, that we perish not."

X

CASTING THE LOT

JONAH i. 7

" And they said every one to his fellow, Come, and let us cast lots,
that we may know for whose cause this evil is upon us."

> "*The lot is cast into the lap: but the whole*
> *disposing thereof is of the Lord.*"—
> PROV. xvi. 33.

THE narrative does not inform us what response
Jonah gave to the shipmaster. His best response,
no doubt, was silence. To the rebuke addressed to him,
however severe, he could offer no objection—"What
meanest thou, O sleeper?" And as to the proposal
made to him,—"Arise and call on thy God, if so be
that God will think upon us, that we perish not,"—he
could scarcely very readily promise compliance with it.
A prophet and true servant of the Lord though he was,
he had, at present, and in so far, retired from his standing as one in communication and in communion with
the King, and assumed the position of a rebel. It is
not, indeed, our works of obedience that *secure* our

prayers being heard; and our works of disobedience, repented of and confessed, forsaken and abandoned, shall not *prevent* our prayers being heard. But it is obviously right and inevitable that a state of disobedience continued in, a course of rebellion pursued, should cut off the transgressing one from the fellowship of his God. Prayer, indeed, is an appeal to God to accomplish concerning us the things which He hath promised; to carry out in our experience and history, in our state and prospects, *His own will.* But the man who is following out, not the Divine will, but his own, is thereby in a position the very reverse of that which is taken up by the soul in true prayer. Hence, not merely does God refuse to hear the prayer of the impenitent; but really the impenitent refuse truly to pray. The first true prayer that comes from the transgressor begins with a resignation of his rebellion. Your coming over to God to ask Him to fulfil His will—and prayer is the offering up of our desires to God for things agreeable to His will—implies the giving up, the surrendering of your own will to His. It implies your return to submission, allegiance, loyalty, obedience; and, though it is not the merit of this return to obedience which secures the hearing of prayer, this return to obedience is implied in the very offering of true prayer.

In his present flight, therefore, from God's presence, and his continued refusal to perform God's will, Jonah has shut against himself the door of prayer. To pray in faith is to pray in submission to the Divine will, and on the warrant of the Divine Word; but for Jonah to

attempt to profess to do so, lays him open immediately
to the rejoinder of his own conscience, How canst thou
pretend such submission, when thou art carrying on this
war against God's will, and fleeing from the obedience
of it? Above the voice of conscience, thus protesting
his hypocrisy in pretending to pray, Jonah, till he
repent and return to his allegiance, cannot rise. Conscience is too mighty for him. His attempt at prayer
is strangled in its very beginning. He has the witness
in himself, against himself. And it is simply in accordance with what conscience testifies, that God also testifies, when He refuses in such a case to hear prayer.

To the Jews, continuing to refuse obedience to the
will of God, Jeremiah was required to speak thus, in
the name of the Lord:—" I earnestly protested unto
your fathers, saying, Obey my voice. Yet they obeyed
not. And now a conspiracy is found among the men
of Judah; they are turned back to the iniquities of their
forefathers, which refused to hear my words. Therefore
thus saith the Lord, Behold, I will bring evil upon
them, which they shall not be able to escape; and
though they shall *cry unto me, I will not hearken unto
them*" (Jer. xi. 7–11). In like manner, by Isaiah, does
the Lord contend with a gainsaying and disobedient
people: " When ye spread forth your hands, I will
hide mine eyes from you: yea, when ye make many
prayers, I will not hear: your hands are full of blood "
(Isa. i. 15).

Does this, then, form any exception to the blessed
truth that God is the hearer and answerer of prayer?

No. But it proves that He is the hater of hypocrisy. The man who, in known disobedience to any command from God, approaches to pray, defies the Divine omniscience, as if God did not know his sin. Or he denies the Divine authority over him, as if God had no right to claim obedience in that particular; no right to be displeased though obedience be refused; no right to complain; no right to count this a reason for interrupting peaceable and friendly relations. The very attempt in such a case to pray is an insult to God. It is a cool and impudent attempt to proceed as if all were right, as if nothing had happened. Should God, in such a case, be inquired of? Should the Most High consent to allow His rebellious creature to reduce Him to so degrading a position; to assume over Him, what simply amounts on the sinner's part to an overbearing attitude of dictation?

You sin against God. You knowingly refuse obedience to some particular of His clearly-revealed will. And, without repentance, and return to a better mind and a better course, you approach Him with your prayers and expect that He will answer them? You expect that He will wink at your sin; allow you to take your own way; indulge you in your disobedience; and permit you in this matter to be a god to yourself: thereby consenting, in so far, to cease Himself from being God? And all this is implied in His continuing on a friendly and prayer-hearing relation to you in the midst of disobedience! Nay: "I will go and return unto my place, till they acknowledge their offence, and seek my face: in their affliction they will seek me early " (Hos. v. 15).

It appears, then, that repentance is necessarily implied in all true prayer. "Then shall ye find Me, when ye seek Me with all your heart:"—when, subjecting all your will to My will, and in nothing continuing to rebel, ye can " delight yourselves in God," *then* shall ye find Me; then will I "give you the desires of your heart." Not that repentance is the meritorious reason for our prayers being heard; they are heard in the mere and free grace of God, and in the name and merit of Jesus. But repentance is implied in an application to that grace —the grace of Him who is the High and Holy One of Israel, the supreme and sovereign God. It is implied, also, in all real resting on the righteousness of Christ. Hence, while we are heard solely in the name of Jesus, we may see the meaning of the apostle's declaration— connecting, as it does by a sure link, the prayer of faith with unreserved obedience—" Whatsoever we ask, we receive of Him, because we keep His commandments, and do those things that are pleasing in His sight" (1 John iii. 22). Without repenting, then, and returning to his duty, Jonah's prayers could not be heard. Nay, rather; truly, and from heart, Jonah could not pray.

To bring him to repentance, however, so that at last his prayers may be heard, is the very purpose of God's strong-handed dealings with him : and these dealings, before they secure the end, must become more strong-handed still. It is another step in this discipline of chastisement and correction which we are called to consider in the seventh verse. "And they said every one to his fellow, Come, and let us cast lots, that we may know for whose cause this evil is come upon us. So they cast lots, and the lot fell upon Jonah."

Now, in this procedure, there are two things to be attended to:—*First*, The fact that each man by making this proposal and going into it disowns the guilt: and, *second*, the method by which they propose to discover it. It is taken for granted that there is guilt involved. It is felt that God, or the gods, the Supreme Being, or superior powers, are displeased. Guilt has been contracted. A guilty party is in the ship. That guilt, that guilty party, God is pursuing by this storm; for the storm is extraordinary, marvellous, if not miraculous. They are forced to believe in some marvellous, some extraordinary, and unwonted reason for it. This reason they think they find, in the supposition that some great crime lies concealed among them—some deadly offence, such as may be righteously pursued and punished by this great and marvellous tempest.

I. The mariners, for their part, one by one, disown this guilt by the very proposal to discover it by lot. Far from being ready in meekness and lowliness of spirit, to say, each one in his own conscience, 'Is it I?'—we find them boldly refusing the charge of criminality, refusing an appeal to their own consciences as a means of discovering it, and proposing to discover it by an appeal to God.

Now, no doubt, as it happened, the anger of God was pursuing, not them, but Jonah. That fact, however, was not discovered to them till afterwards; and so long as they were in ignorance of it, their conduct is to be examined in the remembrance that they *were* ignorant of it. What, then, are we to say of their denying any guilt that could explain or justify on God's part, so to speak, the strong tempest that now lay upon them? Did they not acknowledge themselves to be sinners? Would they have boldly stood up and contended that they were so righteous that God, or the gods, would be unrighteous in sending any trouble upon them? Nay; they would at once have admitted that they were sinners; that ordinary calamities and trials no doubt were righteously enough sent upon them, and were what they could not complain of; and had this storm been merely an ordinary one, they would have been all ready to admit that the trial it brought with it was no excessive punishment of their offences. But it was a tempest so marvellous, indicating so clearly the special and great indignation of God, that it indicated a great and special controversy—great and special sin. Such great and special guiltiness, deserving such great and special punishment—this is what they deny by submitting the matter to the discovery and disclosure of the lot.

Now, here we have an exact picture of the extent to which men are by nature willing to admit that they are sinners; indicating also the point where their admission ceases. They will admit that they are sinners so far as to acknowledge the justice of the smaller trials that they are called upon, in Providence, to endure. But depict to them the eternal wrath of God, the second death, banishment from the presence of the Lord and from the glory of His power, and consignment with lost angels to the lake that burneth, and ask the worldly, unconverted man,—Are you a sinner to that extent? guilty to that degree? do you admit you are a sinner to such extent as justifies God in appointing *that* as the wages of your sin?—and the carnal mind revolts from making any such admission—revolts from honestly acknowledging guilt that would explain, or account for, or justify, a judgment so terrific, a vengeance so conclusive—eternal! Let there be nothing very extraordinary —extraordinary, terrific, or damning—in the storm, the tempest, the punishment; and the sinner will not stand —will not think it worth his while to stand debating the matter and justifying himself. He will admit his sinfulness; but then, in his sinfulness, admitted in these circumstances, he admits nothing extraordinary— nothing extraordinarily sinful, base, or ill-deserving. Yes: and this admission he can make without any great humiliation; without needing to make any application, and without, in point of fact, making any application to God for any signal act of grace, or placing himself under any great obligation to God. His trials and punishments being nothing very extraordinary, he can contrive to bear them; to stagger on under them. He can contrive to outlive the commonplace, ordinary storms of the deep; to put the ship in order, and *lie to* till the tempest abate. But let the tempest become absolutely intolerable—let the anger that sends it rise in its terrors till it become evident that the Almighty has a quarrel which He will not quash, and which the sinner can neither bear nor outlive; let there be denounced upon him a punishment, a penalty, a wrath, a death, not measured by his capacity of endurance, but by the infinite power and glory of the God whom he has dishonoured and disobeyed; ask him now, Are you a sinner to this extent? so great a sinner that, in this, "God is just in speaking and clear in judging," and appoints you nothing but your righteous and mere desert? Ah! you ask him to pass a sentence of condemnation on himself as final, as condemnatory,* as sweeping, as humiliating and complete as that eternal death is finally destructive; and you show him that the only possible escape must be by receiving deliverance as a signal act of grace—a magnificent act of stupendous and unbounded grace; so that he becomes indebted to his offended God for an undeserved kindness and compassion as inconceivably tender, and great, and lasting, as that death is lasting and great and terrific from which it saves him. The natural man is prepared neither so to condemn himself, nor so to be indebted or obligated to his God. To consent to condemn himself as worthy of any such punishment—to feel so great sinfulness in sin as to justify God in appointing for it such a punishment;—this, on the one hand, implies a heart renewed by the Holy Spirit; and, on the other hand, the same newness of heart is realised when a

sinner is made willing to own that his escape from
eternal death is due to the pure favour of God; that it
lays him under inconceivable obligations to God; that
it calls for unmeasured gratitude to God; unreserved,
adoring, loving devotion to God for ever.

Have you come to this acknowledgment of guilt and
grace; guilt on your part—grace on God's? Have you
come to feel that God's sentence of condemnation to
eternal death is simply righteous; and that, therefore,
His gift of eternal life is simply gracious—of mere
grace; mere, amazing, unclaimable, inconceivable grace,
deserving celebrations of endless and adoring praise?
Ah! you do not know the sweet gratitude for grace, if
you do not know the unreserved and guileless acknowledgment of guilt—the guilt even of eternal death, the
guilt of "the wrath which is to come." And in that
case, you cannot speak, with the Apostle's rapturously
fine and tender feeling, of—"Jesus who delivered us
from the wrath to come."

Behold, by the aid of God's holy revelations, the
everlasting mansions of the guilty and condemned! The
storm waxes fierce. The lake of fire burneth. O
sinner, are you for casting lots to ascertain for whom?
Are you still asking, For whom could such doom be
righteously prepared? Are you putting away the
question, "Lord, is it I?" Are you putting away the
answer—the answer that God, by His word and Spirit,
by *His* law and *your* conscience, gives—"Thou art the
man"? What! have you never faced this question?
Is it new to you? What! and you a professing Chris-

tian! And never humbled, broken-hearted, self-condemning; justifying God's simple righteousness in
condemning you; owning His mere grace, so free, so
boundless, so lovely in giving salvation by Jesus!
Know you not these first principles even of Christian
experience? Ah! if you know not, and own not, these
things—the justice and majesty of law; the inexcusableness of sin; the righteousness of hell; the undeservedness, and freeness, and sovereign majesty of grace
—you know not what it is to " awake and arise from the
dead " and come to Christ's " marvellous light." Be not
deceived by temporary, and trifling, and easily disposed
of feelings with respect to sin. Thousands admit that
they are sinners, and listen to hear of salvation, who
know not and own not the hell-deservingness of sin, and,
therefore, cannot know the undeservedness and grace of
salvation, and can neither manifest nor feel the gratitude
which, for such salvation, is due. Ah! when I look
even to that lake that burneth, and that worm that never
dies; and when, by the Spirit of light and strivings, the
storm in my conscience, as to my relation and feelings
and doings towards God, waxes more and more tempestuous, let me not cast lots to ascertain to whom such a doom
could be righteously assigned—for whose sake such a
storm could righteously arise. I am myself the man.
It is I whom sin is finding out. Let me own that God
is not unrighteous. Let me confess I have given Him
good and righteous cause for anger. Let me no more
extenuate my offence and justify myself. He is righteous, and I am not. " Against Him, Him only have I

sinned, that He might be justified when He speaketh, and clear when He judgeth " (Ps. li. 4). Especially let me be encouraged unto this confession—yea, let me be generously overpowered, overwhelmed, ashamed and charmed into this confession—seeing that He only requires an admission that my case is simply the guilty one it is, to absolve me gratuitously, fully, and for ever, from all its guilt, and free me, immediately in hope, and soon in glorious fulfilment, from all its misery.

No! I will cast no lots to discover who is " the chief of sinners." The great Prophet of the Church, by His word and Spirit, declares unto me, " Thou art thyself the man." Yes: and when I truly bow in meek submission, and in free, and unreserved, and full acknowledgment, the same Prophet turns not away from me, nor tarries for a moment in his communications till he tells me, with a voice as true, as powerful, as convincing, " The Lord hath put away thy sin " (2 Sam. xii. 7, 13). For " if we confess our sins, God is faithful and just to forgive us our sins, and to cleanse us from all unrighteousness " (1 John i. 9).

The conduct of these sailors implied that they made no confession. They justified themselves as not deserving any such prosecution and punishment at the hands of Divine justice as the threatened destruction implied. And so can sinners own themselves to be sinners, and guilty to the extent of being worthy of such ordinary punishment as they can put up with, and such that deliverance from it would imply on God's part little grace, and demand on their part little gratitude. But

to own, in holy, self-condemning silence, that they deserve the eternal wrath of the Holy One of Israel—a
wrath so great and so righteous that deliverance from it
cannot be proposed on God's part, save in signal, and
singular, and inconceivable grace and love, and cannot be
embraced on their part, save with feelings of unbounded
gratitude and love in return; this is the self-humiliation
to which the old Adam will never stoop, and which,
wherever it is found, indicates the presence of the new
man, and the prior working of God's regenerating Spirit.

II. Let us now consider the method by which they
propose to discover the guilt which they thus disown.
" And they said every one to his fellow, Come, and let
us cast lots, that we may know for whose cause this
evil is come upon us."

We have several instances in Scripture of the practice
of casting lots. It was by a lot—and after prayer to God
to " give a perfect lot "—that Jonathan was discovered
as having transgressed his father's rash and arbitrary
command to the army not to taste food till the going
down of the sun (1 Sam. xiv. 42). It was by lot, and
after special prayer that God would guide the lot according to His will, that Matthias was chosen and added to
the apostleship, filling up the vacancy caused by the
apostacy and death of Judas (Acts i. 26). It was, in
all probability, by the lot that the Lord, the King of
kings, indicated His choice of Saul to be king over
Israel (1 Sam. x. 21); and that the Righteous One,
the Judge of all, discovered Achan as the troubler of

Israel's camp (Joshua vii. 16–18). And we are familiar with the saying of the wise man; "The lot is cast into the lap, but the whole disposing thereof is of the Lord " (Prov. xxi. 33).

The principle implied in casting lots is, that thereby a solemn appeal is taken to the Lord to indicate His pleasure in a matter that cannot otherwise be decided. Or, taking somewhat lower ground, it is a method of avoiding responsibility and shunning occasion of jealousies.

A question arises. When is it lawful to have recourse to the casting of lots? And when would such a procedure be unlawful? What are the limits between a legitimate and improper use of the lot?

Now, because such a question is only one of a class, a large class of cases of conscience, all involving substantially the same principles, and all to be dealt with in very much the same way, let us devote a little attention to it. What are the limits between a lawful and unlawful appeal to the lot?

1. First, then, let me describe to you a case where its lawfulness is obvious. A general of an army is about to arrange his forces for an assault upon the enemy's citadel. The party that heads the attack are exposed to be cut in pieces; the probability of escape to each of them is exceedingly small, the probability of death exceedingly great. They are, alas! 'the forlorn hope.' Overawed by the thought of appointing his fellow-creatures thus to almost certain death, the general, instead of himself fixing on the portion ot his army that shall

lead the van, chooses to decide the matter by casting lots. Clearly he makes a most lawful appeal to the lot in such a case. Whether simply as refusing the responsibility, or as making a solemn appeal to God, he is only embracing a legitimate privilege. He may with a good conscience, as in the sight of God, and in the spirit of prayer, cast lots to settle this very solemn matter. He ought to do it in the spirit of prayer; and, if a godly man, he will. Such is a case where the lawfulness is quite unquestionable.

2. Let us go at once to the other extreme, and describe a case where the *un*lawfulness is equally obvious. A party of men agree to furnish each a certain sum of money to a common store, and then they cast lots to determine to whom the whole sum shall belong. The character of such a proceeding is clear. All such lotteries, raffles, gamblings, are immoral,—profane. They are, in their very essence, atheistic profligacy. The parties themselves may be made quickly to confess that they are. Will you dare to say, we may ask them, will you dare to say that you can ask the Divine sanction on a step like this? Do you think, if you lose in this speculation, that Almighty God will not hold you responsible for the worldly good you thus lose? for you put away what God gave, and what God commanded you concerning, saying, " Occupy till I come." And He will demand an account of it, as what you lost without His providence taking it from you. And if you gain, will He not reckon with you, in like manner, for being in possession of what He never gave? And

will you dare to call Him in to decide and allocate in such shameful transfers? " The lot is cast into the lap, but the whole disposing thereof is of the Lord." And you take that method which most especially involves His finger to settle what He most especially abhors! The reply of course is that any such thought of thus appealing to God is never entertained. And doubtless that is true enough ; for it is evident that the thoughtless agents are acting all too plainly as those that are without God in the world. But it remains none the less true that " the whole disposing of the lot is of God;" and if in such a case it would be blasphemy to realise it to be so, and still persist, it is practical atheism not to realise it at all. For if " the very hairs of our heads are numbered," and " not a sparrow falleth to the ground without our Father ; "—and the falling out of the lot is not more truly, but certainly more obviously, of His sole will and pleasure ;—then if men can use it without thinking of God and His providence, attributing the result rather to chance, or luck, or fortune, or fate, is not this an atheistic exclusion of the Almighty from the affairs of His own world, and only next in its profligacy to the blasphemy which would be involved in saying that they appealed the lot to God, and sought to make Him a party to their dishonourable dealings ? Enough has been said to show the immorality of casting lots in such a case.

We have taken, then, two extreme instances ; one where the propriety and lawfulness are obvious, the other where the unlawfulness and profanity are equally clear. But then, between these two extremes there may range a vast variety of cases more or less clear as they are nearer to the one or other of the extremes, or approach to some middle line or limit between them. A father, for instance, in dividing some little gifts or presents among his children, to avoid jealousies or dissatisfaction, may have recourse to the casting of lots. They *draw cuts*. If this is right, it is clearly not so obviously right as the case of a general drafting by lot the parties to whom in the breach a death of violence is all but certain. Or again, two young people, engaged in an exercise of lawful recreation, may cast lots to determine who shall begin. If this is wrong, it is clearly very far from being so obviously wrong as an appeal to the lot in a matter of gambling. Is the one, then, really right, and is the other really wrong? Where is the limit between the right and the wrong? Where is the line that separates the lawful from the unlawful use?

Now this is precisely the question which we think no intelligent religious teacher will undertake to answer; and that simply because the Bible itself does not answer it. The Bible does not deal with God's people in the way of answering in set terms every question of conscience that may arise. And if God himself does not in set terms answer every such question, it would surely be wrong in us to attempt to do so. We need not say that if every case and question of conscience which might arise along the whole course of time, and amidst the countless multitudes of the Church in all climes and ages, had been, in so many words, provided

for and answered in a revelation from heaven, the
sacred book would have reached dimensions of such
enormous magnitude as would have rendered it perfectly useless. "I suppose that even the world itself
could not contain the books that should have been
written" (John xxi. 25). But apart from that consideration. While God trains His children under certain
clearly-enough announced commandments, and has given
us His moral law in its various precepts as the rule of our
duty, He has not placed us under an unbending martial
drill, under a miserable martinette-like subjection to in-
cessant, and express, and verbal instructions, leaving no
room for His free Spirit to exercise our consciences in
freedom, or to guide us in filial and manly enlargement.
He deals with us, not under a servile arrangement that
would incessantly, and in terms, dictate to us, giving us
nothing higher and nobler to do than to creep along
every moment exactly by the tight line drawn for us
and to square our conduct by dead mechanical rule.
No. Our Lord gives us His holy law which is the
image of His own holy nature, and the expression of
His own holy life; and which bears in it, therefore, the
image and the impress of the freedom of His own free
holy natures, both as God and man. He writes this
law on our hearts; supreme love to God, unfeigned love
to man; when He freely reconciles us, as friends and
children, to the Father. Then He places us in His
vineyard to do His work;—" Son, go work to-day in my
vineyard." That vineyard we find, not bordered, and
hedged, and railed in, on the supposition of our being

infants under tutors and governors. We find in it no
such series of instructions as would allocate the particular duty of each particular hour; and we find no such
arrangement as would ring us off, by bell or token, from
one duty to another, at the exact moment, leaving us
nothing to do but mechanically to wait the summons
and follow the continual leading strings. This is not
God's way of disciplining His people. He leaves them
much more at freedom, and, in a sense, much more to
their own discretion. Nor does He thereby diminish
their responsibility. Very much the reverse. He lays
upon them a far greater responsibility. He gives them
great general rules, and He calls upon them to apply
these rules. Instead of pointing out each separate
thing they are to do, in which case they might do it and
be little disciplined in spirit by doing it, He calls upon
them in terms like these, " Whatsoever ye do, whether
in word or in deed, do all to the glory of God." He
asks them to keep alive on their spirits a sense of responsibility to Him; to walk under His eye, ready to
do His will. He asks them to keep a single eye to His
glory, and a heart submissive to His pleasure. And
having freely adopted them to His love, and graciously
renewed them by His Spirit, He places them amidst
difficulties, no doubt, and trials and temptations, and
in circumstances where their sincerity will be subjected
to proof, and gives them call and opportunity to show
of what spirit they are, by " doing all things in the
name of Christ Jesus " (Col. iii. 17); or doing all things
in a manner " worthy of their high calling from God "

(Eph. iv. 1); by " doing all things to the glory of God " (1 Cor. x. 31); or doing all things "unto the use of edifying " (Eph. iv. 29).

Are you thus reconciled to God? Are you, like Abraham, God's friend? And are there questions that arise, like this of casting lots, or in matters of apparent conformity to worldly custom,—cases of conscience and of casuistry? And have you to inquire, Is this lawful? may I take the step that is recommended to me? does my Christianity require me, in this or that other matter, to act differently from the multitude around me? And have you difficulty in settling a variety of points connected with your actual daily doings in the world? Expect not an exact, minute, verbal statement, in every case, of what you ought to do. Such statement is impossible; and, were it possible, it is not desirable. And beware of getting fretted into a regret that you have not more definite and exact instructions. Look rather to the spirit that dwelleth in you. Are you of the same mind that was in Jesus? How, think you, would Jesus have acted in the case supposed? Are you willing to decide by that test? Bring into mind the great principle, " Whatsoever ye do, do all to the glory of God." How does the proposed line of conduct appear when that rule of duty is applied to it? Can you take this proposed step, and yet glorify God? Rather, can you take this proposed step, and *thereby* glorify God? Will it stand side by side with a reanimated fear of the Lord? Will it consist with the spirit of prayer? Can you engage in it, and your fellowship with God not be interrupted? Let no man say that solemn rules like these, applied to our current and continual conduct, would mar the happy social enjoyments of life, and the innocent recreations of buoyant youth or of fatigued manhood unbending from weary care. It is not so. God hath made us for mutual society; He hath made us so that continual strain on body or mind without recreation is destructive to our health and usefulness. No enlightened conscience will see any inconsistency between healthful and happy recreation, on the one hand, and glorifying God, on the other. These very recreations, and whatsoever he doeth, the enlarged and free-hearted believer can do—to the glory of God. Only let this principle really rule,—' How may I best and to the utmost degree glorify God?'—and all narrow, creeping, bondage-ridden questions, and all symptoms of a timid, hampered, unmanly, faltering, unfree walk with God, will disappear. And without a free, holy, cordial, open, ingenuous walk with God, all minute and accurate and verbal and mechanical rules might most mechanically and accurately and minutely be observed, but the soul of man be not any more trained to the exalted dignity of a free companionship and unfettered friendship with Heaven.

XI

JONAH IN THE SHIP: ACHAN IN THE CAMP

JONAH i. 8, 9

"Then said they unto him, Tell us, we pray thee, for whose cause
this evil is upon us : what is thine occupation ? and whence comest
thou ? what is thy country ? and of what people art thou ? And
he said unto them, I am an Hebrew ; and I fear Jehovah, the God
of heaven, which hath made the sea and the dry land."

> "And Joshua said unto Achan, My son,
> give, I pray thee, glory to the Lord
> God of Israel, and make confession
> unto him ; and tell me now what thou
> hast done ; hide it not from me."—
> JOSHUA vii. 19.

THERE is a strong resemblance between the ordeal
which Jonah is now undergoing for having fled
from the presence of the Lord and the land of Israel,
and that to which a far less distinguished member of
his nation was subjected soon after that land of Israel
was entered on by the sacred people. That land had
been inhabited by transgressors whose wickedness had
grown up to heaven, and on whom God had now resolved to execute a final work of judgment in their

remorseless extermination, side by side with his work
of grace and faithfulness in establishing Israel in the
land promised to their fathers. The first city doomed
to destruction after the believing, triumphant entrance
of Israel on the consecrated territory, the Lord resolved
to destroy in a peculiar manner. He designed to read
His people a lesson, in the very commencement of their
warfare of invasion, to the effect that all their success
depended on the forth-putting of power on His part and
the forth-putting of faith on theirs. It was a trial of
their faith,—their meek submission to the will, their
confidence in the word, their dependence on the power,
of God. For six successive days, the whole camp of
Israel, the armed men, the priests, with the ark of the
Lord's covenant, move round the strong-walled city. Not
a blow do they essay to strike. Not a shout of defiance
do they send towards the fortress. Not a sound of war
is uttered. Not a move do they make towards victory,
or even towards conflict. Not a sound of any kind is
heard, save the seven trumpets of the seven priests before the ark of the Lord. Day after day nothing comes
of it. Night after night, they return into the camp and
lodge there in peace. Jericho also sleeps in peace ; no
advance made whatever towards its destruction ; free to
laugh at the absurd movements, the childish pageantry
and empty procession of Israel's mad and moon-struck
tribes !

Yes ; it was, day after day, an increasing trial to
Israel's faith ;—a strange procedure ; to the men of
Jericho "foolishness ; " "to the Jews," save for their

faith, "a stumbling-block." But "by faith the walls of Jericho fell down, after they were compassed about seven days" (Heb. xi. 30).

Thus singularly given up, by God's sole power, to Israel's single faith, Jericho was to be entirely a devoted thing; a whole and unreserved victim to God's righteous wrath. "And the city shall be accursed." Such were the stern and clear and most unmistakable instructions of the Lord to Joshua, and from the Lord, through Joshua, to the people: "the city shall be accursed,"—or devoted,—"even it, and all that is therein, to the Lord. And ye, in any wise, keep yourselves from the accursed thing, lest ye make yourselves accursed, when ye take of the accursed thing, and make the camp of Israel a curse, and trouble it. But all the silver, and gold, and vessels of brass and iron, are consecrated to the Lord: they shall come into the treasury of the Lord" (Joshua vi. 17–19).

This command Achan disobeyed. And the next solemn move in Israel's camp, the next solemn chapter in Israel's history, after the splendid miracle of Jericho's destruction, opens thus sadly and gloomily: "But the children of Israel committed a trespass in the accursed thing: for Achan, the son of Carmi, the son of Zabdi, the son of Zerah, of the tribe of Judah, took of the accursed thing: and the anger of the Lord was kindled" (Joshua vii. 1). This kindled anger the Lord kept for manifestation in a suitable manner. The accursed thing detained—yea, "stolen"—from the Lord, of the spoils of the first city, shall fatally bar them from con-

quering a second. They flee before the men of Ai.
Joshua rends his clothes, and falls down before God in
broken-hearted alarm and prayer. "Get thee up;
wherefore liest thou thus upon thy face? Israel hath
sinned, and they have also trespassed my covenant
which I commanded them ; for they have even taken of
the accursed thing, and have also stolen, and dissembled
also, and they have put it even among their own stuff.
Therefore the children of Israel could not stand before
their enemies" (verses 10, 11). Directions are then
given by the Lord for the discovery of the offender,
and next day the multitudes of Israel stand forth to be
searched of the Lord.

It is a solemn scene. Every movement in it, as another and another knell, strikes strong, and with ever
mounting force, upon the evil conscience. A first step
—a somewhat distant approach to the discovery, is
made : from the many thousands of Israel, the tribe of
Judah is selected. The eleven tribes breathe free. On
Judah all eyes are bent. By families, Judah now is
tried. The lot falls on the family of Zerah. The
ground is narrowed and narrowing. Justice is hemming
in the guilty one. The family of Zerah, man by man,
passes in review, and the lot falls on Zabdi, and "Zabdi
was taken." "And he brought his household, man by
man ; and Achan, the son of Carmi, the son of Zabdi,
the son of Zerah, of the tribe of Judah, was taken."
For, " be sure your sin will find you out."

Is it not expressly said by an Apostle, speaking at the
mouth of the Spirit of God, that the events of Israel's

history are recorded " for our admonition, on whom the
ends of the world are come"? And what can be better
fitted to speak to us in terms the most overpowering and
impressive, than the very silence, the breathless silence,
with which a scene like this is transacted among the
people whom the Lord had chosen to dwell among
them? And was it not *designed* to produce this solemn
and awful impression, that every one who saw or heard
of it might " stand in awe and sin not," and do not thus
wickedly? Ordinary providence, indeed, oftentimes
worketh in this very way, though without, it may be,
those specialties and miracles that appertained to Jehovah's dealings with Israel. How often has the criminal become a spectacle to a whole camp—the object
of a whole nation's thought and speech! For the finger
of God is in his trial; and that finger of the living God,
itself unseen, yet points to this circumstance and that,
lays them side by side, places and pieces them together,
carries them and places them beneath the eyes of those
staid and anxious men of jury and of judgment; and,
on being asked to read and tell what they have seen,
amidst the silence of a camp, or of a nation, they simply
read what their eyes have seen, because God's finger
had written;—Proven: Guilty!

Let it be observed how tremendously conspicuous a
man may become, solely and alone, by reason of sin;
—as Achan did. No public servant of the Lord; no
bearer of office among his people; no prophet like
Jonah; but in private life, it may be in humble rank,
Achan, save for his sin, had passed in all probability

through life, with nothing to mark him out to others—certainly with nothing to hand down his name to us. But, a look of covetousness flashes from his eye; the ready hand executes the will of the lustful eye; a few hours pass away in secret self-contempt or shameless sin-drugged deep insensibility, or some average feeling midway between these two extremes; and lo! by the finger of God pointing to his sin, he is the spectacle of many hundreds of thousands of eyes, all unanimously, simultaneously bent on him; he is the theme of many hundreds of thousands of tongues, soon as a solemn awe releases them from breathless silence.

There may be worlds in space, inhabited by races of unfallen beings,—worlds far more numerous than the crew of Jonah's ship—yea, far more numerous than the spectators in the twelve tribes of Israel—"the many thousands of Israel"—as they crowd the plain in silent excitement, in the early sunlight of this solemn judgment day near Ai.   And they may be worlds of magnificence and glory, and official dignity one might say, in the grand priestly service of the universe—as far transcending the native place and position or capacity of this small world of ours, as countless priests, and noble warriors, and girded Levites, and princes, and great men in Israel, transcended in talent, in birth, in office, in honour, in fame, the poor and unnoticeable Achan.   But as he, for sin, became the centre of all Israel's breathless regard; so may this sinful world, and thou, O sinner, be conspicuous in the families of the wide, wide universe, solely, aye solely, because of sin.   This is

thy tremendous distinction, O man! thy terrible con-
spicuousness—even that thou hast sinned. Thou art
become wonderful as having dared to rebel—rebel
against the Most High God. Thou art attracting much
attention. Myriads of flashing holy eyes fall on thee.
God's tribes, and families, and households, and holy
ones, look on thee. " I charge thee before God *and the
elect angels*." Oh! how canst thou stand their gaze?
How canst thou see them, silent and breathless concerning thee? Get thee to thy hiding-place; to that " man
that is an hiding-place ;" that God-man, for whose sake
thou shalt be infinitely more conspicuous to the holy ones
than even sin against the Highest can make thee. Get
thee into Him. Make Christ thy all; while the Father
makes Him thine. And thus release the holy ones
from breathless silence. Give them leave—give them
cause—O man! to sing, " This our brother was dead
and is alive again, was lost and is found." Yea! lest
the tribes stone thee with stones, and burn thee with fire ;
lest the angels, binding the bundles, bind thee among
them, and cast thee into everlasting fire; yea, lest the
ship cast thee out into the raging lake that burneth.
For whether thou be Jonah, high in name and labours,
or Achan, mean and unknown, if thou meet the judgment and the lot impenitent; if thou " stand in thy
lot in the ends of days," thy sin not till then finding
thee out, thy true and engrossing sorrow for sin only
then beginning; thy sorrow shall be sorrow unto death,
and thy sin be unhealed and eternal.

Let thy sin find thee out now ; *now*, while thy Saviour

seeks thee—thy Saviour who came to seek and to *find*, —and who is offended, disobliged, defeated in a loving, longing wish, if He is not gratified in being allowed to succeed in finding thee;—thee, O trembling, smitten soul; thee, whom thy sins are finding.

Achan was taken.   The lot fell on Jonah.

The treatment to which these two men were subjected immediately on their criminality being revealed deserves especial consideration, and the comparison of the two cases suggests not a few lessons of value.   Thus, in the case of Jonah: "Then said the mariners unto him, Tell us, we pray thee, for whose cause this evil is upon us: what is thine occupation? and whence comest thou? what is thy country? and of what people art thou?" In the case of Achan; "Joshua said unto him, My son, give, I pray thee, glory to the Lord God of Israel, and make confession unto Him, and tell me now what thou hast done, hide it not from me."   Such are the two addresses delivered to the two criminals respectively, in the moment of their detection or discovery; the one by heathen sailors to the troubler of the ship, the other by Joshua, the man of God, to the troubler of the camp.   And they even invite comparison, while they promise to reward it.

I. Compare, then, these respective investigations.

1. First of all, observe the *manner* of them.   Mark the alarm of the heathen; the calm solemnity of the man of God.

See the loss of self-possession on the part of the

Gentile sailors; the alarmed haste, mingling with irrepressible and excited curiosity, as question after question comes pouring forth, each tripping on the heels of the former; "What is thine occupation? And whence camest thou? What is thy country? And of what people art thou?" See, on the other hand, the dignity and deliberateness of the holy Joshua; "My son, give glory, I pray thee, to the Lord God of Israel, and make confession to Him; and tell me what thou hast done; hide it not from me." No one can thoughtfully read these two expostulations to the prisoner, these two adjurations to him to tell the truth, to speak out the fact, without feeling that in the one case there is alarm, selfish fear, ungoverned curiosity, heathen haste: in the other, holy deliberation, reverential solemnity; a far higher governing desire than selfish excitement on the theme or fear of danger; a majestic, peaceful discharge of duty, as of one who puts himself forward only as the instrument and servant of Jehovah. The moral littleness of Jonah's inquisitors comes out, as tossed on a sea of mental anxiety, they have scarcely power or time decently to ask a question,—not to speak of waiting for an answer; but forth flows a torrent of queries, very far in their jumbled haste from the solemn dignity, the grave order of judicial righteousness. The moral greatness of Joshua, on the other hand, is seen in the stern, yet mild and quiet, resolve in which he conducts and carries out the trial. There is righteousness in his manner—righteousness inflexible in his manner, movements, countenance, voice, and word: righteousness so strong that it does not need to brace itself up nervously, exhibiting and revealing its weakness. And there is compassion also—compassion so holy, so true, that it does not seek to prove itself by many words. "My son," he says; "my son," even to the man stained with the accursed thing. With such majesty does holy character naturally clothe itself; holy character, and holy office, held direct and in faith from God.

2. But, secondly, compare the two addresses to the criminals respectively, in regard to the *matter* of them.

There are two things to which an address, an adjuration, a charge or inquiry directed to an offender in these circumstances will have, or at least ought to have, respect. It will, or it ought to be, designed to lead him to an admission of the fact, and to lead him to an acknowledgment of the guilt. Now the two styles of address before us are in marked contrast, as to the prominence or proportion in which these two several elements are set forth. The heathen mariners are almost exclusively bent on ascertaining from Jonah the *fact* of his offence; the *guilt* of it, his feelings as to the guilt of it, his admission of the guilt of it, they scarcely concern themselves about at all. Joshua, on the other hand, while in duty required to search the fact, puts forward first of all, and prominently, his poor prisoner's duty to God to confess the guilt.

Read now, again, in this light the heathen sailors' series of hot and hasty queries. There is not a single question concerning guilt. Not a single word directed to Jonah to strengthen his conscience towards confes-

sion unto God of his inexcusable transgression. They
are quite in a lower sphere with their questions altogether. The event, the fact, the action,—not whether
there be *that* in it which adorable rectitude cannot
but relentlessly and righteously pursue; but the act,
the incident, the fact itself: give them *that;* satisfy them
about *that.* Yes, satisfy them upon the fact; not, glorify
God concerning the guilt of Jonah and God's righteousness in thus pursuing Jonah. Tell us, we pray thee, for
whose cause this evil is come upon us; what is thine
occupation? and whence comest thou? what is thy
country? and of what people art thou? Give us the
facts; these bear on us—bear on us and on our safety.
Not, Own the guilt to God; the guilt that bears on Him;
that bears on Him and His rights; that has been touching and tampering with His glory. To this higher
and holier element in the case, the heathens do not rise.

It is otherwise with Joshua. With him this element is in the foreground. "My son, give *glory* unto
God, and *make confession* to him." Thou hast troubled
us, indeed. For thee, our victorious march has been
arrested; our arms soiled with dishonour and defeat;
our brothers vilely driven back and slain, their shields
vilely thrown away; the hearts of the people melted
also, and become as water. Verily thou hast troubled
us and smitten us with grief, making amongst us "many
a sweet babe fatherless, and many a widow mourning."
But while thou hast troubled *us,* against *God,* against
Him, Him only, hast thou sinned. My son, give glory
to the Lord God of Israel, and make confession unto

Him. Tell *me*, indeed, what thou hast done; hide it not: for "a little leaven leaveneth the whole lump;" and the evil leaven, the accursed thing, must be purged away. For against the camp as well as thee, against the camp of Israel by and for thee, is the anger of the Lord God of Israel kindled. Tell *me*, therefore, what thou hast done; but my son, give the glory to God, and make confession of the guilt to Him. The sin, in the *fact* of it, He knows: I know it not; tell it to me. Thy sin, in the *guilt* of it, is not against me; 'tis against Him: to Him acknowledge it. Give Him the glory of confessing to Him,—the true King and Sovereign, the Most High, the Holy One in Israel.

Mark well the difference between the mere fact and the guilt of your sin; and more especially the difference between the admission of the fact and the admission of your guilt. Jehovah comes into the garden in the cool of the day, and brings the criminals from their hiding-place of shame into His presence. The question is: Adam, hast thou eaten? Eve, hast thou eaten? Not to ascertain the fact;—for of that, apart from the Omniscience of the Judge, their every look, every move, every attitude is a sad, and sore, and sufficient demonstration;—but to induce a confession of *sin*, of *guilt*, of inexcusable offence, of righteous liability to anger and punishment. What are the replies? "The woman whom Thou gavest to be with me, she gave me, and I did eat." "I did eat." The fact is admitted. But is the guilt? Nay; if it were, why this preface to the fact; this dwelling so fully on fact, and fact alone; this

brief history of the fact; brief, yet clung to so firmly—
expected to be made so much of? " The woman whom
Thou gavest to be with me, she gave me, and I did eat."
Clearly, the design is, while admitting the fact, to
disown the guilt; to put the guilt on Eve; " She gave
me":—to put the blame, if need be, on God;—"the
woman whom Thou gavest to be with me, she gave
me":—and but for the woman giving me the fruit,
and but for Thee giving me the woman, I had not
eaten—for then it would have been wholly inexcusable.
It is an elaborate effort to disentangle the fact from the
guilt; to acknowledge the one and disown the other.
There is no giving glory to God and making confession
to Him. It is rather throwing over the responsibility on
Him ; laying blame at His door in the enmity of false-
hood : not taking blame to self, and lying down at His
feet in the confidence and confession of truth and candour.

And the woman, she also admits the fact:—" I did
eat." But she too rejects the guilt; " The serpent
beguiled me, and I did eat." Were it not for him
having beguiled me; had I done it without him beguil-
ing me; I would have been guilty indeed, silent, speech-
less, inexcusable, without a plea, and my guilt without
palliation. As it is, I have this to say for myself—
this plea, this answer, this defence, this shield, this
extenuation, this claim against condemnation and death;
" The serpent beguiled me, and I did eat."

What are your repentings? What are your admis-
sions at a throne of grace? Is it merely the fact of
your sin that you admit? Is it the exceeding sinful-

ness of sin, rather, that you feel? The former you may do, and that may satisfy a heathen. It is the latter that satisfies God,—and a man of God. "Give glory unto God, my son, and make confession to him."

Give glory unto God! What glory? and unto what God; or, unto God, under what aspect or relation, shall I give glory? Unto the Lord God of Israel, my son. Unto the God of His people, the God of salvation, standing to thee in Christ in that relation—thy God, O poor offender; the God of thy salvation, notwithstanding all the guilt and blackness of thy sin. Thee He is seeking to save, by this very discipline by which He makes thy sin to find thee out. To number thee among the Israel to whom He is the God of salvation— this is His design in sending forth thy sin—letting loose thy sin—to hunt and harass thee with fear of death, of judgment, of eternal wrath, with present pain of bitter shame and burning conscience. See Him in Christ—too soon thou canst not. Thou canst not too soon realise Him in Christ the God of righteous, holy mercy to thee, the God of thy salvation. And *as such* let Him have glory from thee.

And what glory? Glory, as the heart-searching, all-seeing God: "Thou God, seest me;" "O God, thou knowest my foolishness; and my sins are not hid from thee." Glory, as the Sovereign One, the Ruler, the Lawgiver, the King, the High and lofty One, throned in the court of last appeal, into which, until I come, I never know the greatness and honour of my nature as responsible there. Glory, as the Being who alone can decide on my case: who alone can master all its intricacies; witness, and attest, and understand all its facts; weigh and measure all its criminality; scan and foresee all its fruits and issues: who alone can master and reverse all its evils. Glory, as the Just One, who can do me no wrong; the Judge of all the earth who will ever do that which is right. Glory, as a just God and a Saviour, freely justifying the ungodly who believe in Christ; and who, with His Son's most glorious and evermore amazing cross, and by its efficacy ministered unto me continually by His gospel and His Spirit, opens and searches all my heart, penetrates it with the power of His Son's most terrible but saving death, draws out from their recesses all my lingering enmities, and jealousies, and distrusts, and dislikes, and constraining me to make a clean breast in telling all its foulness, Himself then purges me with hyssop that I may be clean, creates a clean heart within me, and makes me whiter than snow. Yes; let my sin be before me as Achan's was. Let me realise God and His holy ones looking on me—"I charge thee before God and the elect angels"—let me have no door of escape, and above all let me seek none; let me give glory to God, and make confession to Him. Glory be to God, there is room yet for giving glory to Him—vile though I may be in His sight and in my own—though I be of all earth's poor prisoners, and caught ones, and convicts, the very chief. Still I may give Him glory; and He will not refuse it at my hands. Only let me feel that I deserve His anger. And only let the cross of His beloved Son rise, in the Spirit's light, more and more to my view. Oh, that cross of Christ! Oh, the blessedness of perfect expiation of sin effected there, that sin may be forgiven there,—freely, fully, for ever forgiven if I only carry it there! Oh, the dawning, the fast breaking hope that beams and brightens there! Oh, how it makes me honest, how it makes me true, if I really see it! I give glory to God, and make confession to Him at His Son's cross. And the light of His countenance beams even now on me above it; and the glory of His eternal home bursts open for me yonder behind it. What matters the complexion of my lot 'twixt now and then? Weary years of varying, vexing care; sharp, swift trials, following fast on each other; trying duties manifold, it may be; the thousand ills of man's estate in changing combinations, in fast succession, or in slow detail;—I may have to prove them all. But what although, if I have been able only to glorify God in making confession to Him, and He has not rejected the glory, but been indeed glorified in me? It is but a little while, and He shall straightway glorify me with Himself. And even now, if stern, relentless justice should require, as with Achan, that I be offered up a victim to the peace and welfare of the camp; let me only see that it is God who deals with me and demands it; let me only hold fast by His justice, satisfied in atonement by the Lamb— and His love, certified and sealed in atonement by the Lamb—and even still, I can give Him glory; for though I be " delivered over for the destruction of the flesh," and " though the outward man perish," and " I have the sentence of death in myself;" it is "that I may trust in Him who quickeneth the dead," that the "inward man be the more renewed," and "that the spirit may be saved in the day of the Lord." Nay; all lengths can I go through the cross of Christ. Let the Spirit only bring forth upon my heart more and more of the power of that cross, (and its power is altogether endless and supreme), and let me even, if need be—and it is well to study even the extremest case—let me even, if need be, be carried down with Achan to the valley of Achor, and let the people stone me there :— Give me only, still, and always, and there, the cross of Christ, as the Lord still, and always, and there, doth give me; and, nerved anew unto the uttermost of all my need, I have even "the valley of Achor for a door of hope."

In this spirit, as we have ground in holy charity to hope, Achan met and acquiesced in his fate. In this spirit, we know that Jonah more than acquiesced in— himself pointed out—his.

II. Having contrasted the two appeals made to the respective parties in their so similar circumstances, let us in like manner compare their respective answers. And the point of interest turns here again on the relative importance assigned to the admission of the fact on the one hand, and the admission of the guilt on the other.

Thus, in the one case, Achan with much simplicity and meekness owns the guilt against God. "And

Achan answered Joshua, and said, Indeed I have sinned against the Lord God of Israel, and thus and thus have I done." And then, because the case required the minuteness of fact also, in order that the last rack of the cursed thing should be purged away, he goes on minutely to specify every particular, with all the exactness that his preface—" thus and thus have I done "— would seem to promise.

Again, on the other hand, in the case of Jonah, the admission of the fact is out of all comparison the least of it. The fact indeed he admits, briefly, off-hand ; fully, without.reserve ; also without dwelling upon it. What he dwells upon, what he aggravates, is his guilt, his blame-worthiness, his criminality, his ill-deservingness, his entire deservingness of all that God is doing. " And he said unto them, I am an Hebrew, and I fear the Lord, the God of heaven, which made the sea and the dry land." There is the acknowledgment of his guilt. And these are the things that aggravate his guilt. He is " an Hebrew ;" one of the favoured people, of whom he knoweth, and hath had rich experience, that God dealt not so with any nation. And he knows " the God of heaven," and " fears " Him, the God that " made the sea and the dry land," the living God, the Supreme, the Creator, the Preserver of all the ends of the earth, the Answerer of Prayer unto His people, answering them at times by "terrible things in righteousness," yet still " the confidence of all the ends of the earth and of all them that are afar off upon the sea " (Ps. lxv). For such an one to sin, and to sin thus ; for a Hebrew to cast himself out among the heathen; for a believer in the God of heaven, the Maker of the sea and of the dry land, to flee from land to sea, away from the presence of the Maker of both, this indeed was deep-dyed guiltiness and sin. And all this, to his own humiliation, Jonah distinctly speaks out and specifies. The mere fact, the mere admission of the fact, is with him a small matter; all the more so, as his interrogators seemed to count it the most engrossing. With him, the matter of the guilt, the offensiveness, the aggravated and inexcusable criminality, is by far the most important thing calling for admission, for acknowledgment; all the more so because his interrogators made so light of it, so little of it, overlooked it indeed so completely. With him now, in his returning integrity and rising penitence, the admission of his guilt is the great point. He disposes quickly of the fact. Accordingly in our narrative the admission of the fact is thrown quite into a parenthesis, quite into a corner, into the shade, into the background. It is set aside quite in an off-hand way. His telling them the fact is recorded as a matter of course; no attention is concentrated on that. It is not engrossed among the other parts of his reply, but merely stated to have formed a part of it. It seems as if it had been engrossed in the narrative as by a hair-breadth escape: "The men knew that he had fled from the presence of the Lord, because he had told them." In this slight and unnoticeable way,—scarcely for a moment breaking the deep solemnity of the record as it discloses the action of a fallen but godly man's conscience of the guilt,—the mere admission of the deed is disposed of and set at rest. On the solemn owning of the guilt all our notice is concentrated. And not only so in Jonah's original converse on the very scene itself. But, as we are to remember, Jonah himself is afterwards the writer and author, under God's Spirit, of this very record before us. It is he who tells the story. It is he who so quickly disposes of his own acknowledgment of the fact: "The men knew that he fled from the presence of the Lord, because he had told them." And it is he who, on the contrary, recounts and puts on record for all generations the full statement of his aggravated guilt and shame: "I am an Hebrew, and I fear the God of heaven, who made the sea and the dry land." I who have fled from His presence, did so in the face of such light, such privileges, such responsibilities as an Hebrew, a fearer of the living God, alone can know. The admission of the fact is secondary; and both as a penitent groaning under God's hand at the time, and as a prophet writing God's Scriptures afterwards, Jonah brings out its secondariness. He makes no secret of it indeed; but he makes no great matter of it. The great matter—the great point with him is "giving glory" to God; owning his deep guilt; shielding and glorifying, even in his own punishment, God's unspotted righteousness. Is not this the proof that he is, that he is still, that he is once more, a true fearer of the Lord, a leal-hearted son and servant of God Most High? Is not this the action, and test, and proof of filial truth and trustfulness; of a true son's true, and loyal, and holy heart; even amidst sin's acknowledgment; yea, never more truly than in the very fact and moment of sin acknowledged in all its guiltiness, its utter inexcusableness, its exceeding sinfulness? Never is one more intensely a son than in the very act of confession, when confession is heartfelt, ingenuous, true, and full. " Give glory unto God, my son, and make confession to Him."

O fallen prophet! O rising man of God! thou *art* a Hebrew; thou fearest God! Not, Thou didst once fear God, Thou didst once belong to the commonwealth of Israel and covenants of promise. Fallen thou hast greatly; pursued thou art hotly; punished with strong cords of chastisement, by the strong hand of the Almighty. Yet still thou holdest thine integrity; still thou fearest God. O blessed word! " I fear, I do fear, I am fearing, the God of heaven." Yes; hold fast thy fear of God. Hold to it, and protest that still thou fearest God. Say not, I once feared the Lord; once, in days gone by, before I disobeyed Him and fled. The enemy would have thee to put it all to the past, to set it all aside as past. Nay; hold to it that still, disobedient as thou hast been, miserable as thou art, still thou fearest God, truly, reverently, filially, penitently, giving Him glory. Fallen thou hast. Yet let this be thy challenge to the foe: " Rejoice not against me, O mine enemy: when I fall, I shall arise again; when I sit in darkness, the Lord shall be a light unto me." Fallen thou hast. Yet, challenging and defying the enemy, appeal also to the Lord; even as the Lord, by this very punishment, appeals to thee. For is He not appealing to thee? Hark! the terms of His appeal! Jonah, son of Amittai, fearest thou me—me the Maker of this raging sea, and of the dry land? Seest thou not, O Jonah, that thy God is keeping fast hold of thee; and not even thy sin shall pluck thee out of thy Saviour's, thy Father's hand? Seest thou not that He is keeping fast hold of thee, that thou mayest keep fast hold of thine integrity and of Him? Seest thou not that this very raging of the sea, raging against thee, raging against thy sin, is sent forth to keep alive, to quicken, to stimulate, to restore thy true and trusting and obedient fear of God? Doth not every wave, in its tumultuous terror, as it dashes on the ship, cry as from God; "Jonah, son of Amittai, fearest thou me?" A brother of thine in after days, as foully fallen, shall hear a still small voice beside the soft rippling wave of Galilee's lake, say, "Simon, son of Jonas, *lovest* thou me?" And canst not thou reply, somewhat as he shall, "Lord, thou knowest all things, thou knowest that I fear thee"?

Yes; there is uprightness in thee still, O man of God; and by thine uprightness thou shalt rise again, through the mercy of thy God, into righteous peace and dignity, into labours and usefulness still in His service. Cast not away thy fear of God which hath great recompence of reward. Only be true. Only be truthful to man and true to God. Come what may, give God the glory. He can do thee no wrong, even unto eternity. Is He not thy God? And is He not also, O sinning, fallen, troubled, penitent, rising brother, is He not the God of the

sea? That raging sea can never hurt thee, true to thy
God who is also the God of heaven, of the sea, and of
the dry land. Confess to Him. Return to Him. Give
glory unto Him. Come of it whatsoever may, give
Him glory. Though He slay thee, yet still do thou
trust in Him. None of them that trust in Him shall
be desolate.

XII

AGGRAVATIONS OF THE GUILT OF BACKSLIDING

Jonah i. 9, 10

" And he said unto them, I am an Hebrew ; and I fear Jehovah, the God
of heaven, which hath made the sea and the dry land.   Then were
the men exceedingly afraid, and said unto him, Why hast thou
done this?   For the men knew that he fled from the presence of
the Lord, because he had told them."

> "*Hast thou not procured this unto thy-
> self, in that thou hast forsaken the
> Lord thy God, when he led thee by the
> way?*"—JER. ii. 17.

THE answer ingenuously given by Jonah to the hasty
series of questions which the excited sailors poured
upon him, is a sufficient proof that the grace of God
was now bringing him to repentance, as the providence
of God was bringing him to punishment. "I am an
Hebrew, and I fear Jehovah, the God of heaven,
which made the sea and the dry land." Combine this
bold confession of his faith with the full acknowledgment of his fault—" for the men knew that he fled from
the presence of the Lord because he had told them,"—

and we have abundant materials whereby to judge of the frame of mind to which the prophet was now brought. The elements of a true repentance are distinctly before us, as true repentance appears in a believer.

For it is as a child of God that Jonah here repents; and there are elements of sad remorse and contrition in a believer's repentance which have no place in that first exercise of godly sorrow in which the sinner returns to the Lord. The believer sins against all the grace and favour which, as a believer, he has enjoyed; and this goes to deepen the grief and shame which he feels when brought to repentance.

Are you, as Jonah, a true worshipper and servant of God? And are you, like Jonah, overtaken by Divine displeasure in a course of disobedience in respect of some known point of duty? And are you at last humbled to own your guilt? You will acknowledge these three things in the exceeding sinfulness of your sin. You have sinned: *First,* against the knowledge of what God is in Himself; *secondly,* against the experience of what God has been to you; and, *thirdly,* against the consideration of what you have been to God.

These three elements all appear in the guilt of Jonah, and are expressly owned by himself. (1.) Against what God is in Himself, Jonah owns that he has sinned; against "Jehovah, the God of heaven, which hath made the sea and the dry land." (2.) Against what God has been to him, Jonah confesses that he has sinned; "I am an Hebrew:" a member of the people whose God Jehovah is; for whom Jehovah hath done great things; to whom He hath given " the adoption, and the glory, and the covenants, and the law, and the service of God, and the promises, whose are the fathers; and of whom, as concerning the flesh, the Christ should come, who is God over all, blessed for ever." (3.) And, thirdly, against what he himself has been to God, Jonah owns that he has sinned: "I fear Jehovah;" I am one of His true worshippers, His children, His servants; I have been enrolled among the true Israel—a true child of the covenant—a messenger of it also, standing in the counsel and in the secret of the Most High; for " the secret of the Lord is with them that fear him." Yet against this also have I sinned.

By all these three considerations ought Jonah to have been restrained from sinning, and retained in his loyalty to God. The glory of God—the God of heaven, of the sea, and of the dry land—ought to have restrained him. The graciousness of God towards himself ought to have restrained him. And the grace of God in himself ought to have restrained him. And when, in the face of all these three considerations, his disobedience breaks forth and carries him impetuously away, do they not all go to aggravate the guilt which he contracts?

When tempted to sin—to distrust and disobey the Lord—do you, O Christian, keep these three things in view? Do you give these three things due weight? Do you remember the glory of God as He is in Himself? Do you remember His great graciousness to you? Do you give heed, do you give scope, do you give fair play, to the instincts and dictates of His grace in you?

I. Take your stand under the bright canopy of heaven; look above you and look around. The "heaven" above, "the sea and the dry land" below; creation's all; lo! it came from the hand of Him whom now you propose to disobey, from whose presence you propose to flee. How infatuated! How insulting, how provoking to God! His hand, "that made the heaven, and the sea, and the dry land,"—can it not find you, even though you "take the wings of the morning, and dwell in the uttermost parts of the sea?" He that formed all, and continually preserveth all, shall He not continually behold all?—and whither shall you flee from His presence, or how shall you be justified, excused in forgetting it? Are you relapsed so far into that deep ungodliness, that utter death towards God, from which His saving grace aroused you? Are you so far fallen from the sweet enjoyment you once had in looking upward and around on all the wondrous fabric of heaven and earth, and feeding your secret reverence for God your Father by recognising the traces of His goodness, power, and wisdom in the things that are made; by listening—as we delight to listen to the praises of one whom we love—listening to the heavens as they declare His glory, to the firmament as it showeth forth his handiwork? Ah! consider "the invisible things of God" as they are revealed "by the things that are made." When thou considerest the heavens, the work of His fingers, the moon and the stars, which He has ordained, see that thou not only say, "What is man, that God should be mindful of him?" but, What must I be if I be forgetful of God? This is the primary element in your sin. Against the God of glory—against the glory of God—is sin directed. And the consciousness, the conviction, the confession of this, is the primary element in repentance.

II. But, secondly, see what God hath been to you! See His graciousness to you-ward! You are "an Hebrew." Or, which is the same thing, you are a Gentile brought nigh; for the middle wall of partition has been broken down, and you have been adopted into Israel's privileges—engrafted into Israel's goodly olive: and how great are your advantages thence accruing! The revelation of God in the visible Church is unspeakably more tender, and unspeakably more full, than that which the visible creation affords. His glory is seen as in a glass in that Divine word which He hath given in the Church, that testimony which He hath deposited in Israel. They are but dim and shadowy traces of the majesty of God, which the framework of the world bears. The word, as in a mirror, brings the full glory of the Highest to view. There He explains Himself, and speaks familiarly. There He tells the principles on which He rules the world and saves the lost. There He reveals His Son, righteously bearing the condemnation of the guilty, lovingly redeeming them with the price of His life. There He tells of the adoption, and the covenants, the giving of the law, and the service of God, and the fathers, and the coming of the Christ as concerning the flesh. And to you—to you, as substantially an Hebrew, an Israelite, a member of the favoured nation, added to that nation by the taking away of the middle wall of partition—to you He testifies that all these gifts of His grace; the adoption, the glory, the covenants, the oracles of God, the fathers and the glorious ancestry, the Christ and the great salvation;—to you all these things belong—belong as by birthright, insomuch that your living without them can result alone from your rejecting them. Is not this the Lord being gracious to you? And when, in the face of this, you sin against Him, is not your sin highly aggravated? By birth, by baptism, you are an Israelite. You may sell your birthright. You may make void your baptism. But it is by your own act that you make void the one; it is by positive deed of sale that you disparage and alienate and put away from you the other. Humbly and believingly improved, your birthright and baptism would have been seals of grace and pledges of glory. Though they be rejected and abused, you are responsible for them still; and they constitute a grievous aggravation of your sin.

Yes! I believe we have much to learn of the responsibilities that lie upon us simply from belonging by birth to the visible Church; from being, by the removal of the middle wall of partition, exactly in the position of having to say with Jonah, in all the spiritual and substantial import of the confession, " I am an Hebrew."

Nor is our repentance pervaded so fully as it ought to be with the sense of overwhelming, inexcusable, aggravated guiltiness, unless we feel that we have sinned against the great graciousness of God to us-ward in His Church, which is His own house upon the earth.

III. But thirdly; if you are a believer, your disobedience is aggravated by the fact that you fear God—that God's grace is within you. His glory in Himself ought to secure your reverence. His graciousness towards you might be expected to retain you in His love and service. But surely His very grace operating in you; His own Son formed within you; His Holy Spirit dwelling in you; the new creation, the new heart, the new man which the exceeding greatness of His power has in-framed in you; ought to restrain you from knowingly disobeying your Father's will. Surely, when you actually, by grace, do fear the Lord; when the Lord actually "worketh in you to will and to do of His good pleasure;" you may be called upon with special good reason to "work out your salvation with fear and trembling." And if against the power of Divine grace even in your own soul; against the instincts of a new nature; against the claims and promptings of an indwelling Christ—of "Christ in you, the hope of glory;" against the loving movements of the Holy Spirit resting on and abiding in you; you suffer your indwelling sin to break forth and carry the day; oh! surely this consideration may well touch and soften your heart, abasing you in the very dust, and filling you with bitter grief and shame. Let the heathen sin against the glory of God as inscribed on the heavens and the earth. Let false-hearted Israelites sin against God's great graciousness towards them in His word, and house, and ordinances,—His message of grace, His treaty of peace, His offer of eternal salvation. But for you to sin against the glory of God as exhibited to all, and the graciousness of God as testified in the Church, and also against the grace of God dwelling in your very self as in its chosen shrine and temple; oh! this is sin that is " as scarlet and red like crimson."

It hath pleased God to reveal Himself by the works that He hath made,—patent to all. And it hath pleased God to reveal His love and kindness towards man in the Scriptures He hath given; and these are patent to all in the Church—manifest wherever the Church extends. But it hath "pleased God to reveal His Son in you;" to "shine in your heart and give you the light of the knowledge of the glory of God in the face of Jesus Christ;" to "write His law also on your heart and put His fear within you;" and is there any one that can sin under deeper aggravations than you?—just because you truly fear the God of heaven, the God of the Hebrews, the God and Father of the Lord Jesus Christ—your God and Father in Him. Let the consideration of these aggravating elements enter into your repentance, as they entered into Jonah's. Alas! against whom have you sinned? Against the High and Lofty One that inhabiteth eternity, whose name is Holy, and whose glory is above the heavens. Against what a world of

forbearance and grace on His part towards you have you
sinned! And, thou that truly fearest the Lord! against
His own Spirit and work in thy very soul is thy sin
committed. Oh, surely into *your* repentance there may
well enter an element of special grief and mournfulness.
" O wretched man that I am! who shall deliver me from
the body of this death? "

But how important to be able, in believing confidence,
to add, " I thank God, through Jesus Christ our Lord."
Is it not the infinite, free, unchanging love of God in
Christ, which forms the only covert under which you
can repent in peace? Is it not a fresh view of the
bleeding Lamb of God, in the infinite glory of His
Person, and the all-sufficiency of His sacrifice, and the
immoveable sureness of His covenant of peace, which
enables you to hold fast your integrity amidst the deep
consciousness of great and grievous transgression ; which
enables you still to say, and to say with truth, " I fear the
God of heaven " ? For there is in that slain Lamb, that
eternal Son of God, giving Himself in mortal woe a
sacrifice for sin—" there is forgiveness with the Lord, in
Him, that He may be feared." Believing this, you are
set free from the sad snare—the strong temptation which
labours to make void and prevent your repentance—the
temptation to justify yourself, to seek excuses and extenu-
ations, to make out that, considering the circumstances,
your guilt is not so very great. Unbelief, despairing
of forgiveness, and the carnal mind which is enmity to
God, abhorring the deep obligation to God which such
forgiveness would infer, are shut up to deceitful and

disingenuous attempts at palliation and self-defence. But faith—realising the truth and sure gift of a free and full forgiveness, embracing "the blessedness of him to whom the Lord imputeth not his sin "—guilelessly takes home the guilt to self, and prompts that ingenuous, free, and frank, and open-hearted, and broken-hearted penitence in which "there is no guile" (Psa. xxxii. 1–5). Such was Jonah's penitence.

While the prophet's repentance is thus in progress, and before we come to the great catastrophe of the narrative, there are three incidents that transpire in the meantime, to which successively our attention may be directed.

1. In the first place; we are told that on the back of Jonah's answer to their questions, "the men were exceedingly afraid." They were afraid, not now at the storm merely, but at the power and righteousness of the true God, and the distinctness and extent in which He was now manifesting His anger. And this was, doubtless, one of the effects which God's righteous prosecution of Jonah in his disobedience was designed to produce. "When the judgments of God are abroad, the inhabitants of the world will learn righteousness." The bringing of iniquity to light, and to judgment, and to punishment, is an eminent work of God; indicating an all-seeing and righteous Supreme Judge—showing "that His great name is near "—fitted and designed also to cause men to fear and do no more wickedly. The judgment of God upon the shamelessness and profligacy of the sons of Eli

was intended to produce this effect. "And the Lord said unto Samuel, Behold, I will do a thing in Israel, at which both the ears of him that heareth it shall tingle" (1 Sam. iii. 11). And when the case is not a shameless profligate, but a holy prophet, in whom God will not suffer sin to go unpunished, how much more emphatic is the lesson! When He who hath embraced His people into a covenant of pardon and of peace, is seen pursuing their sins—their expiated sins—with evidences of His abhorrence, how solemnising is it! When he "pardons their iniquity, yet takes vengeance on their inventions" (Ps. xcix. 8), and that vengeance is enough to strike awe into the minds of onlookers, how much more terrible must be His vengeance on unpardoned, unbelieving, ungodly men! If judgment begin at the house of God, what shall the end be of them that obey not the gospel? The very fear which these heathen men felt, may well rebuke the careless and insensible. For there are those who see and hear of the judgments of God on the ungodly, and yet are never moved to reverence, and fear, and trembling. The same things that would strike reverence into a heathen will not move a man that is hardened under means of grace. He is hardening himself "as in the provocation;" and all methods of rousing and arresting those that are at ease in Zion, come, in process of time, to be powerless and in vain. "Woe unto thee, Chorazin! woe unto thee, Bethsaida! for if the mighty works, which were done in you, had been done in Tyre and Sidon, they would have repented long ago in sackcloth and ashes. And thou,

Capernaum, which art exalted unto heaven, shalt be brought down to hell: for if the mighty works, which have been done in thee, had been done in Sodom, it would have remained until this day " (Matt. xi. 21-23).

2. We may notice the question which the men put to Jonah. "Why hast thou done this?" Oh! what a rebuke! Fleeing from the presence of the gracious and holy Jehovah, Jonah finds himself impanneled and cross-questioned at the bar of heathen sailors. Could anything he might have dreaded in the path of commanded duty have been half so humiliating as this? Doubtless, in the path of duty a man must take up his cross: and oftentimes it may be painful and humbling. It is well for the Christian to remember, when more generous motives are not likely to prevail, that in fleeing from that path, he lies open to incidents that may be more humbling still: and under them, sustained by no lofty sense of loyalty to God, but with spirit embittered by self-displeasure, he must be destitute of the consolation and dignity involved in bearing the cross. For the cross always carries honour and comfort with it. Always, it is true, that he that humbleth himself shall be exalted, while he that exalteth himself shall be abased. Look at Jonah, for instance. How deeply is he abased! A man whose intellect has been irradiated by the light of God's word and Spirit—who has been exalted to the lofty rank of God's messenger and friend, standing in His counsel, and intrusted with His secret—whose character has been framed of the Spirit for communion with God, and refined and sanctified by His fellowship

and service ;—for such an one to have his duty pointed
out and his offence rebuked by ignorant, unrefined,
rude, yea, idolatrous and heathen men ; how painful is
the retribution ; and how just !

Listen to the question. Suppose yourself in Jonah's
place, and hear the question put to you—put to you, a
man of God, by heathen men. " Why hast thou done
this ? " Did your God provoke you to flee from Him ?
Did He deal so hardly and unkindly with you that you
had no alternative but flight? Were you tired of your
God ? Had you found Him out—as no more worthy
of your trust and obedience ? Had you got to the end
of all the duty that you owed to Him—or of all the
protection or support that He could afford to you ?

" Why hast thou done this ? " If the mission on which
He sent you was difficult, and the warfare heavy, did
He send you on your own charges, so that, being unable
to defray them, you have not dared to face the undertaking? Did He demand your self-denying labour,
and give you no encouragement, no countenance, no
support? Is this the character of your God? Is the
God whom you fear, O Jonah, so hard a taskmaster,
—so unfeeling and severe ?

Ah ! it is well, in your sins and backslidings, to have
this question pressed upon you.

" Why hast thou done this ? " When your heart, that
once found its sweet and chosen pleasure in the Scriptures, in meditation, in prayer, now follows so keenly the
things that perish in the using, and allows itself to be
moulded by the fashion of the world that passeth away ;

—why is this? When you have forsaken your first love, abated the zeal and contracted the extent of your first works;—why is this? Let it not content you to regard the question as a mere vague rebuke—as a mere remembrancer that what you have done is indefensible. Press the question. Accept it as a question under which you may not only well be expected to wince and feel sore—but as a question to be deliberately faced and kept in view, till thorough restoration, and confirmed revival, and zealous return to first love and first works, are again secured.

"Why hast thou done this?" Produce your strong reasons. Has God been a wilderness to you? Have you found a better friend? Have you found a worthier portion? Have you found a sweeter employment than meditation in His word and calling on His name?

"Why hast thou done this?" Have you found Him unfaithful to His promise? Have you discovered that He discourages His people? Will you say that the more you have known Him, the less you have thought of Him? It looks like it, O backslider. It looks like it, if you can remember days when you loved Him more, and served Him better than now.

"Why hast thou done this?" Has the world been better to you than God? Has it been more full, more stedfast, more satisfying, more true than God? Ah! must you not say that the more you have known *it*, the less cause you have had to be pleased with it? But, does it look like it—if you can turn again to its beggarly

elements; and bind in your chiefest thoughts and anxieties with those things that are seen and temporal;
while the things that are unseen and eternal are losing
their hold over you, and not influencing, pleasing, profiting, sanctifying, animating you to love and duty, as
before?

Urge this matter, O backslider, to an issue—to an
answer. Let the case go fairly and fully to trial. As
to the men of the world, the world is their god. No
wonder that they serve it. But why hast *thou* done
this?—thou who art an Israelite and fearest Jehovah—
the God that made the heavens, and the sea, and the
dry land.

3. Let us observe, in the third place, that all the
frankness of Jonah's confession, and all the truth and
depth of his repentance, avail nothing to the removal
of the Divine anger. For we are told that still "the
sea wrought and was tempestuous." Jonah's detection,
and humiliation, and rebuke, and repentance were not
enough. For all this, the Lord's hand was stretched
out still. Confession before God will not always suffice;
—no, nor even confession before man. God may still
pursue His controversy. It is not in any case your
repentance which pacifies His anger, and satisfies His
justice. You never purchase His pardon by the price
of your penitence. That is not in any sense, nor in
any degree, the ground on which the Lord forgives you.
Without repentance, indeed, He will not forgive. To
forgive sin, while still by you cherished and retained—

that is to say, to testify the removal of His anger, while you remove not that which has caused it—would be to declare Himself now reconciled to your iniquity, and no more displeased with the abominable thing. Repentance is required unto forgiveness; imperatively demanded. "Let the wicked forsake his way, and the unrighteous man his thoughts; and let him return unto the Lord, and He will have mercy upon him, and unto our God, for He will abundantly pardon." Still it is not on the ground of the merit of your godly sorrow that the Lord blots out the iniquity of your sin. And therefore, to deepen your repentance and confirm it; to inspire you with a holy terror of like iniquity in time to come; to grave painfully and burningly into your heart, and memory, experiences and recollections that shall rise swiftly to the aid of your integrity and virtue, if tempted to like offence again; God may see meet to prolong the storm that He has awakened, even after it may have been blessed to bring you to repentance.

Even so did He deal with Jonah. It would not have effected the intended discipline, correction, and improvement of his soul, to have now given commission to the waves to be still. Alas! there are more of God's waves and billows to go over him. It is a fearful thing even for a believer to fall into the hands of the living God. For God, even the God of the believing and redeemed, is a consuming fire. It is no mere matter of Divine sovereignty, but a certain and inevitable effect of the Divine holiness, that the storm cannot cease till you cast the offending thing overboard; that the ship can have no peace while the Jonah is in it; the camp no victory till Achan is stoned; and your soul no taste of the peace and love of God till its idols are abolished and abandoned. The whole character of God requires that He should refuse to speak peace to those who retain anything against which He has announced and directed His displeasure; or who neglect anything which He has enjoined as a means of grace, or demanded as a tribute of gratitude. You complain, perhaps, that you find little progress in your religious knowledge, and little joy in religious ordinances; —that you cannot rise to that sweet peace, and sure hope, and lively zeal in duty, which you see by the Scriptures believers are warranted to expect, and which perhaps in a measure you may have yourself formerly enjoyed. Have you examined yourself? Are you sure there is no Jonah in the ship; no Achan in the camp; no idol in the temple; no sin of commission or omission, which as a canker at the root of your religion is spoiling all? Be assured that till it is searched out and consigned to destruction, it is impossible the bright light can shine again on the pages of the word to you; —or the sweet and tender joy of sitting at the feet of Jesus visit you;—or the serene contentment with your lot on earth again compose and strengthen you;—or the full devoted gratitude which makes self-denying duty light, again carry you on ungrudgingly in all the work of the Lord. For the Lord our God is a jealous

God. And many a believer has suffered bitterly from provoking God to act upon that declaration,—so honourable to His own holiness, and to His love of holiness in His people;—" I will go and return unto my place, till they acknowledge their offence, and seek my face : in their affliction they will seek me early " (Hos. v. 15).

XIII

THE CASTING OF JONAH INTO THE SEA

JONAH i. 11–17

"Then said they unto him, What shall we do unto thee, that the sea
may be calm unto us? for the sea wrought, and was tempestuous.
And he said unto them, Take me up, and cast me forth into the
sea; so shall the sea be calm unto you: for I know that for my
sake this great tempest is upon you. Nevertheless the men rowed
hard to bring it to the land; but they could not: for the sea wrought,
and was tempestuous against them. Wherefore they cried unto
the Lord, and said, We beseech thee, O Lord, we beseech thee, let
us not perish for this man's life, and lay not upon us innocent
blood: for thou, O Lord, hast done as it pleased thee. So they
took up Jonah, and cast him forth into the sea; and the sea ceased
from her raging. Then the men feared the Lord exceedingly, and
offered a sacrifice unto the Lord, and made vows. Now the Lord
had prepared a great fish to swallow up Jonah."

> "*Thou answeredst them, O Lord our God ;
> thou wast a God that forgavest them,
> though thou tookest vengeance of their
> inventions.*"—Ps. xcix. 8.
> "*Righteousness and peace have kissed each
> other.*"—Ps. lxxxv. 10.

AS the marvels of this stirring scene heighten to their
crisis, the conduct of all the parties concerned becomes truly noble, and in every respect worthy of much
admiration. In all that is recorded of the prophet,

nothing appears to us so exalted as the combination of godly meekness and godly boldness with which he faces and accepts the tremendous punishment of his transgression.   And it is questionable whether a crew of his own highly-favoured countrymen would have enacted a worthier part towards him than that which was adopted and carried out with so much propriety and dignity by the heathen sailors.   Truly Jonah had even more good reason than Paul to use the language, "The barbarous people showed me no little kindness" (Acts xxviii. 2); while they, on the other hand, as they were about to consign him to a doom which turned out to be a period of "three days and three nights in the whale's belly," might not unjustly say of the prophet, what the centurion said of Jonah's antitype, about to be committed "for three days and three nights to the heart of the earth;"—"Certainly this was a righteous man" (Luke xxiii. 47).

Altogether, there is in this scene, on all hands, an amount of veneration and deference rendered to justice, —to severe, but pure and perfect righteousness,—that cannot fail to render it very impressive to every right-minded reader of the passage.   There is a calm, judicial dignity exhibited by all the parties, which speaks well for their character and bearing in a crisis so fitted to alarm and to unman them.   And it forms a striking proof of the fact that it is righteousness alone that will bear men through the most fiery trials.   Amiability, kindliness, capability of gentler and refined emotion, may grace and adorn the man; but it is righteousness, the love of truth and justice, which forms the foundation and the solid pillars of his character. In the hour of peace, and of gentle, undisturbed serenity, the amiable may be more acceptable than the sternly just. Nevertheless,—though it is true that, whereas " scarcely for a righteous man would one die, peradventure for a good man some would even dare to die,"—in critical hours of destiny it is righteousness that towers aloft above the storm, and—somewhat even like unto God himself—is " mightier than the noise of many waters, yea, than the mighty waves of the sea."

I. In this view, consider, first, the righteous procedure of the sailors in consulting with Jonah himself concerning the steps that were now rendered necessary. Something must be done—and they put the matter to the prophet. " Then said they unto him, What shall we do unto thee, that the sea may be calm unto us? for the sea wrought, and was tempestuous." The storm ceaseth not: the ship can hold out no longer: the cause of the storm has been revealed; for God hath disclosed it by the lot, and Jonah confessed it from his own conscience. And now that the cause is known, what shall be done for removing it? Evidently something must be done, if they are not all prepared to perish together. And they consult Jonah himself.

It says much for them that they do. He had been something more, and something worse, than a thorn in their side. And they might have been expected, as heathen men, to have had little scruple in taking brief-handed measures, and making short work with the troublesome stranger. For a perfect stranger he was to them. No ties of friendship, or acquaintance, or kin, or country could he plead; and the subject of a strange but strong God, bringing down his God's wrath on them—verily, they had little to thank him for! And why make any difficulty in getting rid of him?

1. But God has imbued responsible man with a natural and profound horror of shedding his brother's blood. Nor is this confined to those who are in possession of the Scriptures, those holy writings in which God said—at the very constitution of the world and of society, on rearranging that constitution after it had been obliterated by the flood—"Whoso sheddeth man's blood, by man shall his blood be shed." It is a feeling that has gone down all time, with all the families of Noah; and that, whether the covenant with Noah—whether the Scripture, or that special command in it—has gone down to them or not. However much extreme hardening, through indulgence in sin, may sear the conscience, and go far, apparently, to obliterate this horror at the guilt of murder, it is more proper to say that such searing and hardening rather overpowers than obliterates it. For it abideth still; and it affords one of a multitude of harmonies between the religion of the natural conscience of man and the religion of the revealed will of God. For,—whatever may be said by some who would seem to seek a character for good feeling higher than God himself,—as it is apart from and prior to the Bible, or any precept there, that man instinctively abhors the sin of murder;

so, it was prior to any particular dispensation—any Mosaic economy, for instance, or Jewish theocracy—and as applied to all lands and all times, that God, in starting the world anew in the ark-saved family of the patriarch, gave forth the unrepealed command, " Whoso sheddeth man's blood, by man shall his blood be shed." Nor should it be forgotten, as sufficient for ever to silence the advocates for the abolition of capital punishment, that God has not only given an unrepealed command which He might have been pleased to rest on His own authority and will alone, but He has condescended to give the ground and reason of it; and so long as both the command remains unrepealed and the reason remains a fact, so long is the proposed abolition of capital punishment a daring insult against the Most High. God hath given us the reason why the shedding of man's blood must be avenged by the murderer's death—" for in the image of God made He man." And until this truth becomes untrue, that is, until man cease to be a free, intelligent, responsible being,—fallen, indeed, and in a vast multitude of cases, alas! unrenewed, yet still responsible, intelligent, and free,—capital punishment, both by God's commanding will and by God's assigned reason, is the murderer's doom. And nature and reason sanction the sentence.

It was nature and reason, working in this very direction, that induced these sailors to pause ere they rid themselves of the source of their danger by casting their fellow-man to the waves.

2. But there was omething more than this, doubtless,

at the bottom of their judicious and righteous deliberation. They might be irritated by the rebellious subject of a strange God bringing all the anger of his God upon them in this fashion ; but, behold, how great this new and strange God is! Evidently He is a strong God. May He not be the true God?—the one living and true God? Let them, therefore, pause and weigh well their doings, while evidently the prophet's God is near.

For, have they ever found such a God among their own gods? Have they ever found a God who sitteth above the floods, and ruleth in the raging of the sea, and telleth by lot with whom He is displeased, and followeth up His displeasure with quick and quickening tempest? Is it not a new experience to them? That this great God is near unto them, His marvellous works are emphatically declaring. They feel this. They will stand in awe and sin not. They will do nothing rashly to provoke His anger against themselves. They will rather consult His prophet.

3. For, disobedient though he may be, Jonah, they perceive, is His prophet, and His servant still. Revering his God, they respect *him*. They feel that it is a solemn thing to have to do with anything that this God marks as His own—marks as His own even by His displeasure. Hence they pause. "With the well-advised there is wisdom."

For these reasons, then, the mariners put the matter to Jonah himself. If something painful has to be done, they will at least consult with himself. If possible, they will secure his own concurrence. It may be they shall receive his own directions.

This generous and handsome style of procedure; how fitted was it to touch a chord in the prophet's heart, and make him bitterly regret bringing danger and risk of death on men who could deal so nobly with him! Stimulated to rival the righteous and dignified procedure of those on whom he had brought such impending ruin, and who,—in the very crisis of it, when they have discovered the instrument of that ruin and now have him in their power,—so forbearingly and respectfully abstain from retaliation, revenge, hatred, or haste; under the humbling and rectifying influence on his own mind which this fair and honourable treatment exerts; Jonah now seeks to emulate their rectitude and do them justice, as they are so disposed to do justice to him.

II. Hence his magnanimous proposal in reply: "Take me up and cast me forth into the sea; so shall the sea be calm unto you: for I know that for my sake this great tempest is upon you."

Could anything be more noble, upright, honourable? There is, first, a renewed acknowledgment—frank, free, and full—of his own obnoxiousness to the Divine anger, and of himself as the source and occasion of the present danger: "For I know that for my sake this great tempest is upon you." There is, secondly, an unreserved surrender or appointment of himself to death, as the means of solving the appalling difficulty, and stilling

the raging of the deep: " Take me up, and cast me
forth into the sea." And there is, thirdly,—what
may be valued as coming from a prophet of that God
" which made the sea and the dry land "—a prediction
that the expedient will be efficacious: " So shall the
sea be calm unto you."

In small compass, how complete is Jonah's reply!
It meets the case; it meets all the case. Yet it has
all the brevity of a sentence of judgment delivered from
the bench.

And so, indeed, it is. Under God, and at the mouth
of God, Jonah becomes judge in his own case; and he
judges, even in his own case, with all the relentless
righteousness which the sternest judge in any case could
exhibit. No half measure, no compromise, no delay,
no alternative; the one clear, immediate, complete, irre-
vocable, final doom : " Take me up, and cast me forth
into the sea."

Now, try and conceive of the height of true moral
grandeur to which Jonah at this moment rises. He is
clearly and consciously facing Eternity; and, oh! how
very far is he from doing so in the revolting blasphemy
of one who can take the infinitely awful movement as
one would take a leap on chance and in the dark! No:
he " fears God." He has been a regular, habitual fearer
of God; and he truly fears God still. He has offended
the Most High of late. He has fled from Him. He
has seen, for some time, little of the light of His countenance. He has tasted little that the Lord is gracious.
Nay, rather, the Lord's wrath has waxed hot against

THE CASTING OF JONAH INTO THE SEA   229

him; His hand hath pressed him sore. At this very
moment he hath terrible experience of the power wherewith his Almighty God can prosecute an offence against
His honour, and bring the offender to punishment.
"Deep calleth unto deep, and at the noise of God's
waterspouts all his billows go over him," while he flees
in disobedience "from the land of Jordan." And yet
he will "remember the Lord from the land of Jordan,
and of the Hermonites, from the hill Mizar." And he
will take no crooked way of dealing with God, or
evading His hand and justice. The storm is to him
the voice of God; awful as to Adam in the garden
in the cool of the day; crying, "Jonah, where art
thou?"—more terrible than the still small voice on
Horeb after the strong wind, after the earthquake, after
the fire, "What doest thou here, Elijah?"—"What
doest thou here, Jonah?" Yet Jonah's integrity quails
not. He denies not his own guilt. He denies not the
Lord's righteousness.

When he entered the ship,—his conscience tumultu-
ating with guilt, his heart throbbing with the hurry of
his flight,—worn out with agitation and excitement,
and going down like a hunted and harassed one to find
rest in "the sides of the ship,"—how wide the contrast
between the storm in his soul and the placid sea on
which the happy bark, unconscious of its burden, set
sail! Now the sea storms and is tempestuous: but the
contrast is as great. For, as the result of repentance
and returning duty, Jonah's soul is placid, meek, and
mild as a weaned child—calmly strong in righteousness

also, as a mighty man of power rising above all impending evils.

Are you thus upright before the Lord? Are you truly penitent for all sin; for the sin that doth more easily beset you; for the sin which God may be pursuing with His displeasure? Do you own the justice of all His dealings with you? Do you indeed yield the victory to God, according to that oracle, "Yea, let God be true and every man a liar; as it is written, That thou mightest be justified in thy sayings, and mightest overcome when thou art judged"? You can do so only through the intervention of the great atonement and your faith therein. Never can you face all righteousness till you flee to the cross of Jesus. There, He by whom all things were made, both in heaven and in earth, whether they be thrones, or dominions, or principalities, or powers, suffered under the hand of Divine justice, and satisfied Divine justice. That cross is the only school where an immortal, responsible man can face all righteous questions, and solve them, and accept the true solution. Have you been there and settled all your own case with the Judge of the quick and of the dead; settled it on the terms that are so honourable to the character of God, and that must now and ultimately be so remedial to yours? Have you fled for refuge to the hope set before you in the Gospel? Have you the anchor of the soul within the veil, designed and fitted to enable you to ride out the storm? In one word, have you peace with God on the righteous footing of an imputed righteousness, and a perfect reconciliation by sacrifice? Then see that you evermore face what is righteous, and turn to no crooked way, no evasion, no subterfuge, no refuge of lies, no path of compromise or of deceit. Walk humbly, yet walk boldly and firmly, with God. Though He slay you, still trust in Him. Your chiefest trials are designed to teach you this. Your agony of conflict with infirmities is designed to teach you this. The apparent contradiction between providences very sore and promises most sweet is designed to teach you and train you to this. Though the fig-tree shall not blossom, though there be no fruit in the vine, though the labour of the olive fail; though your house be not so with God; though heart and flesh faint and fail; though God himself slay you with His sore displeasure: still it is a faithful saying and worthy of all acceptation that His own Son died for sinners and rejoices to save them; that he that believeth in Him shall never die; nor from such an one shall the covenant of God's peace or the promise of God's presence and protection be removed, world without end. Therefore, in any circumstances, never doubt that the path of duty, —though it seem to be the path of anguish, of agony, of darkness, or of death,—is yet the way of life, light, and comfort; and however to flesh and blood it may be hard, hold to the motto which men of the world may have devised and may admire, but which men of God alone can rightly go through with, 'Let justice be done, though the heavens rush to ruin.'*

"It is the Lord: let him do with me as seemeth good

* *Fiat justicia, ruat cælum.*

in his sight." It is the Lord: the same who hath
counted me faithful and put me into the office of His
prophet: the same to whom I have been unfaithful;
from whom I have fled; from whom I have deserved so
ill. " Righteous art thou, O Lord; yet let me talk with
thee of thy judgments." Yea, let me ask from Thee
faith and courage and strength to bear them. It is the
Lord; the Judge of all the earth: and " He will do that
which is right." It is the Lord: and if His hand is
strong to smite, 'tis also strong to save. Let Him do
with me as seemeth good in His sight. Though He
slay me, yet will I trust in Him. " Take me up and
cast me forth into the sea."

III. This emulation of generous and righteous and
extremely handsome action between Jonah and the
mariners goes forward yet another stage. The mariners
admirably meet the prophet again. If he responded
generously to their righteous and dignified deliberation
in consulting with himself, or rather in leaving the
matter in his own hands, they reciprocate no less beautifully to the meek and subdued spirit of the prophet
when he prescribes his own death as the only means of
appeasing the sea.

Touched with kindliest feelings of humanity, and
touched with admiration of the mingled solemnity and
righteous boldness with which the prophet can propose
the sacrifice of his own life to their safety, the men evidently resolve that only in the last and direst extremity
shall they act as he has indicated to them; and that

extremity, they rule, has not yet come.   Till then, they
will make every effort.   " Nevertheless, the men rowed
hard to bring it to the land ; but they could not : for the
sea wrought, and was tempestuous against them."

It was well that it was in their heart.   The Lord denied them their desire ; but it was well that it was in
their heart.   It showed their humanity ; their solemn
fear of shedding innocent blood ; their profiting under
that fear of God which Providence had been inspiring
into their minds.   It gave Jonah the opportunity of
being still more satisfied that the proposal he had made
was the only one that could meet the case.   And it
brought more clearly to light the solemn fact that God
was indeed pursuing this matter to His own appointed
issue, and would allow no effort, however well meant,
to baffle His purpose.   God had righteously destined the
prophet to be cast into the sea ;—yea, we may say, to
suffer death for his offence in fleeing from his duty.   For
however God interposed at a later stage, and miraculously
saved the prophet's life, it was nevertheless so much an
interposition of miraculous goodness and miraculous
power, that his restoration from the deep was more
a resurrection than an escape.   For certainly it is one
clear inference we may draw from the analogy suggested
by our Lord ;—" As Jonah was three days and three
nights in the whale's belly, so shall the Son of Man be
three days and three nights in the heart of the earth ; "—
that it was a resurrection-life that Jonah afterwards
possessed, as well as the Son of Man.   Surely Jonah,
like the Son of Man, was appointed unto death.   With

death, then, we say, had God resolved to punish
Jonah's sin. And the strength of the Divine purpose is the more terribly brought to light when every
effort to save Jonah's life comes to nought. " The
men rowed hard to bring it to the land, but they could
not."

No; they could not. For the counsel of the Lord,
it shall stand; and He will do all His pleasure. And
the Lord executeth righteous judgment.

Young man! bear this in mind. You may go certain lengths aside from the ways of wisdom, integrity,
temperance, truth; and to some extent, and in a certain sense, your friends may interpose and bring you
off. Hearts beating somewhat towards you like God's
heart—" How shall I give thee up, O Ephraim!"
—may be at your service, even in your evil plight.
Prayers and intercessions, counsels and rebukes, and
kindliest efforts of righteousness and love, may take
your feet out of the net, and place you in a somewhat
even path again, giving you a fresh start and a new
chance for better things. But beware. Embrace it if
it is so. Embrace it *now*, and improve it. Thank God
for it, and improve it. Cast yourself on Him—His
grace, His word, His Christ, His Spirit, His providence, His fatherly love and righteous will. "As for
me, I will serve the Lord." "Depart from me, ye evil
doers : for I will keep the commandments of my God."
And let this be vigorous; in lively fear before the
Lord; in humble penitence and firm faith of that

mercy which is in the heavens; and let it be daily, dutifully, faithfully, manfully followed up.

For, turning aside again, or going certain other
lengths, may land you, ere you are aware, in a position from which no one will bring you off. However
many more true friends you may have than you deserve, and with whatever zeal and love they lay all oars
in the water in your service, it may utterly baffle them
to bring you off. For there are laws physical, social,
moral, from the effects and influence of which no one
can bring you off. Remember that word of the Spirit :
" Every man shall bear his own burden." To your own
master, in the long run, you must stand or fall. Bless
God that He is able to make you stand. But also,
when finally provoked, He is able to seal your doom.
And if you so provoke Him, then,—as to the interposition and efforts of friends,—" The men rowed hard to
bring it to the land, but they could not " !

IV. The admirable bearing of all parties in this
drama becomes, if possible, still more engaging.

It becomes manifest that Jonah's doom is inevitable;
that Jonah's hour is come. " The sea wrought, and was
tempestuous." And its " tempest," and its " working,"
and its demand were—for *him*. Doubtless, while the
men had betaken themselves to pains, Jonah had secretly
been engaged in prayer. But the pains taken by them
are useless; for still " the sea works, and is tempestuous."
And to the prayers of the prophet every thundering

billow,—as "the sea works and is tempestuous,"—gives him back his stern and ominous answer, as if saying for God, as God himself said to Moses,—" Speak to me no more of this matter, for thou honouredst me not."

So Jonah's hour is come.

It is a solemn moment. Apart even from some of its most appalling circumstances, it is a solemn moment. The funeral of the *dead* at sea is solemn. Though the waters around and the heavens above be all serene, it is a trying hour when the remains of the much-loved friend, or of the mere acquaintance, or even of a very stranger, have to be committed to the deep. And hardened indeed must that heart be that can pass unmoved through the hour when, with mournful funeral service, and from the hands of comrades or of crew, the sea receives another to " the dead that are in her." But when we try in imagination to stand on the reeling deck beside this man of God, offending, yet honourable and honoured, and see alike the firm resignation, combining meekness and moral majesty, with which the prophet faces the waves roaring for him as the lion ravening for the prey, and the mournful admiration and regret with which these heathen men look upon their guest,—revealing that high appreciation of his character which, even though known to them only in connexion with his offence against God and his occasion of extreme distress to them, they have irresistibly been drawn to entertain,—we are overpowered with the impression that high above the floods sitteth an unseen One who is carrying out a righteous award, and who, while He hath said, " Touch not mine anointed, and do my prophets no harm," would appear to have said so, not merely to procure them protection when they are right, but because He Himself will chastise them when they err.   Silence is our best expositor here.   Another such funeral service truly neither the sea nor the dry land ever witnessed. For here are men, not accustomed to call on Jehovah's name, and from whom little, in a sense, could be expected, going through with a duty the most agonising that can ever fall to a creature's hand, in a spirit of godly deliberation and—one almost feels constrained to think—of truly gracious prayerfulness; and following it up with sacrificing and vowing to the Lord ; as if they now gave themselves as wholly to His grace as they have given His offending servant to His justice.   " Wherefore they cried unto the Lord, and said, We beseech thee, O Lord, we beseech thee, let us not perish for this man's life, and lay not upon us innocent blood : for thou, O Lord, hast done as it pleased thee.   So they took up Jonah, and cast him forth into the sea : and the sea ceased from her raging.   Then the men feared the Lord exceedingly, and offered a sacrifice unto the Lord, and made vows."

Thus did these men.   They awoke to know the living and the true God.   They prayed to Him.   They appealed to Him.   The storm, they clearly saw, was in His hand : a reason for it, they saw, was in His heart. And that reason they saw as clearly as they saw the storm.   His hand, they saw, was almighty.   His heart, they saw, was righteous. In brief time, they learned not a little of the living and the true God. They felt this anger. They even became executioners of His wrath. They emphatically justify their deed as being constrained to become executioners of the wrath of the living God. It is a solemn initiation into the knowledge of His name.

And now their guest, their passenger, is gone. The sea has closed over him; and the sea has "ceased from her raging." Yes: if they doubted that a Living One was moving the storm by the power of His hand and according to the purpose of His heart, they can now at least doubt no more. The sudden appeasing of the tempest tells its own tale. They fear God in the calm "exceedingly,"—more than in the tempest. And now, under no stress of weather, under no strain of terror, they vow, not an extorted, mercenary vow, but a free and voluntary dedication of themselves to the Lord. One would fain say these men were converted to the God of Israel. One would fain hope they lived and died in His fear and in His favour.

*   *   *   *   *

It is a calm. The clouds have parted. The waves are hushed. The heavens are beautiful and blue. Onward the strange vessel flits, beating her quiet tack; unconscious of her matchless story; but her crew aware "that a prophet of the Lord has been among them"!

And thus died Jonah. To them, at least, thus died

Jonah;—the death of a criminal pursued by justice; yet
the death of a repentant and righteous man; in death
triumphing over death; committing himself to God in
singular meekness and faith; acknowledging the justice of his doom, and relying on Divine pardon and protection; committing his body to the sea and his soul
to the God whom he feared,—the God of heaven, and of
the sea, and of the dry land.   Thus died Jonah.

So the story reads.   And—save 'for the inspiring
Spirit of God continuing His revelations—so the story
would end.   To all this the mariners could bear witness; and here their witness-bearing, *their* story would
end.   And in this there is a precious lesson.

In God's people and His prophets, their offence and
their chastisement may be capable of being reported;
the knowledge of them common property.   For, their
offence and their chastisement may be upon the surface;
and upon the surface there may be nothing more.
But the story may not end thus.   There may be deliverance, forgiveness, marvels of grace and prayer and
love and joy and communion with God, beneath the
surface or behind the scenes.   Beneath the surface and
behind the scenes, there may be such salvation as the
world shall never know.

'Thus died Jonah;'—so these mariners, on reaching
land, and rehearsing the story, would say as they
brought the marvellous narrative to a close.   Literally,
beneath the surface, God carried on the marvellous
story more marvellously still; bringing in His own
unique, peculiar work of—Life in the midst of death;

His ever glorious work of justice satisfied by being executed, and grace reigning through righteousness unto life from the dead. " Now the Lord had prepared a great fish to swallow up Jonah."

Oh, fear the Lord at *all* times. There is no want to them that fear Him. Accept no deliverance at the expense of righteousness or truth or duty. There is a better deliverance for you. On, therefore : on, rather : fronting the righteousness ; facing your duty ; trusting your God. Is anything too hard for Him ? and is not His faithfulness in the very heavens ? Not His dark dispensations, but His clear and ever bright word of covenant grace and truth, is the ground and warrant of your faith. And, therefore, though He slay you, you may trust in Him still.

On His face,—a frown of deep displeasure for your offence ! In His hand,—a raging storm, relentless, waiting for you ! Could your case well be worse ? Thus much upon the surface. Thus, to sense and reason.

But to faith—what ? Beneath the surface, while He holds the storm in His left hand, with His right hand " the Lord has prepared " a deliverance. And behind the frown, in the depths of the Lord's heart—what ? Protecting, redeeming, life-giving love ! " Righteousness and peace have kissed each other."

Oh, all ye that fear the Lord ! keep ye judgment at any cost : the Lord hath " prepared " His salvation. "Thus saith the Lord, Keep ye judgment, and do justice : for my salvation is near to come. I bring near my righteousness ; and my salvation shall not tarry."

XIV

JONAH'S PRAYER : THE CONFLICT OF FAITH AND SENSE

JONAH ii. 1–9

"Then Jonah prayed unto the Lord his God out of the fish's belly, and said, I cried by reason of mine affliction unto the Lord, and he heard me; out of the belly of hell cried I, and thou heardest my voice. For thou hadst cast me into the deep, in the midst of the seas; and the floods compassed me about : all thy billows and thy waves passed over me. Then I said, I am cast out of thy sight; yet I will look again toward thy holy temple. The waters compassed me about, even to the soul : the depth closed me round about, the weeds were wrapped about my head. I went down to the bottoms of the mountains; the earth with her bars was about me for ever: yet hast thou brought up my life from corruption, O Lord my God. When my soul fainted within me I remembered the Lord : and my prayer came in unto thee, into thine holy temple. They that observe lying vanities forsake their own mercy. But I will sacrifice unto thee with the voice of thanksgiving; I will pay that that I have vowed. Salvation is of the Lord."

"Deep calleth unto deep. . . . Yet the Lord will command his loving-kindness ; . . . and my prayer shall be unto the God of my life."—Ps. xlii. 7, 8.
"I had fainted, unless I had believed to see the goodness of the Lord in the land of the living."—Ps. xxvii. 13.

THE prayer of Jonah is an illustrious instance of the conflict between sense and faith. And it will give unity to our meditations on it, if we keep *this* in view,

and use *this* as the key to its interpretation ; namely, that
it discloses the action and reaction in the prophet's soul,
of sense and faith ;—sense prompting to despair ; faith
pleading for hope, and procuring victory.

To the unawakened soul, that knows nothing of the
anxieties and anguish of the spiritual mind, this whole
contemplation may be altogether uninviting. At best,
it will be to such an one merely a very curious theme ;
but one in which he can discover nothing in common
with his own heart-history or feelings.

The poor and contrite, on the other hand, who know
something of the terrors of the Lord, the trials of an
awakened spirit, the haunting anxieties of their own
disobedience, and the great power of their own sins,
will look on this wonderful prayer with lively interest,
and find in it much to encourage, to rebuke, and to
instruct them. The essential feature of this prayer—
as a prayer of faith in circumstances that, save for faith,
were altogether desperate—will commend it to every
exercised believer, as a prayer to the proper understanding of which he will derive some light from his own
experience, and which, when properly understood, will in
its turn reflect light on his own experience back again,
and tend to purify and strengthen that experience too.

For this prayer of faith, though in unparalleled circumstances, and spiritually noble in a marvellous degree, con-
tains in it nothing but the ordinary principles of all believing prayer ; and though we may not equal it in degree,
if our prayers are not the same in kind, they are false.

Is not this the very trial of faith; namely, to have circumstances to contend with which appear to extinguish hope, yea, which viewed in themselves, not only appear to, but actually *do* shut out all hope whatever? Take the case of Abraham, and the character and commendation of his faith. And do so, bearing in mind that he is the father of the faithful, and that all believers walk in the steps of the faith of our father Abraham. And what is the brief view given of the nature and action of his faith? It is as vanquishing and outliving the contradictory influence of sense. "Against hope he believed in hope" (Rom. iv. 18). Appearances were all against him. Sensible realities all contradicted, and in themselves alone, destroyed his expectation. Had his hope rested on sense, on reason, on nature, on time, it must have failed and sunk for ever. But he did not rest on nature; he did not draw upon the region of sense; he did not lean on the power of reason. He believed. He did not perceive. He did not argue. He believed. "He *believed* in hope." And so strongly did he believe in hope, that his faith destroyed the hope-destroying power of sense. For sense would have destroyed his hope; but this hope-destroying power of sense, his faith destroyed. "Against hope he believed in hope."

This is the true place and action of faith. This is the victory which faith has to achieve. Surrounded by incidents, events, circumstances, influences, powers, all adverse to your deliverance and salvation; and with your hope, as far as this region of the things seen and temporal is concerned, utterly cut off; your faith discovers another region, a realm and kingdom unseen, "the heavenly places," the sphere of "the things that are unseen and eternal." Your faith draws upon *them*. Faith finds them all good and true, precious and powerful, suitable and superior. For these unseen things are of God. They are the promises and pledges of God, and of His Word. For their *truth*, you have no evidence of sense. The evidence of sense is supposed to be all the other way. But you have the evidence of your Creator's word. You receive that as good and sufficient, as the very highest evidence possible. You receive it as simply true. You prove that you receive it as true, by actually proceeding on it, and perilling precious issues on it. You peril your hope, and happiness, and peace upon it. You peril your soul upon it for ever. You believe in hope, when you *see* no ground of hope. You believe in hope, even when all you *see* is against your hope. Circumstances, nature, creation, sight, sense, plead for the giving up of all hope: and their pleas are strong; their statements, in themselves, are true. But over against all these you place, in solitary, unapproachable, surpassing majesty,—God. You say; "The mighty God, even the Lord, hath spoken." And inclining your ear and hearing Him, you *believe* Him, in opposition to *all*. "You hear, and your soul doth live." You outlive—you live down—your despair. "Against hope you believe in hope."

This common principle of the conflict between sense and faith, Paul states in a series of striking contrasts in

a passage with which the believer is familiar. "We
are troubled on every side (according to sense); yet
(by faith) not distressed: (as to sense) we are perplexed;
but (through faith) not in despair: persecuted; but not
forsaken: cast down; but not destroyed: always bearing about in the body the dying of the Lord Jesus,
that the life also of Jesus may be made manifest in our
body. For we which live are alway delivered unto
death for Jesus' sake, that the life also of Jesus may be
made manifest in our mortal flesh" (2 Cor. iv. 8–11).
In another passage, he speaks of the opposition to all
hope which sense presents, as designed to compel us to
draw on the supports of faith: the region of sense
becoming as it were perfectly intolerable, that the soul
may be constrained to flee into the realm of faith, the
heavenly places, as its own and only congenial home.
"We have the sentence of death in ourselves, that we
may not trust in ourselves, but in Him that quickeneth
the dead" (2 Cor. i. 9). And if any lesson is to be
learnt from the matchless story of Jacob wrestling with
the angel, it is this: that God may clothe all circumstances, and all His dispensation towards us, with
appearances of opposition and hostility, in order that
we may flee to the anchor of His pure and simple
Word, and lean on it without any other help, or rather
against all adverse power. The Angel of the covenant
Himself wrestled with His servant and opposed him.
The Lord put forth His strength against Jacob, to
refuse him his desire. If Jacob would believe nothing
more, nothing different, nothing higher, than he saw

and felt, and had experience of, he must have fainted, and failed, and let the Angel go without leaving the blessing behind. He must have succumbed; been conquered; been no prevailing prince with God. But, like his father Abraham, "against hope he believed in hope." He felt the pain of the Lord's opposition. He saw the resoluteness of the Lord's efforts against him. He felt the blow that struck the hollow of his thigh out of joint; and millions in all future ages would have justified him as having yielded with a good grace indeed, had he at that point resigned the conflict, giving up the palm of victory to his opponent. But Jacob believed. He had ground for believing. He had the covenant promise for the ground and warrant of his faith. That word of God was the authorised exponent and explanation of the mind of God. It had been given him that he might read the heart of God by means of it. Outward events and dispensations are not given for that purpose. The written Word is. By it, therefore, we ought ever more to hold. By the word and covenant Jacob held—the covenant word—" I will bless thee and make thee a blessing." Because of that word did he exclaim, " I will not let thee go except thou bless me." " And he blessed him there " (Gen. xxxii. 24–29). Thus faith triumphs over sense. This is the victory that overcometh.

Now, in examining the operation of this in the illustrious case of Jonah, let us *first* view his position from the side of sense, and *secondly*, from the side of faith.

I. On the side of sense. And was ever a case so fitted to call forth utter despair? The facts are stated so quietly, with such simplicity, and with so little comment, that we are apt to miss the impression which a story so singular should produce. "So they took up Jonah and cast him forth into the sea. Now the Lord had prepared a great fish to swallow up Jonah. And Jonah was in the belly of the fish three days and three nights."

But to acquire some deeper sense of his dreadful condition, let us learn of himself, as he speaks in his marvellous prayer; and let the three following things be attended to.

Mark (1.) the case in which he finds himself; (2.) the hand to which he traces it; and (3.) the immediate effects produced by it on his mind.

1. Mark the case in which Jonah finds himself. He calls it generally one of affliction :—"I cried by reason of mine affliction." And then, to specify the affliction, and to indicate its absolute extremity, he uses unparalleled language like this :—"Out of the belly of hell, or of the grave, cried I." Then, entering more minutely on the description of his awful position, he says :—"Thou hast cast me into the deep, in the midst of the seas; and the floods compassed me about: all Thy billows and Thy waves passed over me." Nor does he stop at general expressions of the fact that he is submerged in the mighty deep. His descriptions beeome so particular as almost to fill us with horror while we read them :—"The waters compassed me about even to the soul: the depth

closed me round about, the sea-weeds were wrapped about my head." Nor hath he rest in his living grave: —" I went down to the bottoms of the mountains." And nowhere in all this matchless monstrous journeying is any path of escape discovered: all doors of hope are barred:—" The earth, with her bars, is about me for ever."

Who can imagine the terrors of this unheard-of grave? Oh! if he found courage or composure amidst circumstances like these to address his soul in prayer, and that too believing prayer, to the Lord, how great a marvel or miracle of grace must that prayer be! But it is far more so, if we consider,—

2. In the second place, that the mere circumstances constitute a very small part of the hindrance to the prayer of faith which Jonah now had to overcome. Consider the hand to which he traced his unparalleled calamity. He saw the Lord's hand in this judgment that was come upon him; and he felt, that sore and terrifying as his position was, it was a hundredfold more so as assigned to him by an angry God.

Had his present wretched case befallen him by what is usually called accident, or in the ordinary course of providence in a world of trial, it would have been sufficiently alarming and staggering. All the dark and dreadful circumstances which imagination finds it so difficult to realise, might still, without much wonder, have produced a shock above which his faith might only with the greatest difficulty have risen. But the matter was far otherwise and far worse. God had clothed Himself towards Jonah in all the insignia of a judge,—an incensed judge. He had followed out, with His erring servant, a solemn judicial process. He had summoned him to His tribunal, and witnessed against him. He had sentenced him to death, and seen to the execution of the sentence. His God was indeed pursuing him as an enemy. And though He had prepared a great fish to swallow up Jonah, the terrified prophet might naturally in the meantime have preferred death itself to the world of horrors of the deep, amidst which he was now tumultuously and helplessly hurried up and down.

A mere accident, which may fall on a believer with crushing weight, at the very time when his soul is prospering and in health, and while the light of his Father's countenance is upon him, may be borne. But alas! when terrors like those Jonah now suffers are inflicted in the following up of an angry controversy on God's part with His servant! "THOU" hast cast me into the deep: all "THY" billows and "THY" waves are gone over me, —it is this that aggravates them unutterably. Terrible in themselves, they are a hundredfold more so, coming as messengers of the Divine anger,—executioners of the sentence of God's displeasure. The soul cannot be alive to its relation to God, without feeling them to be intolerable when regarded as proofs of His indignation. The blow may be very painful in itself; but as the blow of *Thy* hand, I am consumed by it. The stroke may be sore: but as *Thy* stroke—oh! remove it. If this is come upon me, well may I mourn: but if *Thou* didst it, I am dumb. "I was dumb, I opened not my mouth; because *Thou* didst it. Remove *Thy* stroke away from me: I am consumed by the blow of *Thy* hand" (Ps. xxxix. 9, 10).

3. Consider the effect which all this produced in his soul; the state of spirit into which all this cast him, and above which his faith had to rise superior. The disspiriting influence and effect of his dreadful condition is indicated particularly by two expressions in the fourth and seventh verses :—" I said I am cast out of Thy sight:" "My soul fainteth within me."

(1.) "I said I am cast out of Thy sight." Such was the impression, the despondency,—the almost despair produced in the agitated prophet's soul. My heart was hot within me: while I was musing, the fire burned; then spake I with my tongue: my anguish overflowed whether I would or no, and I said, "I am cast out of Thy presence." Such is the dictate of the flesh, triumphing for a moment in the varying turns of this sore inward conflict. And what feeling could be more dreadful? To be cast out of God's sight; to be cast away; thrust away from him; how terrible to a really awakened soul! To be banished from the light of the sun; shut up in the depths of ocean, among the roots of the everlasting hills; is terrible beyond description. Yet if God is still propitious, forgiving, favourable, in due time all shall yet be well. But if that can no longer be hoped for; if God is mine enemy; if He and I are separated and put asunder; if He finally has done with me, and has " cast me out of His sight; " then infinite darkness begins to settle down on my soul—irretrievable wreck for eternity is befalling me. In Thy presence is fulness of joy; out of Thy presence, is the second death for evermore.

Ah! if you are asleep in sin, you may think it no terrible calamity to have to dwell away from the presence of God; but if you have aught of the light of life in you, you will feel that to be *cast out* of God's sight is unutterable and everlasting ruin. Why, it is promised as the only thing that can sustain and support an awakened soul :—" Him that cometh unto me, I will *in no wise cast out.*"

(2.) But Jonah expresses the extremity of his despondency in other terms. He says, " My soul fainted within me: " literally, " My soul infolded itself in me." Thought rolled on thought. No outward prop, or sign, or token for good could I discover. My soul collapsed and fell in upon itself; and rolling itself up in its sorrow and anxiety, having nothing to look to without, and nothing to lean on within,—" without were fightings, within were fears,"—my soul fainted in me!

Such were the circumstances in which Jonah's agitated soul had to fight the good fight of faith. (1.) Outwardly he was begirt with terrors unspeakable. (2.) These were the tokens of the anger of God. (3.) His soul under these calamities was brought to the verge of despair. He had to struggle, *first*, against horrors in their own nature unparalleled. He had to struggle, *secondly*, against these, regarded as the messengers of an angry God. And he had to struggle, *thirdly*, against the faintness, the heart-sick faintness of spirit, which they could not fail to produce.

II. It was in these circumstances that Jonah's faith rose in its strength and triumph—that "faith not of himself, but the gift of God." For however tossed and afflicted we may be, even tossed and afflicted inwardly, which is far the worst, we ought still to pray : to pray of course in faith, for there is no other kind of prayer binding on us ; no other kind of prayer allowable ; no other kind of prayer, real prayer. The very verge of destruction is ground for prayer—and that not random exclamation, but believing and assured petition. And it is expressly in such a case that the Hearer of prayer receives the true pure glory due to His name,—the glory due to His omnipotence, His all-sufficiency, His infinite wisdom, His amazing grace, His faithfulness which is in the heavens.

And indeed what can stand us in any stead in such an hour, but the prayer of faith? The case is supposed to be in every light desperate. The circumstances are altogether hopeless. They indicate an angry God. They dry up the soul's springs of strength. There is no entrance of any light, any hope, any relieving influence, except from a new world or region, different from sense, and far transcending it,—yet equally near, or rather nearer. That region is the region of faith. Let it be opened : "Oh! set ye open unto me the gates of it." Let it be entered. Let its truths, and powers, and promises, and hopes, tell upon the soul. Let the Word of God, in short, come in. Let God by His word, His believed word, command the tempest of the soul; forbid the destruction threatened and feared: and a new power comes to bear upon the case, fitted to carry it almightily through to a happy issue; fitted in the meantime to sustain the heart, till an issue of peace and of deliverance comes. Such a time is the very crisis for faith. It is of all times the best for making a clear, thorough, unmistakable experiment in the line and direction of true faith. When every prop is driven out from beneath your feet; when you see not your signs; when all you know is that God is infinitely holy and you are wholly sinful; when your marks and tokens of grace seem to have misgiven, and you are left without one single trustworthy feature in your case to lean upon, or keep company with, or draw hope from till the day should dawn; when inwardly all strength is gone, and outwardly all things are against you: then is the time for the trial whether God's solitary unsupported word alone be enough ; whether God's unattested word, —certificated or countersigned by no one, by nothing in the world without, and nothing in the world within; yea, contradicted by trembling conscience within, and by terrific providence without—whether that word of your God be still true and tried, and to be depended on. It was easy for you to believe in Christ's promise when you did not see the evil of sin;—when you felt not the rigour and righteousness of God's law;—when you knew not the deceit and wickedness of your own heart;

—when you had no insight into, no experience of, the masterful, unconquerable power of your own corruptions. But now is the time for faith, for the trial of your faith; now, when assaulted, baffled, overwhelmed by besetting sin; laden and agitated in conscience, by the guilt of it; seeing the frown of the Lord's displeasure, because of it; feeling the pursuit of the Lord's anger, in His avenging of it; and reading its hatefulness in the mirror of God's pure and holy law, of God's pure and holy nature, of God's dear Son's pure and holy character and example—and above all, of that dear Son's cross. Now is the time for the proof of your faith's genuineness, your faith's truth and power. Now is the need for a faith that shall be "not of yourself, but the gift of God."

It was thus that Jonah's faith was tried: and it stood the test.

The hinge of this conflict between sense and faith, and of faith's triumph in it, is in the fourth verse: "I said I am cast out of Thy sight; yet I will look again towards Thy holy temple." Here is the turning point. But let us trace faith's victory step by step.

1. In the first place, then, we see the truth and power of Jonah's faith in this conflict, in that he betook himself to prayer at all. He cried unto the Lord. Not only so; but "he prayed unto the Lord *his* God" (ver. 1). He gave not up his covenant interest in God. He still maintained that the Lord was his God. He knew that the Lord hateth putting away. Shall we say, he knew that God, on the contrary, was bringing him back? This

indeed was what the Lord designed by His whole procedure: and this design He was securing. And he said:
"I cried by reason of mine affliction unto the Lord;
out of the belly of hell cried I" (ver. 2).

Yes! his affliction constrained him to pray. And
how often after backsliding or disobedience is the true
tone of prayerfulness restored only through the aid of
affliction. For, oh how grievously does known or
special sin derange the power of prayer and the principle of faith! It induces hardness and insensibility
of heart. It seals up the heart and lips from God. It
tends to produce coldness, artificiality, distance, and
estrangedness of feeling in the believer towards his
Father in heaven. There is a sort of proud shame that
dislikes to come to the point; it rather deals in vague
generalities. Immediately there is guile in the soul.
The eye of the child falters and quails before its
Father's eye. There is misunderstanding. Cordiality
is gone. Intercourse is constrained: the sweetness and
refreshing power of prayer is departed from it. The
Spirit of adoption is grieved. Formality takes the place
of living, heart-breathing supplication.

But the stroke of affliction comes. Anguish overflows
the spirit. The child cannot, will not, brace up its own
strength against a Father's rod. It breaks down rather.
Formality now is gone. Necessity constrains truth and
earnestness. Necessity impels to seek a near approach;
a full confession; a free and thorough reconciliation.
Prayer again becomes real; the cry of the poor and
needy; an appeal of exquisite and touching power that

always tells on the heart of the God and Father of Jesus Christ.

Thus it was with Jonah. The adverse and terrific aspect of affairs; the too clearly announced anger of his God; the fainting of his soul within him;—under all these his spirit at last breaks down at his Father's feet. Oh! then comes the true prayer of faith. Out of weakness the child is made strong. Back from unbelief he comes afresh—a believer as before.

2. Jonah set before himself the certainty of Jehovah's reconcileableness, his promised forgiveness, his sure accessibility. It is this that is twice indicated by the expressions:—"I will look again towards Thy holy temple;" "My prayer came in unto Thee, into Thine holy temple" (verses 4 and 7).

For, why this reference to the temple? Is it in the infantile absurdity of ritualism or formalism, building its churches and saying its prayers—facing to the East? I trow not. Away with the carnality that ties the mind down to earth and sense, precisely when only by rising to the things that are unseen and eternal can any relief, refreshment, or reinvigorating power come! Jonah thought of "the temple;" and why? Because God had placed His name there. Because there He gave the symbol of His presence as a God of love, and especially a God of propitiated favour; a God dwelling between the cherubim,—God on the blood-sprinkled seat of mercy, on the throne of grace. Not as confined to temples made with hands, did Jonah think of his God. "I fear the God of heaven, that made the sea and the dry land"

(i. 9). But this God everywhere present, Jonah knew, from the revelation of Him in the temple, as a God of grace; a " God waiting to be gracious, exalted to have mercy; a God of judgment : giving his blessing to all that wait upon him " (Isa. xxx. 18).

And if the symbol of Jehovah's reconcilableness was so precious to Jonah, how ought our faith to rise triumphant over all evil, and amid all affliction,—now that Christ, by the temple of His body, hath effected the perfect reconciliation for ever. In that temple God is now Immanuel, God with us. There is nothing deeper, nothing truer, nothing more abundantly, finally, conclusively proved, than that God is reconcilable, accessible, forgiving ;— gracious to all that will come to Him in the way of His appointment. He has sealed no other truth as He has sealed this. He has proved no other fact as He has proved this. And the proof and seal are permanent. In the midst of the throne there stands " a Lamb as it had been slain." There is " an Advocate with the Father, Jesus Christ the righteous, who is the propitiation for our sins." While this is true, God's holy temple, the most holy place, is the place of free and open access to a sinner *as a sinner*, with all the weight and all the weariness, with all the guilt and shame and pollution, that attach to him. " I said, I am cast out of Thy sight; yet will I look again towards Thy holy temple."

Let faith, then, conquer sense : faith, pleading the proved and the eternal. It has a conflict to carry on. But, in the treasury of heaven, it has the true sinews of the war. A few hours of terrific trial; a few years of weary, vexing care; a limited amount of light affliction, which is but for a moment; a temporary combination of providences, sorely afflicting my body and my spirit;— these may be the proof to flesh and sense that God is displeased at mine iniquity, and will by no means clear the guilty. But the permanent abiding of the Lamb in the midst of the throne; the ever-living and unchangeable priesthood of Him who is at the Father's right hand; is to my faith the surpassing, all-conquering proof that He *forgives* iniquity, transgression, and sin. "I said, I am cast out of Thy sight, yet will I look again toward Thy holy temple:" "and my prayer came in unto Thee, into Thine holy temple." Let the Holy Spirit only reveal and apply the truth; and, in the promise of the Father and the righteousness of the Son, there is enough to be the ground of a faith that shall rise in its unflinching and unbounded triumph above all billows and floods —above the blazing deluge yet to come, the final deluge of fire itself.

Oh, to be exercised in the holy place within the veil! Oh, to direct our prayer to God's holy temple! "For, seeing that we have a great High Priest that is passed into the heavens, Jesus the Son of God," we may well "hold fast our profession. For we have not an High Priest who cannot be touched with the feeling of our infirmities; but was in all points tempted like as we are, yet without sin. Let us therefore come boldly to the throne of grace, that we may obtain mercy and find grace to help in time of need" (Heb. iv. 14–16). Thus did Jonah.

3. And, thirdly, he did not do this in vain. For observe how he is answered in the progressive strengthening of his faith, even while his trial lasts. Hear the noble language of faith, while still he remains, to the feeling of sense, in his horrid grave: " Thou *hast* brought up my life from corruption, O Lord my God." I know nothing more sublime in all the range of recorded human utterances. What could dictate assured and triumphant language like this, but marvellous, miraculous faith? His deliverance is not yet come; yet faith speaks of it as if it were. O noble faith! it is in thy power to bring in the deliverance that is still future, with the sweetness of that which is already present, and the sureness of that which is already past. Weltering still in anguish unspeakable, in dangers and distresses inconceivable, a soul in which *thy* power dwells, gives glory to God for deliverance from them all!

And is not this of the essence of the life of faith? " O wretched man that I am! who shall deliver me from the body of this death?" Who *shall* deliver me. The deliverance is future. It is only on the way. But it is *surely* on the way. Therefore, though the deliverance is future, my gratitude should be present. Not; I *will:* but; I do thank God through Jesus Christ:— " Who *shall* deliver me?" "I *thank* God through Jesus Christ." " For we are saved—already saved—in hope. But that which is seen is not hope; for what a man seeth why doth he yet hope for? But if we hope for that we see not, then do we with patience wait for it;" —and already do we with joy give thanks for it.

4. And now this, in fact, is the last step in Jonah's victory of faith: "I will sacrifice unto Thee with the voice of thanksgiving; I will pay *that* that I have vowed. Salvation is of the Lord." Thus Jonah, delivered from his guiltiness and evil conscience; reconciled to God in peace; washed from his sins, and made again a recognised king and priest, and so recognising and presenting himself before God in His holy temple by faith; offers the sacrifice of thanksgiving. Shut up still in his darksome grave, in the deep, in the shadow of death, we hear him nevertheless singing marvellously —far more marvellously than Paul and Silas in the prison—singing in his darkness, as if he said: "God is the Lord who hath shown me light: I will bind the sacrifice with cords, unto the horns of the altar" (Ps. cxviii. 27). Light! What light has Jonah? He has the light of faith;—the light that shineth in the darkness;—that lighteth up the shadow of death. And amidst the light, he cometh to God's altar to offer the sacrifice of thanksgiving. He cometh unto God,—unto God his exceeding joy.

You will praise God joyfully, O downcast and disquieted believer, when once He shall have given you the deliverance you desire? Your song will begin when God hath done for you all that you ask? Ah! your song in that case shall be grounded in sense, not springing from faith. For observe: while your trial still lasts; while your vexing thorn still goads you; while your much-loved hope seems plunged in the depths of ocean, and no sensible sign yet appears of its being restored; while still there is need of patience, and still there is need of faith; if God give you warrant for faith, even His promise, is that not ground of *immediate* thanksgiving? And if this warrant of faith beget faith; if this promise of deliverance be embraced in faith; will your gratitude tarry all the time till the promise be fulfilled? What would that mean? You will not praise God till the actual accomplishment? Why? Would it be cutting before the point? Would it be giving vent to your feelings of relief too soon?—dangerously soon? Ah! what is that but unbelief?—unbelief, with its maxim, uttered or unexpressed,—a maxim not known in the kingdom of Christ,—'A bird in the hand is worth two in the bush.' Your gratitude and praise would be premature! You distrust the issue! Are you not in the snare of unbelief?

But, be it that the trial lasts; and that, to sense and reason, all is dark. Let in the light of faith. Let Jehovah's word be true, and every man a liar. " Who is among you that feareth the Lord, that obeyeth the voice of His servant, that walketh in darkness and hath no light? Let him trust in the name of the Lord, and stay upon his God." Let in the light of trust; of faith; of God's promise—God's promise all-sufficient, free, eternal;—and ought not praise to spring up immediately? Will not praise spring up immediately? Will there not be " peace and joy *in believing* " ? The man that walks by sense can sing when the deliverance has come. It is faith's prerogative, and faith's peculiarity, to sing before that :—faith's all-distinguishing peculiarity;

faith's all-surpassing prerogative; faith's all-vanquishing power. O most noble grace of faith! "Thou art not of ourselves; thou art the gift of God"!

And then, according to our faith—our faith proved by our thanksgiving—according to our faith it is done unto us. "And the Lord spake unto the fish, and it vomited out Jonah upon the dry land."

XV

NEW TESTAMENT COMMENTARIES : NO. I

THE TYPE

JONAH i. 17 ; ii. 10

MATT. xii. 40.—" For as Jonas was three days and three nights in the whale's belly ; so shall the Son of man be three days and three nights in the heart of the earth."

> "*He was delivered for our offences, and was raised again for our justification.*"—ROM. iv. 25.
> "*Therefore are we buried with him by baptism into death: that like as Christ was raised up from the dead by the glory of the Father, even so we also should walk in newness of life.*"—ROM. vi. 4.

WE have now the light of New Testament commentary to bring to bear upon the history. And the Lord himself is the commentator. We will afterwards find that His comments set forth an analogy between himself and Jonah in three points of views; in respect of a type—a contrasted parallel—and a sign. At present, we confine our attention to the consideration of the type.

It is evident, then, that our Lord invites a comparison, discovers a resemblance, institutes an analogy between the marvellous dealings of God with the prophet, and His own burial and resurrection. And this resemblance or analogy is, as we shall see, of that peculiar kind which we call a type. Now, in comparing the two—these two great interpositions of Godhead with Jonah and Jesus respectively—it is a matter of indifference which of them, in any particular point, is employed to throw light upon the other. The type, for the most part, will illustrate the antitype. But there may be points in which our clear knowledge of the antitype may be carried back to illustrate the type. This remark holds good in the case of the very first element of resemblance which we notice.

I. In both cases there is a death and a resurrection.

The analogy which Christ institutes between His own experience and Jonah's carries this in it: that, substantially, Jonah was in the judgment, and by the hand of God, put to death and brought to life again. His life was forfeited; it was cancelled; and when, after three days and three nights in the whale's belly, he was placed again on dry land, it was a new and fresh life on which he now entered. Substantially, Jonah underwent a death, a burial, and a resurrection. It is very remarkable indeed that Jonah speaks of his burial in the very same terms in which Messiah speaks of

His :—"hell" and "corruption." "Hell,"—*hades*, or in other words, the state of the dead ; the unseen world, the world of disembodied souls,—on the one hand ; and "corruption," the pit, the grave, the prison of the untenanted body, on the other :—these are the terrible expressions which Jonah himself employs to describe his condition. For, in the first place, we hear him in the second verse saying :—"I cried by reason of mine affliction unto the Lord, and he heard me ; out of the belly of *hell* cried I, and thou heardst me." And, in the second place, in the sixth verse, where his faith is triumphing in his deliverance as if it were already come :—"the earth with her bars was about me for ever : yet hast thou brought up my life from *corruption*, O Lord my God." Hell and corruption :—these are the terms by which Jonah designates his penalty—his penalty of three days and three nights in the whale's belly. And in what language does the Son of man speak in the Spirit concerning His endurance of three days and three nights in the heart of the earth? "Thou wilt not leave my soul in *hell ;* neither wilt Thou suffer Thine Holy One to see *corruption*" (Ps. xvi. 10). It is the language of burial and resurrection in both cases. Jonah's life, then, was forfeited, cancelled, taken away and restored. It was a new life that Jonah had thereafter ; newness of life. He was a new man ; he was another creature ; he was raised from the dead.

II. But secondly ; in both cases, the death and burial are judicial processes.

They are not in the ordinary course of nature : neither are they mere physical miracles; that is the least of it, in these tremendous movements. Each of them is a special, signal, judicial procedure ; carried out by God, acting simply and strictly, as a judge, guarding the demands of justice, seeing to their execution and fulfilment. In one word : each of the processes is an atonement; an expiation; a sacrifice : pacifying the Divine Judge; satisfying Divine justice : abolishing guilt; restoring peace ; effecting reconciliation.

Now the bringing out of the analogy, in this respect, will be helpful in showing that the death and resurrection of Christ constitute a proper, real, perfect, and proven satisfaction to the justice of God for the sins of His people ;—a doctrine, which almost all the theological heresies of the present day are, with more or less subtlety and refinement, labouring to overthrow.

It is assailed, for instance, by those who, under various coverts, deny that the law of God has any penalty, properly so called.

A penalty is that which is inflicted in satisfaction for a precept broken. Moreover, through the intervention of penalty, responsible beings are left free to obey or disobey ; and the majesty of law, and the claims and supremacy of the Lawgiver, are still maintained, still kept consistent with the moral freedom of the subject, whether he continue in subjection or not. Save for this, —the existence and infliction of penalty,—subjects may preserve the honour of the Lawgiver if they choose to obey: but the Lawgiver cannot preserve it Himself, when they disobey. In the former case, therefore, even, it is to *them* that He is indebted for His Sovereignty; as is proved by the fact, that in the latter case He cannot maintain it. A state of things like this, were the destruction of moral government and the dethronement of the Moral Governor. A result so shocking, which would make all the universe a hell, is prevented through the maintenance of unbending law—law with its alternative of precept on the one hand, and penalty on the other; law, which ruling inflexibly says, " Do this, and live "—or, alternatively, "The soul that sinneth shall die."

The death thus threatened is penalty, not chastisement; designed simply to uphold the law, not to reclaim the rebel; to satisfy the justice of God, not to correct and purify the sinner. Those we speak of, would make all suffering remedial; corrective; keeping in view the reclaiming of the offending transgressor: not penal; expiatory; satisfactory to the justice of the offended Ruler. This doctrine is followed out most naturally, and most consistently, in the desire and the demand for the abolition of capital punishment. For if punishment is to be purely corrective, humbling, alterative, and purifying to the criminal, then by all means, whatever he has done, spare his life; place him under discipline; mitigate the severity of his suffering, as his evil disposition is ameliorated; and having kept him from damaging others, and done your best to benefit *him*, watch the moment when your process has been so successful that he can be trusted loose again; watch that moment, and liberate him immediately :—for, if you carry the process one iota farther, you as much violate your principle concerning punishment, and inflict that thing which you hate,—a penalty,—as if you had taken away his life. The nature of punishment, as penalty, becomes obvious, in the case of capital punishment,—in the taking away of life; and this is the reason why it is objected to. Anything short of death may and ought to be inflicted in combination with efforts to benefit the criminal. And so, on account of this combination, the element of penalty may be lost sight of. And hence, the punishment of crime, in its strict, original, pure, and proper import, is always capable of being misunderstood, where it amounts to something short of death. But *death* is obvious and simple penalty; not even professing to promote the good of the criminal, but to preserve the glory of law, and satisfy the justice of the judge. Hence perhaps we may see a reason why all the misery inflicted by God in penal vengeance on sin, is gathered up under the one title, " death ; "—" The wages of sin is *death*." In that case, there is no escaping the conclusion that the punishment is penal, retributive, satisfactory to justice ; and not remedial, corrective, beneficial to the sinner.

The doctrine that destroys the very notion of penalty must, of course, subvert the very idea of an atonement; an atonement properly so called ; a real and proper sacrifice for sin, a true satisfaction to justice.

The truth and reality of the atonement are equally subverted by those who acknowledge nothing more specific in the nature and design of Christ's death than a striking exhibition of God's hatred of sin,—an expedient by which He can pardon iniquity, without detriment to His own character, or rather reputation, for holiness.

The death of Christ does indeed strikingly exhibit God's hatred of sin, and very awfully illustrates His character as the Holy One. But it accomplishes these results, only in so far as it is, and just because it is, an atonement—a true and proper infliction of the penalty of the law—a true and proper satisfaction to the justice of the Divine Judge. If God's hatred of sin be held to lie open to doubt or suspicion in connexion with the pardon of sin, and if His holiness is supposed to be obscured by His taking sinners into His friendship, it is vain to point to the Cross and say;—No; behold there, and in the sufferings of His Son, the Divine hatred of iniquity, the Lord's indubitable and unspotted holiness. I say, this is utterly a vain and ineffectual reply, if the Cross is merely an expedient for illustrating God's character and protecting God's reputation for holiness, and not a true satisfaction for sin. Nay, more: if it be no expiation of sin, but a mere scenic representation of holiness;—a scenic representation of God's hatred of sin, got up to save God from *mis*representation when He abstains from punishing sin;—a scenic representation, where there is real suffering, but no real satisfaction; real suffering inflicted and endured, but no real satisfaction rendered or accepted:—then I say, *this* is fitted to misrepresent the character of God; to misrepresent it unanswerably, hope-lessly, blasphemously. For, if the dying Christ, suffering unsearchable woe on the tree, suffers and dies in such circumstances, the character of God both in respect of righteousness and love, is overthrown. Is it conceivable that He should pursue His dear Son to the dust of death, merely to save His own reputation in the eyes of His creatures, and to wipe away an objection which they had taken to His procedure?

For mark this also. If there be no real satisfaction to Divine justice in the Cross, and no such satisfaction necessary; if God may pardon sin without a sacrifice of expiation and atonement; then the objection to His doing so is false. He does it without detriment to His holiness, or to any element in all His glorious character. In that case the objection against which the Cross is pleaded as a reply is groundless. The objection is based on a mere delusion. And is God's dear Son to agonise in body and in soul on the tree of Calvary, in order to furnish by His groans and death an answer to a false and groundless objection? Is that a procedure of Divine love? Is that a dictate of Divine righteousness? Is that like the way of the Divine wisdom? Could not God rather have directly enlightened the blinded minds of the objectors, and shown them the groundlessness and untruth of the objection? Nay rather; having the hearts of all men in His keeping, could He not have prevented the objection ever rising to their fancy at all, seeing that (by the supposition) it is false and groundless? Surely the *expedient* needful on God's part in such a case is plain enough; namely, one or other of two very simple alternatives;—a more effectual ruling of men's minds, or a more effectual revelation of His own. In either of these two ways this false objection might have been dealt with, and not only answered but annihilated or prevented. Then, if so; and if, therefore, the inexpressible agonies of Christ crucified are brought in merely to provide an antidote to a misconstruction and misrepresentation of God's procedure, into which none but the ignorant could be misled, and which they would abandon when properly instructed and enlightened; are we not compelled to raise now the very objection in resistless force, which in a form having in it no force at all, the Cross has been needlessly introduced to remove?— an unanswerable objection to the righteousness of God now, when we see Him punishing the innocent as a stroke of policy merely, and because it is expedient!

If the Cross is to be represented as an answer to an objection at all, it is a forestalling answer. It is an answer to an objection which, without the Cross, would be well-grounded and *true;*—an objection which, instead of needing increase of light to remove it from the minds of the ignorant, the enlightened and the holy would feel the force of, just in proportion to their light and holiness. Nothing can so tremendously confirm that objection to the forgiveness of sins as "Broad School" evasions of the propitiatory nature of Christ's death; and nothing can more gloriously remove it than the old evangelical doctrine of the Cross. The cross of Christ, as a real and proper atoning sacrifice, is not designed to dispel a mere ambiguity about the holiness of God, but primarily and immediately to meet a real claim of His justice, and to constitute a real satisfaction to His justice. It is not merely necessary that God should *appear* to be just, but that He should *be* just in pardoning iniquity, transgression, and sin. A mere *expedient* to save *appearances* is degrading in Divine transactions; most of all degrading as an explanation of that grandest Divine transaction that lights up the character of God from eternity unto eternity. By the ever-wondrous cross of the Son of His love, God secures no appearances. He achieves the reality. By that cross it is not merely represented, but *achieved*, that God is just in justifying the ungodly who believe. But it is as a true satisfaction for sin that the Cross achieves this glorious result, and confers on Him who died upon it the name of " JESUS "—SAVIOUR. He is not our Saviour, on Broad School principles. On their own showing, He may in some sense be the Saviour of God's reputation, but in no sense the Saviour of men's souls. On their views, man can be saved without Him, and saved too without any detriment to God's character, though God's reputation might suffer in the eyes of some of His creatures. How shocking! The Evangel which these men would overthrow makes the cross of Christ a school of light, overflowing with the knowledge of the glory of God in the face of Jesus Christ. But it does so, by making that cross a real atonement—a true, and proper, and perfect propitiation. Obliterate this view of the Cross, and we know no instrument so powerful as that very cross itself by which to bury in eternal darkness both the character of God and the hopes of men.

Now this feature—this fundamental feature—in the atonement, as an infliction of real penalty; no mere scenic representation of holiness, but a real satisfaction for sin—is well illustrated by the resemblance, the type, which we are now considering. For manifestly Jonah's being cast into the sea—his being " three days and three nights in the whale's belly "—was of the nature and had the effect of expiation, atonement, sacrifice, satisfaction, in the true and proper meaning of these terms. Jonah's crime offended Divine justice. Justice pursued, afflicted, detected, exposed, demanded the criminal. Every effort of his own to conceal himself, and every effort of others to save him, were useless. Justice had its one simple, unalterable, inflexible demand. Justice demanded *him*. And when the demand was met, justice was satisfied; " the sea ceased from her raging." Here is the true and proper notion of a sacrifice for sin, an atonement, a satisfaction to Divine justice, a pacification of Divine anger. The idea of substitution also comes in to complete the resemblance; for though at first sight it does not seem to hold good, but rather the contrary,—seeing that on the one hand, Jonah was guilty and the crew innocent, and on the other, Jesus was holy and His people guilty,— yet in reality it does hold very exactly, the force of the type being held to begin as it ought to do, after Jesus is supposed to be embarked with us; united to us;

made sin for us that we might be made the righteousness of God in Him.

But the power of the analogy is not yet fully brought out by any means. And its full strength comes out just at that point where a little more examination might seem to prove that it breaks down. For it may be said, If you make Jonah's sufferings a real atonement and satisfaction, then it seems to follow that he needed no forgiveness for his offence against God in fleeing from His presence; he needed not to draw upon the Divine mercy, for he satisfied Divine justice; and bearing the penalty in his own person, he offered a sufficient sacrifice for his own sin. And thus in bringing out the clear resemblance between the type and the antitype, we would place them on a level with each other, and make Christ's own atonement not the only one. But is it not a clear doctrine of Scripture that there is but *one* sacrifice for sin, and that no other atonement can be accepted? that no sin can be forgiven save on the ground of that atonement alone?

Certainly the one only expiatory, guilt-removing sacrifice of atonement is that of Christ; and any view of Jonah's sufferings inconsistent with that doctrine must be false. Any discussion, also, of the type which would make it supplemental to the antitype, and thereby argue the antitype imperfect, must proceed on some grievous error.

To preserve the perfection of the antitype, shall we then deny the reality of the type? Shall we say that the type was not a real atonement, but merely a repre-

sentation of an atonement? With all submission, this
would seem the very worst method of illustrating and
maintaining the perfection of the antitype. For the
perfection of the antitype implies *reality* in the type;
but a type in which atonement is not real, but only representative and scenic, would be a poor means of exhibiting an atonement that is real and perfect. It was
real—not scenic or pictorial—healing; real healing,
though in a lower sphere—the sphere of bodily disease
—that the brazen serpent conveyed. And without this,
it would have but poorly conveyed instruction concerning *real* healing in the higher sphere of moral remedy
and spiritual salvation.

The fact in the case before us is this. Jonah's being
" three days and three nights in the whale's belly " was
true and real satisfaction to justice and expiation of
offence, *in a lower sphere ;* and thus becomes a true type
of real and perfect expiation in the ultimate and highest
sphere, the moral government of God; expiation effected
by the sacrifice of the Son of man, and sealed by His
being " three days and three nights in the heart of the
earth."

God, be it observed, may carry on one government
within another. There may be His universal government, embracing heaven and earth and hell,—all responsible beings. It is the law of this government that we
have violated by our apostasy and sin. It is the law of
this government which God maintains, consistently with
the forgiveness of sin, in His dispensation by Jesus Christ
and Him crucified. Through that mediatorial dispensa-

tion, the anomalies of the world's history will at the judgment-day be brought into final harmony with the simpler elements of God's universal government, as these are exhibited in heaven, the home of the holy; in hell, the prison of the wicked. That Saviour, in whose person and work salvation and judgment are stored up, is the head of all principality and power. Personally He is God, God manifest in the flesh; and officially He is head over all things unto the Church, which is His body. And having stood in the room of the body, the Church, made sin for them that they might be made the righteousness of God in Him, He expiated their sin, pacified their offended Judge, satisfied Divine justice, magnified the Divine law, reconciled the Divine Father. Those who acquiesce in this arrangement, and, owning righteous liability to wrath, are content in faith and gratitude to take this expiation and satisfaction for their shield and their glory, stand right with Divine justice and are justified by the Divine Judge freely by His grace, through the redemption that is in Christ, whom God hath set forth to be a propitiation through faith in His blood. Entitled hereby to the favour and blessing of God, they obtain the Divine Spirit to purify and refine their moral nature into the Divine image, and are ultimately advanced to the Divine fellowship in glory among the principalities and powers of light. Those, on the other hand, who reject the great salvation and live ungodly and impenitent and unbelieving, have their portion assigned at last in hell among the principalities and powers of darkness. And thereafter the universal moral government of God—

simplified from the elements with which the anomalous estate of the human race as under a dispensation of forbearance at present complicate it—will move forward ; unmingled love resting on the holy, unabated wrath on the wicked. Meantime, through the atonement of the Cross, the real and proper satisfaction for the sins of the elect, God is righteous in prolonging the probation of an apostate race; righteous in forbearing with the wicked ; righteous in condemning those who reject the redemption; and righteous in forgiving and justifying them that believe. And in reference to His universal government; in relation to Himself as the universal and Eternal Judge, and to His *necessary, universal, unchangeable* Moral Law ; in respect of guilt, in its strict and ultimate and essential nature, as consisting in liability to the wrath of the Eternal Judge and to condemnation under the penalty of the eternal law; it is impossible that there can be any atonement besides that of God's Eternal Son in human flesh upon the cross. " By His one offering He hath for ever perfected them that are sanctified " (Heb. x. 14).

But while, in regard to the universal government of God, against which all sin in its essential nature is committed, there can be but one atonement, that of Christ upon the tree, is it not quite conceivable that there may be minor governments conducted within the universal one, quite consistent with it; highly fitted to illustrate it; having laws of their own ; these laws penalties of their own, penalties which may give scope for atonements also ; atonements as real as these penalties, these laws, these governments are; atonements which, just by being thus real and true and proper inflictions of penalty, satisfactions of law, and in maintenance of government, become not scenic representations but typical realities, real types of the true, real, and all-perfect atonement by the death of God's Eternal Son? On this principle, the whole system of atonements under the Levitical economy is to be explained; and their illustrative, and especially their demonstrative and typical value brought out. And it is this principle that will show the full force of the type of Jonah. As universal Moral Governor,—Governor of all the universe, of all responsible beings, and among others, the human race,—Jehovah was Governor of the children of Israel regarded as *men*. But besides this, and besides all that in this capacity He revealed of Himself, He condescended to come into another and more specific relation towards them as *Israel*. He set up among them and over them as Israel, another government more peculiar. He became their local, national King. Their government was a theocracy. God was at the head of it. It remained, however, the *Jewish* government, though God was at the head of it. It was embraced under, but not identical with, His great moral government over all. That government, local and national, like any other local and national government,—not any less because Jehovah was the national King,—had laws peculiar to itself; these laws, their penalties. Satisfactions, therefore, might be rendered, or sacrifices and atonements brought in, if such were the will of the King; and these atonements, though they left the element of offence against God as universal Ruler unatoned for, might really atone for offence against the *minor* government; and thereby really typify, to spiritual intelligence, a coming atonement satisfactory in relation to the *universal* government,—and greater, as that government, embracing all the universe and all eternity, is greater than the local and temporary government over Israel, ranging, as it did, over only a few miles in space and a few years in time.

And thus indeed it was. Jehovah, besides their Governor in the sense in which He is the Moral Governor of all, was the national King of Israel. His throne, and court, and camp were amongst them. And this fact is sufficient to remove the calumny which shallow infidels have often brought against some portions of the Jewish code, as sanguinary and severe. Why should God doom to death the man in Israel who should have dealings in witchcraft? Simply, because Jehovah was King, special King of the nation; and to seek knowledge and counsel—knowledge of fact, or counsel and instruction for duty—from other invisible power was treason; a crime punished in every kingdom with death. Why should God pursue Achan with death, not turning from the fierceness of His anger, till the offender was stoned, and a heap of stones raised over him? Because Jehovah was King: and the King had taken the field; and His subjects were an army, and were under martial law: and the plain instructions of the King, the Generalissimo, being violated, the summary and brief procedure of martial law was the

order of the day,—as in any other army, and under any
general maintaining discipline among his troops, it would
have been. And why should God pursue Jonah even
unto death, for the sin of fleeing from His presence, and
refusing to carry His message to Nineveh? Because
Jehovah was King : and Jonah, His *aid-de-camp* under
orders, became a vile deserter ; and under any king
would have been in like manner, to the utmost of that
king's power, pursued, arrested, and subjected to de-
sertion's penalty, which is death.

It is this very simple, but valuable view of God's
Jewish, local, national, temporary government, as within
His government universal and eternal, which enables
us to see in Jonah's sufferings a real and proper expiation
of a real offence against a real government and law ; and
yet a type—yea, thereby, a real and true type—of the
one only atonement which satisfies for the breach of the
eternal law, and satisfies the demands of eternal justice.   Jonah's primary and ultimate guilt against God,
as the universal Moral Ruler, could be removed only by
the great atonement, of which his own sufferings were a
type.   In the sphere of that government, there is but
one atonement; and it is complete : for in the sphere of
that eternal government, the Eternal Son in human
flesh, through the Eternal Spirit, offered Himself without
spot to God.   In the limited and local sphere of the
national and temporary rule that God instituted over
Israel, the particular and additional element of liability
to Divine anger, resulting from the particular and additional element of Jonah's sin being not only an offence

against the universal government of God, but against the Jewish theocracy,—*this* might be atoned for, justice in *this* respect might be satisfied—by Jonah's own anguish in his marvellous burial and baptism of wrath— his marvellous and living grave in the deep. Hence the final argument from the analogy takes this form :—If in the sphere of the limited and temporary theocracy in Israel, three days and three nights' burial in the deep cleansed an offender from the guilt of his offence against God as Israel's king; then, in the universal sphere which embraces all worlds,—all earth, and heaven, and hell, and an eternity,—how much more shall the blood of Christ, who through the Eternal Spirit offered Himself without spot to God, cleanse our conscience from dead works, to serve the living God ? For as Jonas was three days and three nights in the whale's belly, so was the Son of man three days and three nights in the heart of the earth. For " He was delivered for our offences, and was raised again for our justification " (Rom. iv. 25).

III. The burial and resurrection of Jonah constituted the gate by which the word of Jehovah passed forth from the Jewish to the Gentile world. And in like manner in the antitype. The death and resurrection of Christ was the breaking down of the middle wall of partition.

In point of fact, it was only by his burial and baptism in the deep that Jonah became a prophet to Nineveh. That work of God, as matters stood, could not be accomplished otherwise. The obstacle to it could be removed only in this particular way. But this was successful. It was the means of carrying forth, from the limited and local Jewish theocracy, the message and revelation of God to a wider sphere. And thus the temporary and national government showed symptoms and capacities of world-wide expansion. But the perfection of this is found in the antitype. For an apostle, speaking of this expansion of the Church, thus testifies to Gentile converts: "Remember that when ye were without Christ ye were aliens from the commonwealth of Israel, strangers from the covenants of promise, having no hope, and without God in the world: but now in Christ Jesus ye who sometimes were far off are made nigh by the blood of Christ. For He is our peace, who hath made both one, and hath broken down the middle wall of partition between us; having abolished in His flesh the enmity, even the law of commandments contained in ordinances; for to make in Himself of twain one new man, so making peace; and that He might reconcile both unto God in one body by the cross, having slain the enmity thereby; and came and preached peace to you which were afar off, and to them that were nigh" (Eph. ii. 11–17).

The carrying forth of the message to the Gentiles is thus attributed to the death of Christ. In a parallel passage in the similar Epistle to the Colossians, Paul refers more distinctly to the burial and resurrection. "*Buried* with Him in baptism, wherein also ye are *risen* with Him through the faith of the operation of God, who hath *raised* Him from the dead. And you, being dead in your sins and the uncircumcision of your flesh, hath He quickened together with Him, having forgiven you all trespasses; blotting out the handwriting of ordinances that was against us, which was contrary to us, and took it out of the way, nailing it to His cross" (Col. ii. 12–14).

Always have the Gentiles been indebted for the Divine message to a prophet three days and three nights under the penalty of death : in the case of Jonah, with Nineveh; in the case of Jesus, with the world.

IV. The analogy holds further in this respect, that the experiences of Jonah and Christ constitute, each in its own sphere, an enforcement of the message which each brings to the Gentiles. Our Lord himself informs us that Jonas was a sign to the Ninevites. He not merely speaks of "the sign of Jonas" as something which should be given to the generation to whom He was then addressing Himself; an idea for which there might be some apparent ground if we had only Matthew's statements to go upon : "An evil and adulterous generation seeketh after a sign ; and there shall no sign be given to it, but the sign of the prophet Jonas" (chap. xii. 39 ; xvi. 4). But in the Gospel of Luke we have this particular added, namely, that Jonas was a sign *to the Ninevites :* "For as Jonas was a sign unto the Ninevites, so shall also the Son of man be to this generation" (chap. xi. 30). And in what respect was Jonas a sign unto the Ninevites? Clearly in the analogous respect in which the Son of man was to be a sign to that generation who heard His doctrine, and should hear His future history; in respect, namely, of His three days and three nights' endurance of the penalty of death.   This is the sign of the prophet Jonas, repeated in the case of the Son of man: in this sense he was a sign to the Ninevites. Clearly, therefore, it follows that the Ninevites were informed of the prophet's marvellous experience, as condemned and delivered unto death for offending the God, the King of Israel, and raised again in justification. The prophet himself has left no record of the fact that he gave them this information: yet the Lord is the best of commentators; and it is argued by " good and necessary inference " from the Lord's method of employing and improving the history of Jonah as His type, that Jonah proclaimed to them the terrible death which he endured, and the blessed resurrection which he experienced; and these events as transpiring in such intimate connexion with his bringing to them the solemn message of death,—" Forty days, and Nineveh shall be destroyed."   And can we for a moment doubt that while the message spoke of nothing but death, of wrath, of destruction; and while the prophet would enforce the terrible certainty of retribution by narrating the inflexible pursuit of himself, even unto death, which this God conducted when he refused obedience ; can we doubt that the mercy and miracle of their prophet's resurrection was at once the ground and the gleam of hope which they caught hold of, as an encouragement to repent and call upon the Lord ?   The message, indeed,

was all for death; and the sign alone contained a ground
of hope, while a seal of death was in it too.   Yet "the
men of Nineveh repented at the preaching of Jonas."

How is it, now that "a greater than Jonas is here"?
The death and resurrection of Christ are to us the sign
and evidence of the truth of His mission, the seal and
enforcement of His message.   Apostles uniformly
grounded their appeals to Jews and Gentiles on the
burial and resurrection of the Lord.   The hinge of
Peter's sermon on Pentecost was this : "Him hath God
raised up, having loosed the pains of death."   And
again : "This Jesus hath God raised up, whereof we
all are witnesses."   It is in like manner the burden
and the strength of Paul's sermon at Antioch.   "God
raised Him from the dead."   And both Peter to the
Jews, and Paul to the Gentiles, quote and comment
upon that 16th Psalm, so evidently the experience of
Messiah's soul, and expressive of Messiah's hope and
triumph, while it seems to have afforded Jonah a
vocabulary of expression too :—"Thou wilt not leave
my soul in hell, neither wilt Thou suffer thine Holy
One to see corruption."   Sealed, attested, and enforced
by this Divine prophet's burial and resurrection, there
comes a message to us, as there came a message to
Nineveh.   It is a message not of death, but of life:—"He
whom God raised up saw no corruption.   Be it known
unto you, therefore, men and brethren, that through
this Man is preached unto you the forgiveness of sins:
and by Him all that believe are justified from all things
from which ye could not be justified by the law of

Moses." What say you, brethren, to the message, which in the name of the risen Jesus we bring; which rather the risen Jesus himself brings by our word and witness-bearing? If the strait message of death to Nineveh seemed to have one small glimpse of hope faintly gleaming or glimmering upon it from the mercy and the power of God in raising up the witness-bearer from the deep, shall the message of eternal life, sealed by the resurrection from the dead of the Son of man, and irradiated with infinite glory and infinite love, have no weight with you? Oh, do not you who embrace it glory in it as a message of unmingled and eternal life, because you see all the death already suffered by the Son of man? And ye who reject it, Oh, do you not see that there can remain nothing but a fearful looking for of vengeance—a vengeance which though threatened strongly on Nineveh was loosed by their receiving the risen Jonah; but which in your case must be sealed eternally by your rejection of the risen Christ? "For the men of Nineveh shall rise up in the judgment with the unbelieving ones among *you*, and shall condemn you: because they repented at the preaching of Jonas; and, behold, a greater than Jonas is here" (Luke xi. 32).

V. Jonah's experience was his preparation for new loyalty and obedience; and in the kingdom of Christ, Christ's risen life is the source, in like manner, of newness of life and service.

Contemplate Jonah as he stands again on the dry

land, on the margin of the deep. He is a new man; he is another creature. He has a new life; a new position towards God; a new career opening up before him. Any obstacle to that new career, any drawback on this new life that might be supposed to arise from the past, is gone; for the past itself is gone. His old life is entirely cancelled; all its guilt obliterated; all its sin atoned for; all its evils, interruptive of Divine fellowship and blessing, abolished—left behind in the depths of the sea. For he is dead to the past: and it has no more hold upon him; no more dominion over him; no more evidence against him; no more wrath in store for him. Oh the blessedness of sacrifice, of atonement!—a blessedness depending on atonement being real, proper, and perfect—the blessedness of satisfaction to justice; the satisfaction that is given in death, accepted and sealed in burial, witnessed and proclaimed by resurrection. Blessed is the man whose sins are covered, to whom the Lord imputeth no iniquity; in his spirit surely there need be no guile. Freed by perfect death from guilt—"for he that is dead is freed from sin"— the path of life is before him. The pulse of life beats strong within him. A new career opens to him. A charmed life now is his. "Lord here am I: send me."

Thus would Jonah feel. Thus did Jonah give himself now to newness of service and in newness of spirit; —his risen life free from the load of guilt; lightened of the dread embargo of death and condemnation; elastic, infallible, bounding, free! What though the city be exceeding great and wicked? What though the message be mysterious and sad ?   Jonah hesitates not, nor halts any more.   It is the risen, redeemed, charmed, infallible life of God's reconciled child.   " Lord, here am I; send me."

And is not this, O believer in a risen Christ, is not this the type and fashion of your life of faith ?   For as Jonas was three days and three nights in the whale's belly; so have you in Christ been three days and three nights in the heart of the earth : and your life now is a risen life.   There is no new life, no spiritual life, in all the race of Adam, save that which accrues from partici- pation in the risen life of Christ.   If you are quickened, it is in Christ.   If you are raised up, it is together with Christ.   If you sit in heavenly places—in the sphere of the spiritual and redeemed life—it is in Jesus Christ.

And in what does the risen life of Christ consist? and what is its source?   And in what does it differ from His life in the days of His flesh ?   In the days of His flesh He rather lived our life than His own.   He lived under the law; in our relation to the law, and under its condemnation; and He might well have said, " Be- hold, I die daily."   For us He bare the wrath of God ; and just as in His favour is life, so in the wrath of God is death.   For us, all the days of His flesh, He was made sin; and the wages of sin is death.   But He died the death to an end—He died it all—He died it out. He died death dead, and done.   The Son of man was three days and three nights in the heart of the earth ; but God loosed the pains of death, because it was not possible that He should be holden of them; and as it began to dawn towards the first day of the week, He was raised from the dead by the glory of the Father. And as He rose, no bond of law kept hold upon Him any more; no condemnation laid its taint upon Him any more; the glory of His Father's unmingled and eternal favour shone upon Him now for evermore; and in His Father's favour He had life, His risen and eternal life. O poor and contrite sinner! that life was for thee, and is thine. That glory of the Father; that favour which is life; that loving-kindness which is better than life; are thine. This is thy risen life in Christ. For " we are buried with Him by baptism into death : that like as Christ was raised up from the dead by the glory of the Father, even so we also should walk in newness of life " (Rom. vi. 4).

Oh! with what freshness,—as of the morning light of an eternal Sabbath; and with what force,—as of the eternal power of Messiah's resurrection; may that blessed appeal now break upon our ears : " If ye then be risen with Christ, seek those things which are above, where Christ sitteth at the right hand of God " (Col. iii. 1).

Note.—In a volume like this, it would have been out of place to deal much more fully with the various Broad School evasions of the Atonement. They all embody a denial of its nature and design *as a Propitiation.* And when that is denied, it is of no consequence what is set up as a substitute for it. All these evasions are thoroughly excluded by the Westminster Confession, chap. viii., *passim*, and chap. xi. sec. 3. They destroy all evidence alike of Righteousness and Love in the Divine administration. And, so far as they are embraced, and their legitimate spiritual influence is not counteracted, they render true conviction of sin, gracious contrition of heart, and conscious reconciliation to God, impossible. Their prevalence cannot but move every intelligent reader of Holy Scripture to the deepest grief.

XVI

JONAH RESTORED TO OFFICE

JONAH iii. 1

" And the word of the LORD came unto Jonah the second time."

> "*I shall not die, but live, and declare the works of the LORD. The LORD hath chastened me sore: but he hath not given me over unto death. Open to me the gates of righteousness.*"—Ps. cxviii. 17–19.

RESTORED to the land of the living, the prophet is restored to office also, and furnished anew with the Divine commission to Nineveh.

It is indeed a signal instance of Divine grace when the rebellious servant is not only pardoned—personally restored to favour—but even replaced in office, and allowed again to serve the Lord in special duty in His kingdom. It would have been a very conspicuous instance of gracious condescension and forgiving love, had the Lord simply forgiven the penitent prophet his great sin in disobeying the heavenly command and flee-

ing from the presence of the Lord: and though the
intimation of his pardon had been accompanied with
an injunction to return to his native land, and abide in
the comparatively narrow sphere and seclusion of private
life—never henceforth being permitted to aspire to the
honour of glorifying God in the prophet's calling—we
would have felt that the mercy of the Lord, as extended
to the penitent Jonah even in this degree, was very
eminently illustrated, and worthy of all celebrations and
praise. But the work of the Lord is perfect. And in
bringing His erring servant to repentance, and reinstat-
ing him in favour, He reinstates him in office also; sealing to him the assurance of his own personal forgiveness by the restoration of his holy calling. Jonah is
to have cause to say, "To me who am the least of all
saints "—" who am not worthy to be called " a prophet,
because I fled from the presence of the Lord—" to me
is this grace given that I should preach among the
Gentiles " the word and message of God. Thus also,
in Peter's repentance and restoration;—the crowning
seal of the Lord's approbation is affixed when the
shepherd's crook is again put into the penitent's hands,
and the gracious command given to him: "Feed my
sheep."

How gracious is the Lord! Yea, our God is merciful.
His thoughts are not as our thoughts, neither are His
ways our ways. He stints not the liberality of His
grace; He places no limits on what He is willing to
bestow, or we warranted to ask. Rather, He will do
exceeding abundantly above all that we can ask or

292 JONAH RESTORED TO OFFICE

think. His design, indeed, is to "show in the ages to come the exceeding riches of His grace in His kindness towards us by Jesus Christ" (Eph. ii. 7).

Most righteous and unanswerable would His procedure have been, both with Jonah in the Old and Peter in the New Testament times, had He set aside His fallen servants from ever intromitting with the public work of His kingdom—from ever again putting their hand officially to His cause upon the earth. Forgiving their iniquity personally, yet taking vengeance on their inventions by taking from them their office and giving it to another, He might have left upon them a mark of His displeasure under which they would have gone mourning all the days of their lives.

But He dealt not with them as they had sinned. He wholly obliterated the remembrance of their transgression. He cast it into the depths of the sea. He was perfectly appeased. He was wholly reconciled. He readmitted His penitent servants and children to His perfect confidence. He placed them again in His counsels. He set them high in His confidence and service as before. He took them near to His person afresh. He had work for them still. He could commit His honour to their keeping once more. He could take them unreservedly again into His confidence, and generously repose confidence again in them. He does not put them to a distance. He does not put them on probation, and require them to purge themselves from all suspicion of insincerity, or do penance for past transgression, by serving in some menial work, and proving themselves

to be true, in some humble place.   But taking them at
their word ; accepting their confessions of guilt and their
expressions of grief ;—" being very gracious, and owning
their sincerity ; "—He looses all their bonds, He exceeds
all their hopes, He sets aside all their fears : and by a
full and free forgiveness, a full and free reconciliation,
He puts away all their sin wholly, and remembers
against them their iniquity no more.   They had forsaken His way, and kept not His commandments : and
He had visited their transgression with the rod, and
their iniquity with stripes : nevertheless, His loving-
kindness does He not take from them, nor suffer His
faithfulness to fail.   And the plenitude and perfection
of His manifested favour, in investing them anew
with their high and holy function as His prophets, is
the seal which His infinitely generous grace bestows
in token that He has returned unto them once more, in
all the riches of His love.

The prophet's prayer has been heard.   He is delivered from His living death in the deep.   " The Lord
spake unto the fish, and it vomited out Jonah on the dry
land."   So far the Lord's wrath is turned away.   Jonah
breathes forth his gratitude and gladness in a song of
thanksgiving.   He rejoices in the mercy of God.   He
glories in his reconciliation to his God anew.

But is all well ?   Is the remembrance of his offence
cancelled for ever ?   Will it never be mentioned to him
any more ?   Is all between him and his God again,
exactly as if this sad offence and its dread penalty had
never been ?   Or will the Lord keep up the remembrance

of his rebellion, and brand him henceforth as not to be trusted in His service?

Are these, or such as these, the prophet's fears for a moment? Does he doubt, whether, after sin like his, he can find *such* favour again in his master's sight as to be trusted once more with the high honours and responsibilities and confidence of his master's service? Is his anxious heart waiting to be set at rest on this point also?

He has not long to wait:—" The word of the Lord came unto Jonah the second time, saying, Arise, go unto Nineveh, that great city, and preach unto it the preaching that I bid thee."

Now, let us trace the effect of Jonah's late experience in qualifying him for his coming work. For the Lord had been dealing marvellously with him. *And His dealings are designed as preparations.* When the Lord painfully chisels and polishes a living stone, it is for some special place in the temple: and it will be seen to have acquired under His hand a special fitness for its place.

In the present case, Jonah would resume his commission with a new obedience; with a meekness, a faith, a courage; to all of which his punishment and pardon had been the signal means of disciplining him. He would resume his work and mission with another spirit: (1.) As a sinful man whose sin had been eminently forgiven; (2.) As a prayerful man, whose prayer had been eminently answered; (3.) As an afflicted man, whose affliction had been eminently blessed.

I. As a sinful man whose sin had been forgiven, he could not fail to accept, at the hand of the Lord, the mission now assigned him in a spirit of reverence, and dutifulness—of gratitude, submission, and obedience. He would be ready to say with the Psalmist, " I will run the way of Thy commandments for Thou hast enlarged my heart." Subdued, not more by the mighty power of God in pursuing him with punishment, than by the tender kindness of God in abundantly pardoning, he would hold himself in readiness to prove his thanksgiving by prompt and loyal obedience. Rejoicing in the sweetness of a fresh and full reconciliation ;—lightened in spirit by tasting in God a mercy larger than he could ever formerly have thought of ;—cleansed from the darkness that brooded over his soul, and the countless images of terror and of evil which rose up before him while he was fleeing from his God in rebellion, and his God was pursuing him in wrath ;—enjoying the unutterable blessedness of him who, after griefs and fears unspeakable, has God's own warrant for saying, " Return unto thy rest, O my soul, for the Lord hath dealt bountifully with thee ; "— Jonah would not only be prepared, but desirous to be engaged again in his Master's service.

There are two distinct principles that prompt the forgiven soul to serve the Lord. There is gratitude— one of the finest and most healthful and animating emotions of which the heart of man is susceptible—gratitude for the grace, the generosity, that forgiveth unreasonable offence. And this blessed principle is called into special exercise by forgiveness bestowed on the gospel scheme; " For the love of Christ constraineth us : because we thus judge, that if one died for all, then were all dead, and that He died for all, that they which live should not henceforth live unto themselves, but unto Him which died for them, and rose again" (2 Cor. v. 14, 15).

But there is reverence also. For in forgiving iniquity, transgression, and sin, God is not only gracious but sovereign. It is as a Sovereign that God forgiveth. It is in all the majesty and glory of the King of kings; in all the authority of the Lord of lords. It is as the Judge that God dealeth with sin at all, whether in avenging or in forgiving. Till I see His sovereign glory as the Lawgiver, the Governor, the Judge, I never know my guilt in resisting and rebelling against Him. Till then I never have any adequate idea of my position as a sinner. Till then I never go into God's presence, to deal with Him anent my sin, with any adequate or holy impression of sin's exceeding sinfulness. It is with God as the Sovereign Ruler, the God of infinite authority and infinite majesty, that I must deal, when I seek the remission of sin. It is against the Sovereign Lord of all that I have sinned. In that character I must own Him in confessing my sin. In that character will He have Himself owned in pardoning it. He will, in the very transaction of my forgiveness, cause me to see His glory. His right to deal authoritatively anent my sin, His right to remit the penalty of eternal death, implies an infinite glory on His part—the glory of infinite, sovereign, authoritative right to rule—infinite, sovereign, authoritative right to dispose of me. If I sincerely acknowledge that He has the right to settle eternally my standing before Him; if it be acknowledged, as sincere confession does acknowledge, that it lies with Him to pronounce me condemned, or acquitted and accepted in His sight; if, whether in condemning or acquitting, He is seen to act as the Supreme Judge, from whose bar, even unto eternity, there can be no appeal; and if, in forgiving my sin and announcing my relation to Him to be that of one righteous in His sight, He eminently acts in His character of Lord and Sovereign, making known the riches of His glory on a vessel of mercy which He had afore prepared unto glory;—then I cannot intelligently enter into this transaction without having, in the very essence of it, communion with God as my Lord and King. My forgiveness does not merely prepare me for beginning to see that He who has forgiven me is now entitled to be my Lord; but my forgiveness is my Lord's glorious manifestation of His Lordship,—His majestic act of sovereign authority concerning me and over me. There is forgiveness with Him that He may be feared. And to stretch forth my hand to receive His gift of pardon, is to stretch forth my hand and touch in reverence the sceptre of unlimited, eternal, sovereign, holy government.

Thus a true reception of the true forgiveness fills the soul, in the very instant, with reverential submission, quickening and calling forth a promise and pledge—yea, a longing desire and a loyal endeavour—to obey.

And this, mingled with gratitude, constitutes the

noblest and most ennobling principle that can animate the sons of men; while, under its lively impulse, the believer breaks forth into the joyful exclamations: " What shall I render unto the Lord for all his benefits ?" " O Lord, truly I am thy servant; I am thy servant, for thou hast loosed my bonds." " Lord, what wilt thou have me to do ? "

For any service that the Lord may appoint, a deep experience of His forgiving mercy is a necessary and effectual preparation. But especially is it needful, and especially is it effective, if the service be that of proclaiming to others the character and will of our God.

This is strikingly illustrated in the case of David. In the matter of his great guilt, and of God's consequent controversy with him, there seems to have been nothing in which he was more hampered and hindered than the discharge of his duty as a prophet or a teacher of others; bound, as indeed every believer is, to warn transgressors, and show them the way of life. And there seems to have been nothing which his profound repentance and perfect restoration to Divine favour more abundantly qualified him for, than this duty of testifying to his fellow-men the will and grace of God that they might be saved. " Hide thy face from my sin, and blot out all mine iniquities. Create in me a clean heart, and renew a right spirit within me. Cast me not away from Thy presence, and take not Thy holy Spirit from me. Restore unto me the joy of Thy salvation, and uphold me with Thy free Spirit. THEN—*then*

—will I teach transgressors Thy ways, and sinners shall be converted unto Thee " (Ps. li. 9–13).

Nor is it superfluous to refer to the instance of Isaiah. Melancholy indeed was the commission assigned to that prophet. The gospel is a savour of life to some, and of death to others. It is so in either case in proportion to the fulness and richness with which it is proclaimed. If deadly, it is more deadly the more truly and plentifully it is preached. Among all the prophets, Isaiah testified most emphatically and abundantly of Christ. He is, by way of eminence, the evangelical prophet. Alas! the richer his exhibitions of the coming Christ were to be, the harder were the hearts of his countrymen to become under his ministry. The deadly alternative result was to prevail grievously. He was even to be warned that it would be so. A ministry of judgment was thus to be assigned to him. The terrible commission was to be given : " Go and tell this people, Hear ye indeed, but understand not; and see ye indeed but perceive not. Make the heart of this people fat and make their ears heavy, aud shut their eyes : lest they see with their eyes, and hear with their ears, and understand with their heart, and convert and be healed." A woeful mission for a patriot! a trying, an agonising service to a tender heart! Little wonder if the prophet, in the hope that such a ministry of judgment might be brief, hastens to inquire, " Lord, how long ? "

But, oh, the heart-withering answer! " And he answered, Until the cities be wasted without inhabitant, and the houses without man, and the land be utterly desolate, and the Lord have removed men far away, and there be a great forsaking in the midst of the land."

How shall the tender spirit of the prophet—for with all his terrific energy and force his is a tender spirit still—how shall it be reconciled to go and minister what will thus so extensively, thus so long, prove the savour of death unto death? It is some comfort to him that his people are not about to be cast away; that they are not utterly to be exterminated or disowned. The Lord assures him of a remnant that shall be saved: "But yet in it shall be a tenth, and it shall return and shall be eaten: as a teil tree and as an oak whose substance is in them, when they cast their leaves; so the holy seed shall be substance thereof." Even in the deadly apostasy and deep desolation of "a gainsaying and a disobedient people," there is "a remnant according to the election of grace." But even with this mitigation of the prophet's deep alarm and anguish for his people, how is he to be reconciled to undertake the work of ministering to them an influence which the vast majority shall wrest to their own destruction?

He receives a vision of the Lord—the King—seated on the throne of His glory, high and lifted up. Before Him the seraphim veil their faces and their feet with their wings. Their voices of responsive adoration fill the temple. The posts of the doors shake, and the place is filled with smoke. Prostrate in conscious uncleanness and unfitness for the presence and service of a King so searchless in His might and glory, Isaiah falls at the throne;—"Woe is me! for I am undone; because

I am a man of unclean lips, and I dwell among a people of unclean lips: for mine eyes have seen the King, the Lord of hosts." What is the remedy? What is the reviving cordial? Pardon, pardon; the purging away of sin; the sealing of the Lord's forgiveness and His favour. " And he laid the coal from the altar on my mouth, and said, Lo, this hath touched thy lips; and thine iniquity is taken away, and thy sin is purged." Isaiah sees the King, the Lord of hosts; but intensely terrible as is His glory, intensely sure and perfect is His free forgiveness, His royal and eternal favour. Fear not, O trembling child of the dust! O contrite spirit! conscious deeply of thy sin; thine iniquity is purged; purged, even so as satisfies this King of glory, the Lord of hosts; purged by the power of an altar on which even HE shall lie, wounded for thy transgressions, bruised for thy iniquity: and now thou mayst stand before Him—His servant, His counsellor, His prophet.

And hark! There is a work to be done; there is a servant to be found. Thy redeeming God, in His unsearchable administration, has mysterious work to do; work that might shake the loyalty of an inexperienced, an untried commissioner; service that may not be performed by a novice,—that may not be performed even by a veteran, save in the adoring aquiescence which believes in the rectitude and goodness of the Lord, even when His way is in the great deep and His procedure past finding out. "Also I heard a voice saying, Who will go for us, and whom shall we send?" Who will undertake the terrible commission? Whom

can we safely send on this soul-trying service?   " Then
said I,"—adoring the glory of the Lord, my cup run-
ning over with His grace—" Then said I, Here am I;
send me " (Isa. vi. 1–13).

With like feelings will Jonah now welcome the
mission to Nineveh,—mission of judgment though it be.
Pardoned, and cleansed, and reinstated in the favour
of ·his God, the Lord whom he fears, even the God of
heaven, he will be in meek, adoring, loyal readiness
now to do Him service—even though the duty be sore
to flesh and blood—though it be the work of threatening sore judgment on a great and sinful city.

II. As a man of prayer whose prayer had been
eminently heard and answered, Jonah had a new
qualification with his new call to serve the Lord.

He had obtained singular experience of the faithfulness of God as the hearer of prayer. He had called
upon the Lord in circumstances almost fitted to shut
out the possibility of hope. He had laid his case
before the Lord when it seemed all but desperate. Out
of the belly of hell had he cried unto the Lord. Cast
out of His presence he had yet ventured to look again
towards His temple.

If there be a case on record pre-eminently fitted to
confirm the declaration, "Men ought always to pray
and not to faint," it is the case of Jonah. And if his
experience is fitted to encourage and animate others, how
abundantly must it have influenced himself! Think
you that he would not enter with revived animation

and vigour on the duty of his calling, from his being able to return to it with the new song in his mouth : "I waited patiently for the Lord, and he inclined unto me and heard my cry : he brought me up out of an horrible pit, out of the miry clay; and set my feet upon a rock and established my goings"? Would he not resume his post and his office with livelier loyalty and implicit sense of duty, when he could resume it with the blessed protestation : "I love the Lord because he hath heard the voice of my supplication : because he hath inclined his ear unto me, I will call upon him as long as I live "?

For this blessed experience of prayer heard and answered would brace him for his work in more ways than one. Thus—

1. In the first place, it was a testimony to him of his own sincerity and integrity.

Shocked by his own rebellion, the penitent prophet would not lightly or easily be convinced that his heart was again thoroughly guileless and right with God. The strength and subtlety of its rebelliousness would alarm him. That that rebelliousness was truly subdued he would seek a fresh and satisfactory proof;—a proof coming from without and not from within;—a testimony, not from his own inward consciousness, which might deceive him, but an infallible testimony in which he could not be deceived. Such a testimony he would find in the fact of his prayer being heard. For God heareth not sinners;—that is, He heareth not those in whom sin still reigns. He heareth only the righteous, the true-hearted, the sincere. Uprightness of spirit is essential to true prayer—the prayer of faith which the Father heareth alway. Hence, when prayer is truly heard and answered, the answer is peculiarly sweet, as carrying with it a testimony from God to the suppliant's simplicity of spirit and godly sincerity.

It is thus that the Psalmist in the 66th Psalm interprets an answer to his prayers as the witness of God to his integrity. "Come and hear," saith he, "Come and hear, all ye that fear God, and I will declare what he hath done for my soul." And what is it that God hath done for his soul, and which he feels impelled to publish unto "all that fear" His name? It is nothing else than this; that God had eminently and distinctly heard his prayers, and therein gave him the gratification of knowing that there was no duplicity in his spirit and no evil way within him. "I cried unto Him with my mouth, and He was extolled with my tongue. If I regard iniquity in my heart "— if I cling to any beloved idol, or any besetting sin—"the Lord will not hear me. But verily God hath heard me : he hath attended to the voice of my prayer." He would not have done so, had I been regarding iniquity in my heart. And when He *hath* done so, it is His testimony to me that He who knoweth all things, knoweth that I love Him: yea, "Blessed be the Lord, which hath not turned away my prayer, nor his mercy from me."

Thus assuredly might Jonah also judge that the Lord had graciously attested his returning integrity and uprightness. And how blessed a help would this conviction be in resuming his duty! To know that verily his soul was right with God; that verily his heart was supremely set upon the love and service of his Sovereign; —how would his hands no more hang down, his efforts no more be feeble or fitful! " 'Tis a point I long to know, do I love the Lord or no?"—many an anxious soul is often made to say. Nor among the many reasons that may weigh in leading to an earnest desire for settlement on that all-important point, is this the least; even that then I may take my Lord's work in hand with the blessed and bounding assurance that there is no danger of His meeting me with the alarming demand: "Who hath required this at your hands?" or of His repudiating my service with the stern interrogation: "What hast thou to do to declare my statutes, or to take my covenant into thy mouth?"

Oh! art thou anxious to enjoy a perfect and a sure exemption from this danger? Art thou longing to serve the Lord with the full assurance that verily thou art His servant, and that He himself doth seal and certify thee as such? Go to His throne of grace. Take thy whole case and lay it forth before Him. Thy special burden, difficulty, trial, thorn, fear—*that* do thou specially deal with thy God concerning. And *so* deal with Him; so appeal to Him, in all the earnestness and deep sincerity of Jacob wrestling with the angel; so peril all thy happiness and all thy hope, all thy salvation and all thy desire, upon the graciousness and faithfulness of thy God; so continue instant in prayer—" I will not let thee go, until thou bless me "—and, by faith and patience, *so* put God upon

His word and promise, that He may *manifest* Himself in thy help, and distinguishingly answer thy prayer. Then shalt thou have God's testimony that He counts thee of a perfect heart,—an Israelite indeed, in whom is no guile. Ah! then His service will to thee be exceeding acceptable. Thou wilt ask for thy work; "Lord, what wilt thou have me to do?" And thou wilt do it with love, and fervour, and unselfish diligence. Thou wilt do it in newness of spirit; with all thy heart, and with all thy soul. Thou wilt be in thine element now, in serving the Lord.

So would Jonah resume his calling; eminently heard and answered of the Lord; the Lord testifying that he was of a pure heart, that he was truly His servant.

2. But the answer to his prayer would animate him to return to his duty in another way. It would inspire him with the assurance that he was not returning alone; that he had One for his "shield and his strength," who would bear him safely through all the danger, and successfully through all the duty, to which he was now summoned.

He was about to enter, unprotected, a city, whose inhabitants were pre-eminently wicked and violent; and he was to threaten them in the name of the Almighty with speedy and complete destruction. It was as going into the lion's den. Nothing but an implicit reliance on the presence, the faithfulness, the power, and the protection of God could possibly bear him through, in the calmness and courage befitting an ambassador of God. But surely the late amazing interposition of the

Lord, in saving him from the deep, in answer to his prayer, was fitted to fill him with the requisite confidence, and with the strength and decision needed for the discharge of his duty.

Thus at least did David arm himself against his enemies, feeding or fanning his courage to face them. " Lord, how are they increased that trouble me! There be many that rise up against me. But thou, O Lord, art a shield for me : my glory, and the lifter up of mine head. I cried unto the Lord with my voice, and he heard me out of his holy hill." And what were the immediate fruits of this blessed experience of answered prayer? Calm confidence and calm courage : the calm confidence of a peacefully-sleeping child,—" I laid me down, I slept; I awaked, for the Lord sustained me ; " and the calm courage of a dauntless man,—" I will not be afraid of ten thousands of people, that have set themselves against me round about" (Ps. iii. 1--6).

Yes! to come forth from the holy place, fresh from an audience of the King, and not an audience only, but an answer; to come forth an acknowledged and accepted friend; an answered and successful suppliant; *that* is the preparation for whatsoever future of suffering or of service may be opening up before you. " From henceforth let no man trouble me : for I bear in my body the marks of the Lord Jesus " (Gal. vi. 17). Yes! and let no evil dismay thee, nor over-master thee. " Because thou hast made the Lord, which is my refuge, even the Most High, thy habitation ; there shall no evil befall thee, neither shall any plague come nigh thy dwelling.

For he shall give his angels charge over thee, to keep thee in all thy ways. They shall bear thee up in their hands, lest thou dash thy foot against a stone. Thou shalt tread upon the lion and adder: the young lion and the dragon shalt thou trample under feet. . . . . He shall call upon me, and I will answer him. I will be with him in trouble; I will deliver him, and honour him. With long life will I satisfy him, and show him my salvation " (Ps. xci. 9–16). Glorious promise! May not *that* reconcile you to any trying service? May you not boldly face even a dark and lowering future? " Put on the whole armour of God, ... praying always with all prayer and supplication in the Spirit." So was Jonah armed now.

Thus as a man of prayer, whose prayer had been eminently answered, was Jonah afresh qualified for resuming the prophet's mission.

III. Once more; as an afflicted man, whose affliction had been eminently blessed, he was now peculiarly fitted to receive anew his difficult, but Divine commission.

Before he was afflicted, he went astray; but now he will keep God's word. Chastened and subdued,—of a meek and quiet spirit,—overwhelmingly convinced that no device of man can prosper against the strong hand of the Most High, he would return with a readiness to render implicit and unquestioning obedience to whatsoever the Divine oracle should enjoin. Knowing the terrors of the Lord, he could speak of them feelingly, and with reverence. On this theme, he could speak from personal and profound knowledge. Not any less than the royal Psalmist could He say, "I believed, therefore have I spoken; I was greatly afflicted:" so closely would his speaking for God stand related henceforth to his terrible experience. Or he might address himself to the work of declaring God's message in words like these: "I shall not die, but live, and declare the works of the Lord. The Lord hath chastened me sore: but He hath not given me over unto death." And if it be God's terrible work that Jonah must declare—God's strange work of judgment,—still Jonah himself knoweth both the "goodness and severity of God;" and he knoweth that the Lord's severity is never cruelty—never unrighteous, even should it destroy a city by fire, or a world by a flood. In His own terrible experience, he knows the severity of God; yet he knows also that the Lord is righteous, yea, that his God is merciful.

There is scarcely anything more necessary for God's ambassador to possess, and scarcely anything more difficult to attain, than a thorough ability of spirit to threaten straitly and terribly the enemies of his Lord, and yet to do so with combined feelings of liveliest love and pity for their souls and of profound acquiescence in God's righteousness in threatening them. Either it is difficult to love those to whom we carry what we feel to be the Lord's most due and righteous sentence of His eternal wrath; or it is difficult to justify that terrible doom when called to carry it to those we love. At once to acquiesce in the propriety, the necessity of their threatened eternal ruin; and to love, and pity, and long

after them in the Lord :—to abstain, on the one hand,
from quarrelling with the rectitude of that decision of
the Most High, which we know must sweep those we
love, except they repent, into the fire prepared for the
devil and his angels; and on the other hand, to take a
no less loving and lively interest in them because we
justify God in revealing His wrath from heaven against
them :—*this* is the sore trial which God's servant has to
undergo.   Often he is tempted to be more sparing in
setting forth the terrors of the Lord than fidelity both
to God and man demands.   To sigh after those whom
as yet the Lord assigns to eternal perdition, and to
side with God in unshrinking loyalty in His doing so;
—*this* is the painful trial of spirit which thousands
never think of, but which the pastor who understands
his office and seeks even in some measure to discharge
it, has habitually to face.   It is questionable whether
the high spiritual attainment which it implies and
demands, is ever in any measure very decidedly reached
save through the furnace of affliction, whether external or
spiritual, and more especially the latter.   "I believed,"
said David, "therefore have I spoken; *I was greatly
afflicted.*"   And Paul—entering profoundly into the spirit
of that brief declaration, and realising the profound connexion between speaking for God, on the one hand, and
faith combined with affliction, on the other—has this comment upon the Psalmist's experience, appropriating it to
himself and to the pastoral office generally: "But we
have this treasure in earthen vessels, that the excellency
of the power may be of God, and not of us.   We are

troubled on every side, yet not distressed; we are perplexed, but not in despair; persecuted, but not forsaken;
cast down, but not destroyed; always bearing about in
the body the dying of the Lord Jesus, that the life also
of Jesus might be made manifest in our body. For we
which live are alway delivered unto death for Jesus'
sake, that the life also of Jesus might be made manifest
in our mortal flesh. So then death worketh in us, but
life in you. We having the same spirit of faith, *according as* it is written, I believed, and therefore have I
spoken; we also believe, and therefore speak " (compare
Ps. cxvi. and 2 Cor. iv. throughout).

"Brethren, pray for us;" may the pastors of the
Church well say. The office we have to discharge is
in no respect an easy one. The anxieties connected
with it are manifold. To sit loose to these anxieties,
and suffer them to lie lightly on our spirit, is not the
way to commend ourselves to Him that sent us, or to
be pure from the blood of all men. Especially we have
to tell those who are not in Christ that the wrath of
Almighty God abideth on them. We have unflinch-
ingly to denounce upon them the speedy and the endless
execution of that wrath except they repent. We have
to tell some, that neither we nor any fellow-creature can
behold the slightest evidence that this repentance is in
their case begun; and that they are, therefore, to all appearance ripening for eternal perdition. In delivering
declarations so terrible as these, it behoves us to speak
as those who feel that God will do a righteous thing
in consigning such to eternal woe if they repent not,

and yet to speak as those who at the same time long after them in the bowels of Christ. In denouncing against them this fierce wrath of the God whom they have abandoned, to whom they have never yet returned —the God whom they have offended and insulted, and to whom they have never seriously sued for forgiveness and for reconciliation—we are not permitted even to announce, as Jonah was, a respite of forty days. We cannot offer you one week, one day, one hour, to count upon. We are required to summon you to repentance and surrender—on the spot. But we bless God we have an explicit message of mercy, such as was never put into Jonah's hands; a declaration from the Lord of hosts—whom you have made your enemy, and to whom you have been enemies—that He is prepared to receive you immediately into reconciliation and favour, through a great propitiation, through the sacrifice of Him who was "three days and three nights in the heart of the earth:" and behold! now is the accepted time; behold! now is the day of salvation. Laid hold on in simplicity and truth, with lively and living faith, this word of the Lord shall be the anchor of your soul, sure and steadfast: neglected and despised, it shall be a swift witness against you. Therefore "let the wicked forsake his way, and the unrighteous man his thoughts: and let him return unto the Lord, and he will have mercy upon him; and to our God, for he will abundantly pardon."

XVII

THE COMMISSION RE-ISSUED—AND ACCEPTED

JONAH iii. 1–4

" And the word of the Lord came unto Jonah the second time, saying,
Arise, go unto Nineveh, that great city, and preach unto it the
preaching that I bid thee.   So Jonah arose, and went unto
Nineveh, according to the word of the Lord.   (Now Nineveh was
an exceeding great city of three days' journey.)   And Jonah began to enter into the city a day's journey, and he cried, and said,
Yet forty days, and Nineveh shall be overthrown."

> " *What was I, that I could withstand
> God ?* "—ACTS xi. 17.
> " *If the watchman see the sword come, and
> blow not the trumpet, and the people
> be not warned ; if the sword come and
> take any person from among them, he
> is taken away in his iniquity ; but
> his blood will I require at the watch-
> man's hand.*"—EZEK. xxxiii. 6.

WE have considered the new spirit of dutiful obedience with which the prophet, after his marvellous
and merciful deliverance, would return to the duties of
his holy calling.   Let us now consider—(1.) The terms
in which his commission was renewed; (2.) and secondly,
the manner in which he executed it.

I. In the first place, then, we may consider the terms in which his commission was renewed. "And the word of the Lord came unto Jonah the second time, saying, Arise, go unto Nineveh, that great city, and preach unto it the preaching that I bid thee." And here,—

1. Notice, *first*, the expression employed to indicate the fact that a Divine communication was given to the prophet; "The word of the Lord came unto Jonah, saying."

It is the formula, or phrase, customarily employed to designate the conveyance of a Divine communication to a prophet. It first occurs on the occasion of a prophetic announcement being made to Abraham ; and it prefaces that wondrous interview that Jehovah held with His servant beneath the blue vault of the midnight heavens, and beside the slaughtered parts of the victims, or sacrifices, by which He ratified the promise of the land to his seed : "The word of the Lord came unto Abraham in a vision, saying, Fear not, Abraham, I am thy shield, and thy exceeding great reward " (Gen. xv. 1). From that time the phrase occurs in Scripture in common use. May it not indicate, however, not merely the advent of an audible sound, but the presence of a living person ? May it not point out the Revealer, as well as express the fact of a revelation ? The Son of God receives in Scripture the peculiar name of " the Word." " In the beginning was the Word, and the Word was with God, and the Word was God " (John i. 1). It is He who is the only Prophet and Teacher in the Church. It is exclusively through Him that the communications of the Godhead are made to men. No man knoweth anything whatever of the Father's thoughts and purposes, of the Father's mind and will, save the Son, and he to whom the Son shall reveal them. May it not indicate, then, the intervention of the great Angel, Apostle, and Prophet of the Church,— through whom alone Divine communications have in any age been made,—when the singular expression is used, " The word of the Lord came, saying"? The language is somewhat strange, if the mere phenomenon of an audible sound is indicated. It is singularly appropriate if the advent and utterances of a living person be intended. Moreover it serves to keep prominently before our minds the fact that *Christ* has in all ages been the medium through whom the intimations of the Divine will have been given forth, if we understand that His office, and the exercise of His office, as the great Prophet and Revealer, are indicated, when the expression is employed, " The word of the Lord came."

It is worthy of observation, also, that while there is a special sense in which it may be said that the word of the Lord came to the prophets, inasmuch as they were constituted the public depositaries and heralds of the Divine revelations : there is a sense, also, in which the word of the Lord is come to every one of us. Wherever the Scriptures are read or preached, " The word of the Lord " is come to every one who hears them. And it remains that every such one consider what reception he has given to " the word of the Lord." There is something exceedingly alarming in the idea of giving a

slighting reception to the word of the Lord—of treating
it, when it "comes" as if it were unwelcome, undesirable,
weak, and despicable; as if it were unworthy of being
honourably received, or incapable of avenging the insult.
The whole character of man, in the light of eternity,
depends on the reception that he has given to the word
of God. The unconverted have rejected and despised
it. If it were not so, it would have arrested, alarmed,
humbled, and abased them, and made them turn from
idols to serve the living God. Believers, on the contrary, have received it " in power, and in the Holy
Ghost, and in much assurance; "—they have " received
it not as the word of man, but as it is indeed and in
truth, the word of God, which worketh effectually in
them that believe." And do not think that this word
is ever empty, solitary, and dead? The Spirit of Christ
abides always by His word. Where that word is lightly
esteemed and not admitted to judge, to rule, and regulate
the soul, the Great Prophet, in the person of His
Eternal Spirit, and in the exhibition of His own and
His Father's will, is despised.

Are men aware of the guilt that they contract in refusing that reverence, faith, and obedience to the Word
of God, which believers in a measure alone truly render
to it? Are they awake to the alarming thought that
the King of glory has paid them a visit in the declarations of His Word and in the strivings of His Holy
Spirit; that they have had an opportunity of receiving
and entertaining suitably the eternal Word or Son of
the Most High God, or of rejecting, slighting, and

despising Him? Yet this is the alternative when the Word of God has come, even as it has to all of us. " For the word is nigh thee " (Rom. x. 8).

2. In the commission thus renewed, the word of the Lord distinctly again sets forth to Jonah the greatness of the city : " Go to Nineveh, that great city."

And I think the obvious design of this was to set prominently before the prophet's mind the great difficulty of the work assigned to him. There is to be no concealing from him the arduousness of the task put into his hands. He is made distinctly aware that a work is given him to do, of extraordinary, yea, superhuman magnitude. And the Lord's purpose in thus insisting upon the greatness of the city, and the consequent difficulty of the undertaking, is not hard to discover. He evidently designed to constrain Jonah to despair of his own strength and qualifications, and to shut him up of necessity to the strength of God as his only resource. He would have his service imbued with an overpowering sense of the necessity of utterly denying himself; of laying aside all carnal weapons of warfare ; of conferring not with flesh and blood, but casting himself wholly upon his God that he may be strong in the Lord and the glory of His power. The more the prophet was appalled by the superhuman achievement appointed to him, the more would he feel that he must betake himself to the asylum of his Lord's protection and support; that he could not possibly go alone; and that by faith he must secure and lean upon the presence and the power of Him whose ambassador he was.

And the manner in which God thus dealt with Jonah is substantially the manner in which He deals with every believer ; with every one whom He delivers from the power of darkness and transfers into the kingdom of His dear Son. He calls upon them to count the cost. He puts at their disposal the means of doing so. He will have them clearly to understand that the work and warfare on which they are entering are of such a nature that no qualifications of theirs are in any measure adequate to bear them successfully or safely through.

I do not mean to say that God gives every believer, at the time of his conversion, a view of the whole path of trial by which He means to lead Him to the promised land, or sets distinctly in his eye the series of afflictive dealings or painful conjunctures and ever-varying contests through which the true soldier is to be perfected for his rest. Very much the reverse. The effect of any such anticipation at the opening of the Christian life would, humanly speaking, prevail in many instances to crush the young purpose of believing patience and perseverance. It is often well for the believer to be able to look but a little way before him. The conflict which, when once exercised in the school of Christ, he might be able to bear, might altogether overwhelm him at his entrance ; and few have long known the trials to which a faithful attempt to walk with God exposes His people, without taking frequent refuge in the Saviour's precious declaration, " Sufficient for the day is the evil thereof ; " and in that other promise, " As thy day,

so shall thy strength be." ˉ Nor is it possible to imagine
how many believers have been cheered by the remembrance that—"It came to pass, when Pharaoh had let
the people go, that God led them not through the way
of the land of the Philistines, although that was near;
for God said, Lest peradventure the people repent when
they see war, and they return to Egypt: but God led
the people about, through the way of the wilderness of
the Red Sea " (Exod. xiii. 17, 18).

Still, all this is not only consistent with, but illustrative of, the fact that the whole Christian life is supernatural,—an impossibility to our own wisdom and
strength; and that we cannot take one step, or achieve
one conquest in it, without feeling that it is an undertaking all too high for us. Though God shielded
Israel from the depressing influence of immediate war
with the Philistines, they could be saved from that, and
from Egypt both, only by being led "through the way
of the wilderness of the Red Sea." They are thrown
wholly upon Divine protection, Divine power, Divine
provision. They are taken most completely off from
all self-dependence. They are absolutely shut up to
God. To confer with flesh and blood is useless. Unless God be on their side, they must be swallowed up
quick. Unless by faith they cast themselves wholly on
God, there is neither help nor hope. They are simply
shut up. By faith only can they pass through the Red
Sea as on dry ground. By faith only can they live in
the wilderness. By faith only can they find a path
through that trackless desert. To them, their unseen

Leader, Provider, Lawgiver, and Guide, is "all in all." They must count the cost, and see that their only hope must be in this, namely, that "with God all things are possible."

It is precisely so in all that pertains to our salvation; our fighting the good fight of faith; our working out our salvation with fear and trembling; our abiding faithful unto death. No man knows the tone of mind which is the peculiar essence of all that is truly Christian, who has not seen the superhuman magnitude of an immortal soul's salvation, and of its perfecting in grace and preparation for glory. With man it is impossible. With man it is impossible to recommend his guilty soul to God, or pay a ransom for his sin; impossible to implant in himself the vital principle of all grace and holiness; impossible, even when it has been planted, to maintain it in life, health, and vigour; impossible to conduct to a successful issue the opposition that must be maintained between that vital principle of grace and the remaining suggestions, impulses, temptations, in a word, the lusts, of the flesh. He is wholly cast upon Another for acceptance with the righteous Judge of all the earth; even on a Divine Substitute and Surety. He is wholly cast upon the gracious power of Another to renew his nature and enable him truly to trust in the Lord, and fear, and love, and serve Him; even on the Divine Spirit, creating a new heart and renewing a right spirit within him. He is wholly cast upon the same grace of God in every duty, in every time of need; and he never need make one single effort with the view of

THE COMMISSION RE-ISSUED—AND ACCEPTED 321

"working out his own salvation," save on the believing understanding that "God worketh in him to will and to do of His good pleasure." The Bible continually warns you against undertaking the Christian life and warfare in your own strength. It points out the greatness of the work, and shows you that it is too great for you. It shows you the radical and entire change in which the Christian life begins; the great and arduous contest through which it is maintained in existence, prosperity, and progress, amidst the wickedness that remains in your own nature, the tempting and blunting influences of the world, the insidious, ensnaring, violent, and alarming efforts of Satan : and it distinctly sets forth all the arduousness, perseverance, self-denial requisite, *in order that* you may not fall into the sad snare of imagining that you can either undertake or carry on this work, except in the confiding and appropriating faith of the Holy Spirit's continual power. So clearly are the sore trials of the faithful Christian depicted; and the multitude of graces he has to cultivate,—diametrically opposite, each of them, to what is natural to flesh and blood; and the manifold duties expected of him, if he is to walk worthy of his high calling of God, who hath called him to His everlasting glory and kingdom ; —that it is impossible for a man really to understand the case thus depicted, and be infatuated enough to fancy himself adequate to meet it.

When you read, therefore, in the Divine word, of the great and astonishing expectations that God cherises concerning you; and when you are apt to fall into utter despair of ever being able to realise them ;—when, in your experience, the actual attempt to do so brings you into contact with continual impossibilities ;—behold and believe the Divine purpose with regard to you. The gracious purpose which God has in view is to take you off from all refuges of lies, and shut you up to His own faithful promise and almighty power. When you learn this lesson, and present yourself helpless at His throne ; when you appear before Him in your absolute extremity ; when it will no more hide from yourself that your fancied strength is gone, and you hide it from God no more, but resign and renounce all help, all power, save His ; —you shall then know that with God all things are possible ; that what is marvellous in your eyes need not be marvellous in His ; that the ruin of your own strength is the beginning of your glorifying His ; that when you are weak then are you strong, because you have learned now to be strong in the Lord. Be not afraid, then, though evidences multiply to you continually, of the superhuman difficulties in the way of realising steadily your reconciliation with God, and prosecuting steadily the duties of the Christian life and the cultivation of the graces of the Christian character. You are being taught a lesson without which you will never go from strength to strength. But " wait upon the Lord : be of good courage, and He shall strengthen thine heart : wait, I say, upon the Lord " (Ps. xxvii. 14).

3. The next thing noticeable in the commission delivered to the prophet is the implicit obedience which is now expected of him. His whole mind and will are

now to be in immediate and unreserved subjection to God. And there are perhaps two evidences of this.

For when the Lord says, " Arise, go to Nineveh, and preach unto it the preaching that I bid thee," it may be, as some have supposed, that the Lord did not at this time inform Jonah of the exact message he would have to deliver, but required of him an immediate departure to the scene of his duty, delaying till he had reached it the announcement to him of the specific communication he would have to make. If this be so, then Jonah must have felt himself placed in some respect in a position similar to that of Abraham, when the Lord called him forth from his native land without yet indicating to him the new land of his adoption. "Now the Lord said unto Abraham, Get thee out of thy country, and from thy kindred, and from thy Father's house, unto a land that I will show thee." In either case, there is an immediate duty prescribed; and there is a suspended and delayed communication—delayed and suspended till obedience has first been rendered to the commandment delivered. Thus the Lord tries the obedience of His people. His own authority alone in prescribing duty is the sufficient obligation on His creatures to obey; and irrespective of consequences and of future issues, His simple word alone is entitled to reverence and compliance. Present duty is what we ought to seek to know and seek to do; and when the Lord leads us on in the path of doing it, He will lead us on to larger and more satisfying and more comforting knowledge of His purpose with us. " If any man will do the will of God, he shall know of the doctrine whether it be of God." Abraham is bound to go forth without knowing whether the Lord is leading him; this is the trial of his faith. Accordingly, it is expressly mentioned as the commendation and proof of his believing confidence: " By faith, Abraham, when he was called to go out into a place which he should after receive for an inheritance, obeyed; and he went out not knowing whither he went " (Heb. xi. 8). By faith, in like manner, Jonah must arise and go to Nineveh, to preach there, not yet knowing the preaching, the proclamation, the message that may be put into his mouth. How clearly, in such cases, is faith at once the only instrument of peace, and the only impulse to obedience ! There can come forth, in such cases, nothing but a " work of *faith*."

But be this as it may; whether Jonah was at once put in possession of the preaching that God commanded, or had to wait till he had accomplished his journey and reached the city before he knew what he should be required to address to its wicked inhabitants, this at least is obvious, that Jonah must be simply a minister of the Divine word. He has no discretionary powers. He is to be an ambassador, in the strictest possible sense. He has simply to make known the will and word of God : " Preach unto it the preaching that I bid thee."

Now this is the law of the prophetic, the pastoral, the ministerial office :—to preach the preaching that God biddeth. To this law, Christ himself, the great prophet, was eminently in subjection. That He should be so, was announced to Israel of old, when He was promised as a prophet like unto Moses: "I will raise them up a Prophet from among their brethren, like unto thee; and I will put my words in His mouth; and He shall speak unto them all that I shall command Him " (Deut. xviii. 15). In accordance with this, how often, when that Prophet came, did He disclaim the authorship of all that He said, and assign it continually to the Father! "Jesus answered them and said, My doctrine is not mine, but His that sent me; the words that I speak unto you, I speak not of myself." "For I have not spoken of myself; but the Father, which sent me, He gave me a commandment what I should say, and what I should speak. And I know that His commandment is life everlasting; whatsoever I speak therefore, even as the Father said unto me, so I speak." Again and again, to this effect, does Jesus continually attribute His word unto the Father as the author of it. Himself personally cognisant of all truth, He acts as the Church's teacher under the responsibility and within the exact limits of His office. Officially ordained the Father's ambassador, He confines Himself to a declaration of the Father's words. He preaches the preaching which the Father has assigned to Him. Exactly as the Father hath said unto Him, so He speaks.

And the law of the prophetic office, thus exemplified in Christ, is imposed on all His servants. For herein is His own saying concerning them true—" As the Father hath sent me into the world, so have I sent you into the world." This, indeed, is the source of all their safety, strength, and courage. "The word of the Lord came unto Jeremiah, saying, Before I formed thee in the belly, I knew thee; and before thou camest forth out of the womb I sanctified thee, and I ordained thee a prophet unto the nations. Then said I, Ah, Lord God! behold, I cannot speak; for I am a child. But the Lord said unto me, Say not, I am a child : for thou shalt go to all that I shall send thee, and whatsoever I command thee thou shalt speak. Be not afraid of their faces : for I am with thee to deliver thee, saith the Lord. Then the Lord put forth his hand, and touched my mouth : and the Lord said unto me, Behold, I have put my words in thy mouth " (Jer i. 4–9). Here, also, is the proof of their fidelity and the origin of their success; for in proportion as they preach the very words given them of the Lord, even as the Son himself did, will they have some humble sympathy with the Son in ultimately professing their faithfulness : " I have glorified thee on the earth : I have manifested thy name unto thy people; I have given them the words that thou gavest me : and they have received them, and believed " (John xvii).

The gospel, then, that is statedly preached to you, if in any measure faithfully preached, is the word of the unseen God,—the thoughts and will of the King Eternal, Immortal, and Invisible. They come forth through His own Son as the original, the one only authoritative, the perfect Prophet. They are now delivered—the message is handed on and handed round—from Him to the assemblies of His professing, worshipping people, by the lips of men, chosen from among themselves, and chosen by themselves. This is the singular and glorious treasure, that is deposited in earthen vessels; the word of the only wise God. Unless unfaithful to our office, we preach the preaching that the living God hath bidden us.

But if this be true, mark the deplorable position in which unbelievers must find themselves placed; and every one must be called an unbeliever who does not so embrace the message of alarm and of mercy as to flee from the wrath to come, repenting of his iniquity and turning to the Lord in newness of obedience.

Mark the position in which they are placed. By refusing to believe the preaching that we preach, they are either accusing Almighty God of sending them by our mouth a message utterly useless and trifling; very solemn and awful in its terms, but very senseless in its import; not worthy to be allowed to work effectually in them or produce any change upon their purposes or course: or, they are bringing against us the unparalleled accusation of falsifying the commission given us, and not preaching the preaching that God hath bidden: or, they are laying themselves open to the accusation of making God a liar; of making His word void, so far as their testimony can go; and of giving no more weight to a communication from Heaven than to one from some fellow-creature who holds a low place in their esteem, and by whom they would remain unmoved, say to them what he might. Oh! is it not very obvious that the simple possibility of being capable of treating in this manner a communication of the wisdom and will of the Most High God, indicates a depth and entireness of depravity, such as verifies at once the solemn declaration, "Verily, verily, except a man be born again, he cannot see the kingdom of God "? Were careless and unbelieving hearers of the gospel to rise up in a body, and denounce the exhortations delivered to them by their pastor as a mass of his own self-originated and fraudulent imaginations, there would be infinitely less to wonder at in their refusal to submit themselves to the moulding influence of the doctrines to which they habitually listen. But actually to admit that the sum and substance of the instruction delivered to them is a message of truth coming truly and authoritatively from God, and to live precisely as if such truth were merely fancy, is of all things an exhibition of absurdity and contradiction that exhibits human nature in an aspect most humiliating. But the absurdity and infatuation are equalled by the guilt; for great must be the guilt of men by whom their Lord's word of salvation when it comes to them is rejected and despised. "I am come a light into the world, that whosoever believeth on me should not walk in darkness. And if any man hear my words and believe not, I judge him not; for I came not to judge the world, but to save the world. He that rejecteth me and receiveth not my words, hath one that judgeth him : the word that I have spoken, the same shall judge him in the last day. For I have not spoken of myself: but the Father which sent me he gave me a commandment what I should say and what I should speak " (John xii. 46–49).

Nor can we think otherwise of that coming judgment than that it must be so much the more severe as the rejected message from the Father was gracious. For what is that message, that commandment, which the Son delivers from the Father with such exactness and fidelity? Let the Son himself declare it. "The Father which sent me, he gave me a commandment what I should say and what I should speak. And I know that his commandment is life everlasting : whatsoever I speak therefore, even as the Father said unto me, so I speak " (John xii. 49, 50). Oh blessed mission ; on which alike the living Head and the faithful pastors of the Church are sent ! Oh blessed commandment; to Him and to them alike delivered of the Father !—for does He not " send them into the world, even as the Father sent Him into the world "? Oh exalted motto of the most beneficent office ever executed on the earth ! "I know that His commandment is life everlasting : whatsoever I speak therefore, even as the Father said unto me, so I speak."

Yes ! The continual Divine injunction to the preacher is :—" Preach the preaching that I bid thee." May he not well take kindly to his office ; seeing that, however some may put the commandment from them, he nevertheless knoweth that " the commandment is life everlasting "?

II. Let us briefly consider, in the second place, the manner in which Jonah now fulfilled his mission. " So Jonah arose, and went unto Nineveh, according to the word of the Lord. Now Nineveh was an exceeding great city of three days' journey. And Jonah began to enter into the city a day's journey: and he cried, and said, Yet forty days, and Nineveh shall be overthrown."

The great point, or rather the great principle, of interest and instruction here, is contained in the declaration that "Jonah arose and went *according to the word of the Lord*." Nothing now weighed with Jonah, nothing moved him, but "the word of the Lord." Formerly he had fled from the presence of the Lord, *according* to his own fears; *according* to the multitude of his thoughts within him. Now he arises, and goes to Nineveh, *according* to the word of the Lord. He rests his determination on "the word of the Lord." He clothes his soul with "the word of the Lord." He answers every temptation with "the word of the Lord." Everything save "the word of the Lord" is as nothing in his sight; he looks not to the things that are seen.

Here is the great principle of the trial of faith. As a believer you profess to assign, in your practical regards, a place of absolute, unquestioned supremacy to "the word of the Lord." When God hath spoken, it is enough. You are no more faithless, but believing. You are not disobedient to the heavenly message. Difficulties, dangers, fears, anxieties—all must give place where "the word of the Lord" is against them; where they are against "the word of the Lord." You simply consider them not. You "stagger not at the promise through unbelief." You bid your trembling heart be still and see the salvation of the Lord. Ah! this is "the shield of faith; and by it ye shall be able to quench all the fiery

darts of the wicked one." You resign your own wisdom.
You refuse to be governed by things seen and temporal.
There is nothing too hard for the Lord; and the Lord
hath passed His word. You "believe that what He
hath spoken He is able also to perform;"—that what
you have committed to Him He is able also to keep.
You confer not with flesh and blood. The weapons
of your warfare are not carnal. You are content with
"the word of the Lord." You know that it will stand,
and that it will protect you. You believe that it will
be unto you even as the Lord hath said. You will
venture, peril, trust all on His faithfulness. And
blessed are you in doing so! That word of the Lord
is a secret home in which your soul dwells in peace.
All fears, alarms, obstacles, now are without—outside
the citadel. You look forth upon them in composure.
They cannot reach you. You have a safety and a
peace quite impregnable. You move about in a charmed
atmosphere. Wherever you go, you carry this atmosphere with you. Because of it, the world knoweth
you not. Because of it, you are in the world but not
of the world. Your principle and rule of action is "the
word of the Lord."

Did you ever meet affliction thus?—did you ever face
a trial thus?—did you ever pass through a painful
crisis, a sore probation of your patience, faith, or constancy, keeping in view all the while that your purpose
and procedure, your temper and policy, should be
"according to the word of the Lord"? And did you
fail? No. And you never will fail while the desire of

your heart and the doing of your hand are ruled and ordered thus. This is the essence of Christianity—the essence of faith.

Tranquillity is here—and strength. Fears and alarms shall pass away; but the word of the Lord endureth for ever. Hindrances to duty shall surrender and give place; but the counsel of the Lord, it shall stand. The multitude of the imaginations of man's heart are vanity; but what the Lord hath spoken, that is what shall be. To peril all on what hath come forth from the mouth of the Lord is conformable to natural reason; though it is the attainment of nothing less than spiritual and supernatural faith. "For the law of the Lord is perfect, converting the soul: the testimony of the Lord is sure, making wise the simple. The statutes of the Lord are right, rejoicing the heart: the commandment of the Lord is pure, enlightening the eyes. The fear of the Lord is clean, enduring for ever: the judgments of the Lord are true and righteous altogether." "For all flesh is grass, and all the glory of man as the flower of grass. The grass withereth, the flower thereof falleth away: but the word of the Lord endureth for ever" (Ps. xix. 7-9; 1 Pet. i. 24, 25).

XVIII

NINEVEH'S REPENTANCE: ITS ORIGIN AND NATURE

JONAH iii. 5, 9

"So the people of Nineveh believed God, and proclaimed a fast, and put on sackcloth, from the greatest of them even to the least of them. . . . Who can tell if God will turn and repent, and turn away from his fierce anger, that we perish not?"

"Then hath God also to the Gentiles granted repentance."—ACTS xi. 18.

THE repentance of Nineveh is one of the most singular events in history. A great and proud city suddenly smitten into the most profound humiliation, from the greatest of its inhabitants unto the least of them,—from the king on the throne to the meanest citizen,—is a spectacle to which, I suppose, history affords no parallel. Cities, and countries, and communities have oftentimes, with not a little unanimity, given themselves to humiliation and fasting. But there is no event on record that can at all be compared with the fast and the repentance of Nineveh.

The repentance of Nineveh may be considered, *first*, in its essentials; and, *secondly*, in its circumstantials.

We confine our attention at present to the essentials. And here, the ORIGIN and NATURE of this repentance, will call for our consideration.

I. The origin of Nineveh's repentance. It arose, in the first place, from their faith of the terrible destruction threatened; and, in the second place, in their hope of escaping it.

1. First; this repentance was prompted by faith. " So the people of Nineveh *believed* God, and proclaimed a fast." All originated in their faith. They heard the message of the prophet with astonishment; but not with incredulity. They received him as an agent commissioned of Heaven to declare their coming doom. They believed him to be a messenger from God ; and they believed his message.

Doubtless, the hand of God is to be traced in this, and His power and gracious influence on their hearts. And a very wondrous work it is of the grace of God, that a city such as Nineveh,—great, and violent, and proud, and of a haughty spirit,—should have been so greatly, so suddenly humbled to believe the message of God. Surely God's Holy Spirit was with God's holy word among them: and very powerful, though secret, were His operations. It is impossible to account for their faith without attributing it to the operation of God upon their hearts, and the sovereign mercy of God towards them. Who could have expected that Jonah should meet with any such reception from a heathen, violent, profligate, enormous community like that of

Nineveh? What could have been looked for, but that they should either treat him as a senseless dreamer, —congregating in multitudes to laugh at him as he sped through the town with his ominous and unvarying cry about the coming calamity; or, irritated by his pertinacity, take steps to avenge the insult speedily? What wonder though they had for a time amused themselves with the solemn aspect of the frenzied foreigner; and then—when they could no more maintain even to themselves the charge against him of being beside himself; when the persevering discharge of his sad commission, and the wise, and calm, and holy aspect of the man, forbade to mock him any longer— passed from laughter to wrath, and subjected him to some one or other of the deaths of torture which, alas! the sculptures of the Assyrian capital now exhumed, prove to have been but too common outlets for their cruelty? Assuredly, at least, it is very marvellous that they did not unanimously treat the prophet, as Lot was treated by his sons-in-law. When the angels had announced to that patriarch the dreadful visitation of Divine wrath under which the city of his habitation was to be obliterated, they said unto him, "Hast thou here any besides? son-in-law, and thy sons, and thy daughters, and whatsoever thou hast in the city, bring them out of this place: for we will destroy this place, because the cry of them is waxen great before the face of the Lord; and the Lord hath sent us to destroy it. And Lot went out, and spake unto his sons-in-law, which married his daughters, and said, Up, get you out

of this place; for the Lord will destroy this city"
(Gen. xix. 12–14). You remember the reception which
his mission of mercy met with. "He seemed unto
them as one that mocked." They regarded him as beside himself. Destroy this place! what likelihood,
what symptom of *that?* Or what preparation? The
plain of Jordan is fertile; well-watered, even as the
garden of the Lord, the paradise of peace; or as Egypt,
the paragon of plenty, the granary of the world. The
sky is serene; the fields are rich and beautiful; the
river wends peacefully between its banks as ever; not
a breath of storm stirs; nature smiles in quietness and
promise: and what should bring destruction on the
morrow?

Is it not very remarkable that Jonah did not, in like
manner, seem unto the men of Nineveh "as one that
mocked"? Judging by sense, what forces were in
action, or in preparation, to destroy them in forty days?
From what quarter should the unexplained blow descend? And with a threat hung over them so utterly
indefinite—indicating nothing of the source or nature of
the coming ruin—what wonder if, like Lot's sons-in-law,
they had heard the threat with unmingled incredulity?
But in perfect contrast with the state of mind which
these infatuated relatives of the holy patriarch exhibited,
and which not even all the knowledge they must have
had of Lot's staid, and wise, and holy character could
overcome, an utter stranger to the men of Nineveh
meets with credit at their hands though he delivers a
message as stern and terrible. Surely this was of the

Lord. Surely His Spirit was striving powerfully and successfully with the Ninevites, else Jonah had appeared to them as one that mocked. When the Ninevites believed God, was not this a faith which was " not of themselves "? Was it not " the gift of God "?

Let us observe how their faith wrought. For " faith worketh." Faith is a most energetic and impulsive principle. It leads a man to work. Saving faith— that particular, distinguishing faith which receives the saving love of God in Christ and Him crucified—saving faith " worketh by *love*." For it embraces an infinite, sovereign, undeserved, most tender and eternal love on the Saviour's part; and it works by gratitude, admiration, and love in return. Generally, faith worketh; and it worketh according to the nature of that which is believed. If that which is believed be something dreadful and alarming, it worketh by *fear;* and if any possibility of escape seem left, it prompts to the embracing of whatever means may realise it. Of faith operating in this manner, namely by fear, and prompting to what steps are needful to secure deliverance from dreaded evil, Noah is an eminent instance. " By faith Noah, being warned of God of things not seen as yet, moved with fear, prepared an ark to the saving of his house " (Heb. xi. 7). What Noah believed was in its nature dreadful. He had no evidence of its truth, but the alone word of God. The " things " of which he was warned were " not seen as yet." But he took the word of God for truth. And " faith," or the word of God apprehended by faith, " is the evidence of things not seen." To Noah, therefore, as in every case, his faith was, as it were, a new sense; giving him an undoubting perception of things not otherwise perceptible : and accordingly, perceiving the advent of dreadful evil, he was moved with fear; and, being moved with the fear of evil, he took means to avert it. He built an ark. By faith Noah built an ark. It was his work of faith.

And precisely thus did faith work in the case of the men of Nineveh. They believed God, speaking to them by His messenger. " Warned of God of things not seen as yet "—of a destruction of which no sign nor symptom of any kind appeared—for which they had no evidence whatever, but simply the message of the prophet, which they received as the word of God—they believed God ; and their faith wrought in a manner suitable to the position in which they now found themselves placed. " They proclaimed a fast."

It is to be observed that faith operates differently according to the matter believed. When faith looks to the love of Christ, the redeeming love of Christ, faith worketh by *love :*—" We love Him who first loved us." When faith looks to the infinite wrath of God—to the inexpressible and eternal ruin of lost souls—faith worketh by *fear ;* and we " flee for refuge to the hope set before us ;" like the manslayer speeding to the refuge city because he sees the revenger of blood dogging his heels. When faith looks at Christ bearing in His love the wrath from which He calls us to flee, faith worketh by *grief ;* and " looking on Him whom we have pierced, we mourn." And all these operations of faith—love, fear, grief,—enter into that repentance unto salvation which true faith produces.

The element of fear was the great and leading element in the repentance of the Ninevites. "Who can tell if God will turn and repent, and turn away from His *fierce anger*, that we *perish* not?" The dread of "perishing;" the dread of the "fierce anger" of the Lord; operated powerfully. They were filled with fear. They were "moved with fear."

This is the least noble of the elements that enter into true repentance, or produce it. Saving repentance,—repentance unto life,—certainly has constituent principles in it more exalted, more pure, more generous: lively grief for offending against God, our Creator, Preserver, Saviour;—ingenuous shame in contemplating the moral loathsomeness of sin;—inexpressible gratitude and admiration in beholding the rich grace of God in the gift of His dear Son as our sacrifice and intercessor;—generous and self-forgetting ascriptions of glory, and praise, and righteousness to Him against whom we have unreasonably rebelled. But in exalting the more generous and noble features of repentance, let not the commonplace principle of fear be overlooked. While we call upon you to be grieved and mourn for your provocations against God, we are by no means to omit calling on you to be alarmed at the danger of being overtaken by His wrath. The principle of self-preservation—the combined desire of happiness and dread of evil—is a principle to which Scripture frequently appeals, which it seeks to awaken and to enlist. The rightness and reasonableness of repentance are to be preached; but the plainer and more commonplace theme is also to be preached; namely, the danger to yourselves of continuing impenitent. The high spirituality which would press only the loftier and purer class of motives, omitting all reference to those that seem allied to self-love, is not countenanced in Scripture. In dealing with the impenitent, the Lord speaks copiously of the bearing of their impenitence upon themselves; and seeks to awaken and alarm by the threats of terrible destruction from the presence of the Lord. "Except ye repent, ye shall all likewise *perish*." "Turn ye, turn ye, why will ye *die*." "Fear Him that is able to destroy both body and soul in hell." A slavish fear of God, or a mere physical terror or dread of evil, have little in them to evidence a state of grace. But in the first awakenings of the careless transgressor, they may oftentimes serve no small beneficial purpose. Anything is better than the listlessness, the indifference, the deep slumber, in which multitudes of sinners are steeped. Insensible to the finer motives which might lead them to be ashamed of their ingratitude to God, it were well if the threatenings of God's wrath would sting them out of their unfeeling and hardened condition. "Can thine hands be strong; can thine heart endure in the day that I will deal with thee, saith the Lord?" "If I whet my glittering sword, and mine hand take hold on judgment; I will render vengeance to mine enemies, and reward them that hate me."

What is it that can account for the careless sinner

living unmoved under threatenings and warnings such as these? It is a very sad conclusion to come to, but it is inevitable. He does not believe God. He does not give God and God's word the credit which he would give to a fellow-creature and *his* word. Practically, he treats the threatenings of God as if there were no meaning, no truth, no reality in them. He doth not know; he doth not consider; he doth not believe. God has threatened to cast him into hell-fire, prepared for the devil and his angels; to laugh at his calamity, and mock when his fear cometh; to abandon him throughout all eternity to the unmitigated effects of his wickedness, and to his own depraved desires, to the companionship of those who have ruined themselves along with him, and to the retribution of His wrath and curse without relief and without end. God hath further assured him that as the tree falls so it must lie; and that He may, at any moment, without warning, call him to His judgment-seat, and assign him his portion of intolerable and unending ruin. And yet, in the face of all this, the careless sinner can eat, drink, and be merry; can buy and sell and get gain; can pursue his worldly objects of ambition and desire, with the whole unbroken strength and vigour of his mind. Can it then be thought that he believes the Lord? Impossible. However sad the conclusion, it is obvious that the negligent and prayerless sinner is, to all practical ends, an atheist; he is practically living in a state of infidelity and atheism; and however much he may revolt from admitting this, it is impossible for him by an appeal to his conduct to refute it. So thorough and intense is the depravity of human nature! And so true is the inspired declaration that we are by nature " without God in the world " !

It is the quickening and wakening up of a new sense, or feeling, or sensibility, when the sinner begins to take the word of God, concerning his state and danger, for real and true; and acts upon the supposition of its truth, exactly as he would act on the supposition of the truth of some statement affecting his temporal affairs. Apply to your eternal concerns and to what affects them—we might say to him,—apply to *them* the same line of thought and action that you apply to temporal interests ; and, on the supposition that what God says to you is true, and is by you dealt with as true, you will become altogether another creature. If the prospect of a temporal calamity bestirs you to escape it, you will not fold your hands in the prospect of eternal perdition. If the displeasure of a superior troubles you, you will not sit at ease under the wrath of the Supreme. Believing the truth as to your condition and prospects will work a mighty change in your feelings and procedure. What will you then give in exchange for your soul ?

Can anything more clearly prove the necessity of our being born again, than this amazing infatuation that leads us to deal with God's words as if they were empty wind? Must we not be corrupt in the whole man, in very truth spiritually dead, ere we could be capable of anything so marvellously wicked? The

Ninevites will rise in judgment against us, for " they believed God " and " repented at the preaching of Jonah."

2. We are not, however, to imagine that a belief and apprehension of terrible evil denounced upon them was the only impelling motive to the repentance of the city. Certainly an element of hope mingled, to bestir them to exertion. A slender hope it must have been at the best; yet still most valuable. The absence of hope excludes the possibility of repentance. Despair seals and quickens the sinner's enmity and hatred to God. And it would have done so eminently in the case of the Ninevites. Had they viewed their doom as utterly inevitable, they would have been either paralysed or infuriated. They would have been still more estranged from God. But some hope, evidently, in their apprehension still remained. The word among them was: " Who can tell if God will turn and repent, and turn away from His fierce anger, and we perish not ? "

Now what room was there, in their case, for entertaining this hope ? Did not the strait threatening,— unconditional, unqualified,—run in these terms, " Forty days and Nineveh shall be destroyed " ? And how did this leave room or scope for any hope of mercy ?

There were two things from which the Ninevites might gather hope :—

(1.) There was the general consideration that all threatenings are warnings ; that they are uttered, in order, if possible, that they may not be executed. Had it been the purpose of God, finally and irrevocably fixed,

to overwhelm the city with destruction, it would have
been unnecessary and superfluous to give them intimation. The announcement was given, clearly, if possible,
that the evil might be averted. Manifestly, in the very
sending of a herald to give them warning, there was
mercy towards them. Through the streets of Sodom
and Gomorrah no awakening ambassador wended his
mournful way foretelling the doom that was decreed.
To Lot's sons-in-law, tidings were carried by Lot himself; the angels of the Lord commanding him to do so.
And to them, the commission bore evidence that they
were not so consigned to judgment, but that their faith
and flight would assuredly have saved them. But on
the other dwellers in the doomed cities of the plain,
destruction fell without a warning; for God had determined it without any door of hope. The very mission,
however, of Jonah to Nineveh carried in it some intimation on God's part of a lingering mercy towards
them, a mercy that would warn them how soon justice
must take its course. The Ninevites themselves seem
to have judged thus. Reason taught them that if
God abstained from suddenly and instantaneously
pouring out His wrath upon them, and gave them
forty days' notice, it must be because there was some
space given for repentance, some room for hope. Thus,
under a dispensation of forbearance, threatenings are
employed, not to shut the door of hope, but to awaken
the insensible and compel them towards the gates of
repentance.

(2.) But secondly; the hope of the Ninevites may

have arisen from another cause, or been prompted by another consideration. Our Lord in the days of His flesh was solicited by the unbelieving Jews to show them a sign, and He answered—" An evil and adulterous generation seeketh after a sign, and there shall no sign be given to it, but the sign of the prophet Jonas : For as Jonas was three days and three nights in the whale's belly, so shall the Son of man be three days and three nights in the heart of the earth." And again—" As Jonas was a sign unto the Ninevites, so shall also the Son of man be to this generation." Now it seems very clear, from these sayings of our Lord, that the respect in which Jonah was a sign, was in his being three days and three nights in the whale's belly ; that in this respect he was a sign to the Ninevites ; and, therefore, that the Ninevites must have been made aware of his history—the history of his original commission, his disobedience, his flight, his pursuit, his punishment, and forgiveness. Without their knowledge of his history he could not have been to them, in respect of that history, a sign. But this very story of what had befallen the very messenger whom God had sent them could not fail to impress them, not only with a deep sense of the terrors of God's wrath, but with a lively perception also of His mercy. The fact, also, that the Lord interposed to deliver His servant from the dreadful misery in which he was shut up, could hardly have been imparted to them without some intimation of the place which the prophet's lowly prayers held in the matter. And they could, therefore, scarcely avoid seeing that there is some influence which prayer and penitence exert in averting the threatened wrath of the Almighty; and hence, perhaps, their wise and humble question,— "Who can tell if God will turn and repent, and turn away from His fierce anger, that we perish not?"

Such then was the origin of the Ninevites' repentance. It originated in faith, as indeed every good thing does. And their faith wrought by fear and hope combined. Their fear predominated; but hope was not altogether wanting. The evil dreaded was sufficient to break and humble all their pride; to prepare them to abase themselves to anything that might afford any prospect of escape. And the hope they entertained was sufficient to prevent their fear from turning into despair; sufficient to prevent them from being paralysed out of the efforts to which their fear might reasonably prompt them.

The combination of appeals to these two principles of fear and hope which Scripture makes, in addressing us on the part of God, when it calls us to repentance, is most complete. The evil, by the terror whereof it seeks to arouse us, is terrible beyond conception, and irrevocably certain and sealed on impenitence. On the other hand, the glorious inheritance, by the hope of which it labours to allure us, is equally great beyond conception, and assured even by the oath of God to all who repent and turn unto the Lord. By the terrors of the Lord, therefore, we ought to be persuaded; and by the mercies of the Lord we may well be overcome. If these terrors and mercies both be believed in and dealt with as realities, they will indeed compel and constrain us to turn from all our evil ways,—to turn unto the Lord that we may live.

II. But let us consider the NATURE as well as the origin of their repentance. "They cried mightily to God, and turned every one from his evil way, and from the violence that was in their hands." The city underwent a sudden and striking reformation. "God saw their works that they turned from their evil way." Their haughtiness and pride were abased; their contempt of God was abandoned; their luxury, cruelty, violence, and unrighteousness were given up. And God looked on with approbation. "Is not this the fast that I have chosen? saith the Lord: to loose the bands of wickedness, to undo the heavy burdens, and to let the oppressed go free, and that ye break every yoke? Is it not to deal thy bread to the hungry, and that thou bring the poor that are cast out to thy house? When thou seest the naked, that thou cover him, and that thou hide not thyself from thine 'own flesh?" Such is the fast that the Lord calleth for: not a formal, ceremonious, outward solemnity; but a spiritual and moral reformation, outwardly evidenced and certified by new obedience.

The principle is this: true repentance is a change of mind, of heart, of disposition: it is the making of a new heart and of a right spirit. It originates in regeneration; in our being born again; in our obtaining a new nature and becoming new creatures in Christ by the Spirit. And it flows forth, in unmistakeable manifestations, in

a new course of conduct; in a reformed life; a life aim-
ing at new ends, conducted under a new rule, and
aspiring to attain to a new standard. Repentance,
springing from a true fear of God and a true sight of
sin, manifests itself in a dutiful obedience to God's law
and a jealous abstinence from sin. True and saving
repentance is not a mere shaking off the evil fruit from
the tree, and tying on fruit of a better appearance. It
is the changing of the tree's very nature; and good
fruit is then naturally brought forth, and not artificially
appended. The penitent exclaims, " Create in me a
clean heart, O God, and renew a right spirit within
me." Thus much for the healing of the tree. He obeys
the command, " Cease to do evil, learn to do well."
Thus much for the new, good fruit. " Make the tree
good, and the fruit good " (Matt. xii. 33).

Shall we say that the repentance of Nineveh was
thoroughly spiritual and saving in the light of eternity ?
Alas! there is no evidence to show that thorough conversion to God was effected, at least in the city generally.
True, spiritual, living religion does not seem even to
have taken hold on Nineveh. Idolatry continued to be
practised ; and the ultimate fate of the city may be read
in the prophecies of Nahum—prophecies that have
minutely been fulfilled, and their detailed accuracy
verified before the whole world, in the disinterment
within these days of the buried capital, and the bringing to the light of day, after more than two millenniums,
of its ancient sculptures and records.

It may be inquired, then, why God should have set

the seal of His approbation on their repentance, as we shall afterwards find He did, if it fell so far short of thorough regeneration and conversion? And the answer is, that God's procedure in sparing them is not to be taken as the pronouncing of His opinion upon the goodness, thoroughness, or spiritual nature of their repentance. God is carrying on towards individuals and communities a dispensation of forbearance, subordinately to a dispensation of saving mercy, and with a view ultimately to a final dispensation of judgment. The exigencies of such a procedure imply a large amount of Divine patience. Occasionally, as in the instance of the flood, of the cities of the plain,—and of Nineveh, had repentance not intervened,—God puts a limit to His long-suffering; and, being provoked by flagrant wickedness, sweeps the evil suddenly from the earth which it pollutes. His not interfering to do so with a community, does not, by any means, imply the presence and the power among them, to any great extent, of His true and holy fear. They may be far enough as a whole from that, and yet not be given over to the flagrant iniquity which usually provokes the special judgment of Heaven. And we can easily conceive of a community on the very verge of the limit of God's patience, but, under salutary, and, so far, religious alarm, turning and retreating to safer ground,—repenting in a sense, and turning from their evil ways,—without going over to the ground of true, spiritual, vital godliness, or being savingly, and for eternity, converted. They may take up ground comparatively safe from special and dreadful judgments, without becoming truly living Christians. For, were God immediately to smite with His wrath for the usual ungodliness of unconverted men, He would be continually doing so; and works of judgment would be the ordinary features of His administration. On the contrary, judgment is His strange work; and forbearance is the great leading feature of His present dispensation. And hence we might warrantably enough expect that a repentance, exhibiting a great reformation of manners, without going so far as vital conversion, would secure the favourable interposition of God, and the removal of His threatened and exterminating indignation. The Ninevites, though few of them probably were savingly converted, were sincerely alarmed; they were convinced of their wickedness, and they turned from the evil of their doings. Their daring neglect and contempt of God were abandoned, and they cried mightily to Him. Their unrighteous and unjust actions towards man also were abandoned, and they began to deal in rectitude among themselves. They laid aside, in short, the eminence and distinction in wickedness to which they had attained. And the features of their case that had provoked the Divine indignation being gone, the Divine pity, as we shall see, returned, and a forbearing Providence flowed towards them again in its wonted channels.

But what an evidence does this afford of the unspeakable goodness of God! If even their very imperfect repentance—their turning from their evil ways, though alas! it fell short of turning truly to the Lord—was, nevertheless, regarded by the Lord, how open must His ear ever be to the poor, afflicted soul that turns truly to Himself! We have an instance of God's extreme readiness to be reconciled to us on our repentance in the merciful manner in which He dealt with Ahab. We are told concerning that wicked monarch that " there was none like unto Ahab which did sell himself to work wickedness in the sight of the Lord." Yet when Elijah was sent to denounce the most dreadful judgments on his house, the wretched king, stung with alarm and remorse, " rent his clothes, and put sackcloth upon his flesh, and fasted, and lay in sackcloth, and went softly." There is not the slightest evidence, but the contrary, that this was a vital change of heart. But there was in it true regret; a sincere owning of God's power, and hand, and righteousness ; a justification, in so far, of the justice of God's threatening ; and a public testimony to the supremacy and government of God. And though not accompanied by a renewal of nature and a repentance unto life, it was pleasing in the sight of God in so far as it went. "And the word of the Lord came to Elijah the Tishbite, saying, Seest thou how Ahab humbleth himself before me? Because he humbleth himself before me, I will not bring the evil in his days; but in his son's days will I bring the evil upon his house " (1 Kings xxi. 25-29). He procured a delay of the threatened temporal judgment all the days of his own life. So decided was the regard which the Lord had to Ahab's meek and humble reception of His awful word.

And how very great is the encouragement which this
holds out to sinners to repent and return unto the Lord
with all their heart and with all their soul! A repentance arising only from a regret, however deep, and
producing an outward reformation however valuable,
but without a change of heart, will assuredly avail but
little. God may not count it utterly of no value in the
light or on the platform of time. But in the light of
eternity and of the spiritual world, it can profit you
nothing. We must all appear before the judgment-
seat of Christ. And anticipating that most awful
event, it is ours to rend our hearts and not our garments
—to seek grace that the tree may be made good—that
we may be actually renewed in the spirit of our minds,
transformed in the renewing of our minds, renouncing
ourselves, and putting on Christ Jesus, and living in the
Spirit. But how great is the encouragement to turn to
God and seek the grace which a risen Saviour is exalted
to bestow, and which He proves His readiness to give by
the record of His merciful and pitiful procedure even to
those who fell far short of sorrowing after a godly sort!
Be persuaded, then, to lay deeply to heart, on the one
hand, the terrible wrath of Almighty God against the
unconverted, and the terrible ruin of an unsaved soul.
And lay equally to heart, on the other, the great and
sure mercy and acceptance in Christ open to all who
turn from their evil ways and come unto God by Him.
And seeing that God, who at sundry times and in divers
manners spake of old by the prophets, hath in these
last days spoken to us by His Son, let us bear in mind

that if we are not found among God's penitent, believing, renewed, and redeemed children, the men of Nineveh will rise against us in the judgment; "For they repented at the preaching of Jonas; and, behold, a greater than Jonas is here."

XIX

NINEVEH'S REPENTANCE :—ITS NATIONALITY ; ITS EXPRESSIONS ; ITS EFFICACY

JONAH iii. 6–8, 10

" For word came unto the king of Nineveh; and he arose from his throne, and he laid his robe from him, and covered him with sackcloth, and sat in ashes. And he caused it to be proclaimed and published through Nineveh, by the decree of the king and his nobles, saying, Let neither man nor beast, herd nor flock, taste anything; let them not feed, nor drink water: but let man and beast be covered with sackcloth, and cry mightily unto God; yea, let them turn every one from his evil way, and from the violence that is in their hands. . . . And God saw their works, that they turned from their evil way; and God repented of the evil that he had said that he would do unto them; and he did it not."

> " And Jehoshaphat feared, and set him-
> self to seek the Lord, and proclaimed
> a fast throughout all Judah. . . . . .
> " And all Judah stood before the Lord,
> with their little ones, their wives, and
> their children."—2 CHRON. xx. 3, 13.

CERTAIN circumstances connected with the repentance of Nineveh are worthy of particular notice by themselves. We may notice first, the *nationality* of it; and secondly, the *outward indications*.

I. First, then, we may notice the nationality of this repentance. It was a public, general, royal fast. The king himself set the example. "For word came unto the king, and he arose from his throne, and laid his robe from him, and covered him with sackcloth, and sat in ashes." And he did not merely countenance the proposal of a fast by his example ; or counsel it by his advice. He commanded it by his authority. " He caused it to be proclaimed and published through Nineveh by decree of the king and his nobles."

Of such fasts we have many examples in Scripture. When the children of Moab and the children of Ammon, reinforced by a heterogeneous multitude of the enemies of Judah, came against Jehoshaphat, we are told that on word being brought to him, the "king feared, and set himself to seek the Lord, and proclaimed a fast throughout all Judah" (2 Chron. xx. 3). In like manner, in the days of Joel, we find the Lord calling for repentance, and enjoining a public fast : "Blow the trumpet in Zion, sanctify a fast, call a solemn assembly : gather the people, sanctify the con- gregation, assemble the elders, gather the children, and those that suck the breasts : let the bridegroom go forth of his chamber, and the bride out of her closet. Let the priests, the ministers of the Lord, weep between the porch and the altar, and let them say, Spare thy people, O Lord, and give not thine heritage to reproach, that the heathen should rule over them : wherefore should they say among the people, Where is their God?" (Joel ii. 15–17). And the regard which the Lord mercifully has to such exercises of deep repentance in His sight, is indicated in the promise which Joel was commissioned to connect with them ;—" Then will the Lord be jealous for his land, and pity his people. . . . And I will remove far off from you the northern army, and will drive him into a land barren and desolate."

There are many such instances in Scripture history of great national fasts called by royal decree, and observed by general consent. In our own land, and in our own day, there have been not a few instances of a practice so laudable and impressive—a whole nation at the monarch's call humbling itself before God, confessing provocations, and deprecating His wrath.

Some, indeed, would object to national recognitions of religion, and such royal calls and injunctions to observe its duties. Civil magistracy, they tell us, is a civil, temporal, earthly institution, having under its regulation the affairs of time and the world, and having nothing to do with religion;—and the civil magistrate, or chief ruler, they would accordingly prevent from in any way intromitting with religious matters—matters belonging not to time but eternity, not to this world but the world to come.

There are a number of grievous errors wrapt up here in one. It seems to imply that the affairs of this world *may* and *ought* to be carried on apart from the affairs and obligations of religious truth and duty ;— thus shutting up religion to a territory of its own, beyond which it must not be suffered to trespass. But apart from this; how can religious obligation lie upon the separate individuals of a nation, and yet the nation as a nation be exempt from it? It is certain that nations as a whole may please or provoke God; just as a family may do; just as an individual may do. God deals with a community as a whole, just as He deals with a household as a whole. And as when God is angry with a family, He deals with them in His wrath for their family provocations, so He deals with communities and kingdoms. If a family, therefore, ought to be religious;—in the sense that not only are its individuals to be religious, but unitedly, and as in their mutual relations, they are to observe the duties of family religion;—it ought to be the same in a kingdom. The father of a family is not only to be a pious man himself, but he is to see that in the united worship of his household, and in religious principles being brought to bear on all its movements, there be a household piety—a family recognition of God. For true religion is not a thing to be kept secret between a man's own conscience and God. No doubt the springs of it are deep seated in the inmost soul; and the Christian life is a hidden life. But for that very reason,—by reason of the inmost secrecy, and therefore irrepressible power of its principles,—it will assert and vindicate its influence in all circumstances, and over all the relations in which men stand towards one another. It will therefore guide those in whom it dwells, not merely in their own private relation to God, and in their worship and more immediate duty towards Him, but in the whole influence they can exert over their fellow-creatures,—in all their relations, whether as superiors, inferiors, or equals. But especially as superiors,—where *authority* belongs to them,—where they have it in their power to " *command* their households after them,"—they will arrange that in all the ongoings of these households God shall be recognised, and His authority and will obeyed. They will say with Joshua, " As for me and my house, we will serve the Lord."

It is this element, however, of command, of authority, against the introduction of which in religious observances not a few reclaim. I would *advise* with my household, or any irreligious and wayward member of it; I would advise; I would exhort; I would instruct and entreat: but I can go no farther. I can't make them religious, and I won't command or compel them. But all this sophistry is utterly laughed to scorn by the simple perusal of the fourth commandment:—" The seventh day is the sabbath of the Lord thy God: in it thou shalt not do any work, thou, nor thy son, nor thy daughter, thy manservant, nor thy maidservant, nor thy cattle, nor thy stranger that is within thy gates: " —by the which terms thou art held of God guilty of Sabbath desecration all the same, whether it be " thou, or thy son, or thy daughter, or thy manservant, or thy maidservant, or thy stranger that is within thy gates." Thou wilt not be held guiltless on the plea that thou didst instruct, didst entreat, didst plead. Didst thou *command?* Didst thou bring out, for securing obedience to God, all the authority with which thou art endowed as head of thy household, and which thou dost not scruple, if need be, to bring forth for securing obedience to *thine own* will? To "the stranger that is within thy gates," thou art bound,—when advice, entreaty, exhortation fail,—to give forth thy command; backed by the penalty that, if it be not obeyed, he can be "within thy gates" no longer. With "thy manservant, and thy maidservant," thou art to deal, if need be, in like manner also. Yea, "thy son and thy daughter" are not to abide "within thy gates" and despise the commandments of God. Thou art to command them; and, failing obedience, then thou art to disown them, to cast them off, and cast them out. Eli, alas! acted on the principle that a parent may advise in religious things, but may not imperatively command and threaten. And his house and his name were blotted out for ever!

Have you any influence, any power, any authority over children and dependants which you may use in your own service and work, but which you would refrain from bringing forth on the side of God? What were this, but selfishly to surround the accomplishment of your own will with securities, which you refuse to adopt to secure observance in your household to God's will? And can it be that, in such a case you really honour God? Nay: it is not whole-hearted, sincere, thorough-going, and true honouring of God where your government of your household does not call into exercise, when needful, on the side of God, every influence which you can ever rightly use on your own side. If there be a principle of authority—an element of command—vested anywhere in a family at all, religion lays it under contribution to the cause of the Most High—under call to uphold and promote the observance of His will.

And the same principle holds in a nation. So far forth as a monarch's authority goes, it goes all the length of entitling him to enjoin a fast and a solemn assembly—a public, universal, national recognition of God—the God who is dealing with the nation as a whole, and summoning the nation as a whole to acknowledge Him. Nature itself teaches this truth. It rises up to view in its own native reasonableness in the hour of solemn thoughtfulness, the hour of sad national calamity. All sophistical objections about the impossibility of making men religious by Act of Parliament then disappear. The truth comes obviously to light, and commends itself to reason and conscience. Well was it for Nineveh that its king was not embued with certain modern notions about magistrates and kings having nothing to do with religion. The city's doom had been sealed by them!

Can anything be more plain than the duty of kings and all in authority to promote among their subjects the advancement of true religion and the glory of God, as that duty is enjoined in the second Psalm ;—" Be wise now therefore, O ye kings; be instructed, ye judges of the earth. Serve the Lord with fear, and rejoice with trembling. Kiss the Son, lest he be angry, and ye perish from the way." So that it is not merely a dictate and a duty of natural religion, but a revealed command, that monarchs should reign for the glory of God;—yea, that His revealed religion—His holy Word, as it declares the religion of Christ, the Son of God—should be honoured by them; that they should "kiss the Son." For the Father hath set the Son on the holy hill of Zion—made Him "the Prince of the kings of the earth."

This duty does not, of course, permit them to invade the liberties of Christ's Church as a divinely-organised and divinely-ordered society, free to obey Christ as her only Head. On the contrary, it is the doctrine we are now maintaining,—the duty of kings to glorify Christ, to consult His Word, and consult for His honour,—it is this that will alone ever effectually prevent them interfering with the prerogatives of His Headship or the liberties of His people. When we maintain, therefore, as the Church to which I have the honour to belong maintains, that the civil magistrate has no jurisdiction within or over the Church, God forbid we should set it on the ground that he has nothing to do with religion, or the Church of Christ, at all. Poor foundation, indeed, would that be for the principle maintained! He has so much to do with religion, and is so bound in his public capacity to act under religious obligation and duty to Christ, that he is bound to know and recognise Christ's Church; and *then* to leave her free to serve Christ in all spiritual things. He is bound to know the truth of Christ; to protect those who maintain the truth of Christ; and to promote by every means in his power their labours to circulate and extend it. He is bound to suppress blasphemy, perjury, Sabbath desecration, and all that necessarily tends to the dishonouring of God and the demoralising of the people. He cannot command or compel man to be religious. No commandment can make man religious—not even God's commandment can do it. The gospel of the grace of God, rendered effectual by the free and sovereign Spirit of God, can alone renew the heart of man or make him sincerely religious. Spiritual obedience to God neither magistrate nor parent can secure. But is no authority, on that account, to be exercised? Is no obligation, on that account, to be enforced? Does God's own authority cease? Is the obligation to obey God's commandment at an end? *His* commandment even will never make men religious. Is it, therefore, set aside? No, verily. The assertion of law, obligation, and authority, does *not* rest upon consequences: whether owned or not, the obligation is the same. And be it remembered that while God uses His own authority and gives forth His own commands as means with which He often sends the accompanying grace and power to obey; so a parent or superior may not only use his entreaty, example, persuasion, and exhortation in the hope that God will accompany *them* with His blessing; but may specially put forth his authority and peremptory command in the same hope that God will bless *them* likewise, and secure a true obedience—secure the good and righteous end designed. Let parents, masters, and all in authority make the 101st Psalm the rubric of their household or public procedture. " I will sing of mercy and judgment: unto thee, O Lord, will I sing. I will behave myself wisely in a perfect way. O when wilt thou come unto me? I will walk within my house with a perfect heart. I will set no wicked thing before mine eyes: I hate the work of them that turn aside; it shall not cleave to me. A froward heart shall depart from me: I will not know a wicked person. . . . Mine eyes shall be upon the faithful of the land, that they may dwell with me: he that walketh in a perfect way, he shall serve me. He that worketh deceit shall not dwell within my house: he that telleth lies shall not tarry in my sight." " I know Abraham, that he will *command* his children and his household after him; and they shall keep the way of the Lord to do justice and judgment; that the Lord may bring upon Abraham that which he hath spoken of him."

It is an evil and a dangerous principle that would exempt the rulers of a kingdom from being in subjection, in their public capacity, to the Word of Christ, and from being under obligation in their government to rule for the promotion of *His* kingdom. It strikes at the root of all family as well as national religion; and while it would confine Christ to the separate consciences of individual men, it would refuse Him the right to govern the households and communities into which, in Providence, they are combined. Its universal and perpetual prevalence would prevent the fulfilment of the promise that " the kingdoms of the world shall become the kingdoms of Jehovah and His anointed One;" and would subject all nations to the threaten-

ing : " The kingdom and nation that will not serve
the Church shall perish ; yea, those nations shall be
utterly wasted " (Isa. lx. 12). Again, we repeat, it was
fortunate and good for Nineveh that no such notion
prevailed there. Theirs was a national fast, decreed by
royal authority.

II. The second noticeable circumstance is, that it was
accompanied with many solemn and affecting external
expressions. In these, the king himself led the way
and showed the example. " He arose from his throne,
and laid his robe from him, and covered himself with
sackcloth, and sat in ashes." And he decreed that the
whole city should follow this example. The edict
which, with counsel and consent of his nobles, he proclaimed was to this effect : "Let neither man nor beast,
herd nor flock, taste anything : let them not feed,
nor drink water : but let man and beast be covered
with sackcloth."

How marvellous, sudden, and extreme the change
that has passed on the violent and bloody city !
Severe and singular is the royal decree. Yet extreme dangers call for extreme remedies ; and in
the light of coming destruction, unseen yet credited,
even this procedure itself is that of staid wisdom and
sobriety. In the East, indeed, the manners and customs
went, and still go, to authorise and beget a larger and
more vivid expression outwardly of inward feeling than
in these colder climes we are wont to adopt. The use
of sackcloth and ashes, for instance, in a day of grief,

or in acknowledgment of guilt, was common. Thus when Mordecai learnt that a decree had gone forth from Ahasuerus for the exterminating of his countrymen, he "rent his clothes, and put on sackcloth with ashes, and went out into the midst of the city, and cried with a loud and bitter cry; and came even before the king's gate: for none might enter into the king's gate clothed with sackcloth" (Esther iv. 1, 2). And the same course was adopted wherever that bloody edict was announced. "In every province, whithersoever the king's commandment and his decree came, there was great mourning among the Jews, and fasting, and weeping, and wailing; and many lay in sackcloth and ashes" (v. 3). And so usual were these striking accompaniments of humiliation in ancient times, and in oriental lands, that Jesus speaks of them as if they formed unfailing and integral parts of such exercises of grief, and sorrow, and confession: "Woe unto thee, Chorazin! woe unto thee, Bethsaida! for if the mighty works which were done in you had been done in Tyre and Sidon, they would have repented long ago in sackcloth and ashes" (Matt. xi. 21). But it is not necessary to multiply instances. Every one familiar with his Bible will call to remembrance many of them; and it is the principle of them which is worthy of notice. Of course, as substitutes for repentance, fastings with sackcloth and ashes would be only a hateful hypocrisy, increasing and provoking the wrath of God. As indicating externally nothing more than was truly felt, they were fit accompaniments of solemn, moral, and spiritual exercises. In reference to the spiritual reality, and guarding against the mere external form, the command is very speaking and impressive : " Rend your hearts and not your garments." And where this is not attended to, but a mere round of empty forms and shows is paraded before a heart-searching God, nothing could be more utterly Pharisaical and worthy of reprobation. To this degeneracy Israel, in the days of Isaiah, had too clearly reached, when the Lord could address them in such terms as these : " Bring no more vain oblations; incense is an abomination unto me ; the new moons and sabbaths, the calling of assemblies I cannot away with ; it is iniquity, even the solemn meeting " (Isa. i. 13). The form alone, while the inner spirit in its persistent wickedness belied the profession, God could endure no longer. God is a spirit, and must be. worshipped in spirit and in truth. Yet this does not hinder but where He is thus worshipped in spirit and in truth, the spirit and truth—the spiritual truth, the true spirituality —may be conjoined with and expressed by actions suitable. To some extent it must be so, and always is so. Though we profess to worship God with our hearts, yet we lift up our hands ; we look reverently upwards ; or we stand, or kneel. We assume attitudes or postures which in themselves, it may be said, are of no use or value ; but which, nevertheless, nature teaches us to feel are suitable to the state of mind ; nor could that state of mind be real without prompting these outward manifestations. " The publican, standing afar off, would not lift up so much as his eyes to heaven, but smote upon his breast, saying, God be merciful to me a sinner."

The chief feature in these outward indications of humiliation is this:—they are employed as expressive confessions of guilt, and not merely of a sense of danger. They are all designed to own that the dreaded judgment is righteous; that it is deserved; that we are worthy in justice of nothing else at the hands of the Lord. This is what is implied in these tokens and badges of abasement. They are acknowledgments that all excellence, or beauty, or comeliness, morally and spiritually, have been lost by us; that we have stript ourselves of everything that could recommend us to God; that we are not only in a pitiable condition, but criminal in that we have reduced ourselves to it; and that we own and admit that we are so. This confession the Lord imperatively demands as an indispensable preliminary to the administration of forgiveness; for He will have His forgiveness understood and acknowledged to be what it is—a gracious, free, and sovereign pardon. Till this is admitted, the Lord knows not what to do with His erring people. It is His own declaration that He does not. "Put off thine ornaments from thee,"— said Jehovah to His people Israel, when they had sinned a great sin before Him in making the golden calf and provoking the Lord to jealousy,—"Ye are a stiffnecked people: I will come up unto thee in a moment, and consume thee: therefore now put off thine ornaments from thee, that I may know what to do unto thee." Nor should it be forgotten that the lowly and deplorable appearance of an individual, or a people, sitting in sackcloth and ashes is designed to serve as an appeal to the Divine commiseration; on the same principle on which Jehoshaphat, when the hearths and homes of Judah were imperilled, arranged, in his fast and humiliation-prayer, the artless and touching scene of which we read : " And all Judah stood before the Lord *with their little ones, their wives, and their children* " (2 Chron. xx. 13).

It may be inquired, however, why the insensate brute creation should have been involved in the royal edict, or what good purpose could be served by their being made to share in the austerities and severities of a time of fasting ? " Let man and beast be covered with sackcloth ; " " let neither man nor beast taste anything." To this it may be replied that although the animals are not responsible and guilty with man, yet such, in God's estimation, is the exceeding evil of sin, that because of it the animals suffer for man's sake. Nor can God's judgments, in general, take effect on a community without involving in their sweeping stroke the brute creation. Can there be famine in a land without the animals being very chief sufferers ? What saith Joel ? " The seed is rotten under their clods, the garners are laid desolate, the barns are broken down ; for the corn is withered. How do the beasts groan ! the herds of cattle are perplexed, because they have no pasture ; yea, the flocks of sheep are made desolate. O Lord, to thee will I cry : for the fire hath devoured the pastures of the wilderness, and the flame hath burned all the trees of the field. The beasts of the field cry also unto thee; for the rivers of waters are dried up, and the fire hath devoured the pastures of the wilderness" (Joel i. 17–20). It was thus in the beginning; when man's fall brought much misery,—yea, death,—on the unoffending animals. Nineveh's destruction would have embraced *them* also. Generally, too, " the whole creation groaneth and travaileth together in pain," waiting for the removal of that subjection to vanity which the introduction of sin hath riveted (Rom. viii. 22). It is not therefore to be wondered at that even the dumb brutes should have been arrayed in sackcloth in the days of Nineveh's dreaded ruin and deep repentance. The warrior's steed, in sable plumes and mournful trappings, follows his master's body to the grave; nor, if outward signs of sorrow be at all allowable, will any feeling mind, that hath witnessed *that* one, deny its deep and touching pathos. And if any farther vindication of the Ninevites in clothing the beasts of the field with sackcloth, and conjoining them in the deep humiliation and the fast, is needed, let us pass at once beyond all arguments, and call to mind the fact, that the appeal implied in the aspect of the desolate and fasting cattle went home to the heart of God himself; and in vindicating His procedure in sparing the city, He gave in His reason for doing so no less a place to the interests and claims of these dumb animals than the Ninevites had assigned to them in the fast: " Should not I spare Nineveh, that great city, wherein are six score thousand persons that cannot discern between their right hand and their left hand ; *and also much* CATTLE ? "

It remains that we consider the *efficacy* of Nineveh's repentance. "And God saw their works, that they turned from their evil way, and God repented of the evil that he had said that he would do unto them ; and he did it not." In other words, their repentance prevailed to turn aside the judgment threatened. God repented of the evil which He had said that He would do.

Here, some would say, behold the falseness of the doctrine that God hath ordained all things by a sure, eternal, and unchangeable decree. Nay ; we reply ; behold, rather, the infinite condescension of God in consenting to speak of His own procedure in terms suitable to the weak capacities of man. "Known unto God are all His works from the beginning of the world." Yet the revelation of His secret decree is one thing, and the declaration of His will for our duty is another. Were God always to reveal His sure eternal purpose, He could not carry on a moral government at all. And in carrying on His moral government, He alters His procedure as circumstances alter ; yet He changes not thereby His eternal purpose : for both the alteration of the circumstances and the alteration of His procedure are alike decreed by Him—decreed and brought to pass both. Especially He repeatedly speaks of Himself as " repenting." Thus, at the era of the flood,—to indicate His deep displeasure and disappointment with the sons of men, whom not even the promise of a Saviour, the seed of the woman to bruise the serpent's head, could restrain from ungodliness and violence,—the Lord, on beholding the moral desolation of a corrupt, wicked race, exclaims : " It repenteth me that I have made man on the earth; and it grieved Him at His heart " (Gen. vi. 6). Another instance of the use of this language occurs in the case of the prophet Amos, to whom the Lord threatened to destroy Israel, first slowly and as by a quiet, resistless consumption, under the emblem of the action of grasshoppers or gnawing worms, and then violently and by fire. In each case, Amos interposed with his earnest intercession, and the Lord is said once and again to have " repented." " Thus hath the Lord God showed unto me ; and, behold, He formed grasshoppers in the beginning of the shooting up of the latter growth, and lo! it was the latter growth after the king's mowings. And it came to pass, that when they had made an end of eating the grass of the land, than I said, O Lord God, forgive, I beseech thee : by whom shall Jacob arise? for he is small. The Lord repented for this : It shall not be, saith the Lord. Thus hath the Lord showed unto me ; and, behold, the Lord God called to contend by fire, and it devoured the great deep, and did eat up a part. Then said I, O Lord God, cease, I beseech thee : by whom shall Jacob arise? for he is small. The Lord repented for this : this also shall not be, saith the Lord of hosts " (Amos vii. 1–6). Magnificent and redoubled instance of the truth that " the effectual, fervent prayer of a righteous man availeth much " ! while it is a double instance also of the Lord repenting and turning away from the evil which He thought to do. But perhaps the passage of Scripture, bearing most closely on this feature of the Lord's procedure is that in Jeremiah, where it is distinctly and explicitly announced as being at the foundation of all His moral government, His government by threats and promises, rewards and punishments:—"At what instant I shall speak concerning a nation, and concerning a kingdom, to pluck up, and to pull down, and to destroy it; if that nation, against whom I have pronounced, turn from their evil, I will repent of the evil that I thought to do unto them." And the same holds good on the other side also. " And at what instant I shall speak concerning a nation, and concerning a kingdom, to build, and to plant it ; if it do *evil* in my sight, that it obey not my voice, then I will repent of the good wherewith I said I would benefit them " (Jer. xviii. 7–10).

It was precisely this general principle which came in for the salvation of Nineveh. "They turned from their evil way, and the Lord repented of the evil that he said he would do unto them." And was there any changeableness in God, indicated by this change in His procedure? Nay; this change in His procedure was needful to avert the charge of change in His character, and in the *principles* of His procedure. It was wicked, violent, unrighteous, atheistical, proud, and luxurious Nineveh which God had threatened to destroy. A city sitting in sackcloth and ashes, humbled in the depths of self-abasement, and appealing as lowly suppliants to

His commiseration—a Nineveh like that—*that* Nineveh, He had never threatened. *That* Nineveh He visited not with ruin. He had never said He would. The Nineveh which God threatened to destroy passed away; it became totally another city—far more so, in virtue of this change in moral state, than if it had been translated from its olden geographical position, and wholly transformed in its architectural appearance. Surely its great moral change has made it more truly another place— a kind of new creature, old things having passed away and all things become new—than any alteration in its physical aspect could have done. It really, in God's estimation, is not the Nineveh He threatened at all. The terrific threatening does not apply now. "God saw their works;"—their fruits meet for repentance, namely, "that they turned from their evil way;— and God repented of the evil that he said that he would do unto them : and he did it not."

Of course, it is after the manner of men that the Spirit speaks, when He attributes to God at any time repentance or a change of mind at all. And doubtless He speaks of God after the manner of men continually. For there has been far too much said in the way of accounting for, and explaining, and justifying such an expression as this; "the Lord repented that he had made man;" or "repented of the evil He thought to do;" far too much *on the idea,* or as countenancing the idea, that this expression needs a vindication peculiar to itself. It is not so. It needs no more to be vindicated than a thousand expressions in which God, putting on the person of a man, speaks to us as from the position, and as with the feelings of a man, in order to make His own mind and heart intelligible to us. We are ever to guard against assigning human imperfection to God. But we are equally to guard against assigning to Him such a character or nature as would render living, intelligible, friendly intercourse between Him and His people impossible. But impossible utterly, all such intercourse must be, if I may not speak to God in the same forms, and phrases, and feelings in which I would offer a request, or state my case to a fellow-man, though of course with unreserved submission and unlimited adoration of the Almighty and Holy One of Israel. My adoration unbounded ;—my surrender of myself to God unreservedly ;—these are tributes to the searchless glory of His Godhead which I may not withhold, and yet profess to worship Him. Nevertheless, with these I must be allowed, in condescension to my weakness, to ask God to be " attentive to the voice of my supplication ;" to " behold and visit me ;" to " stretch out His hand " for my help; to " shine upon me with the light of His countenance ; " to " awake ; " to " arise ; " to " draw near ; " to " come and dwell with me." All these expressions and requests are after the manner of man. I must be allowed to spread out my sorrow and my trial before Him, precisely as if my design and expectation were to work upon His feelings, and move and induce Him in His pity to deliver me. I must be allowed, with Hezekiah, to spread out the threatening letter before Him, as if the very sight of it, held before

the throne in my hand, were to make a deep impression
on God's heart, as it implies an artless and sincere
expression of the helpless anguish of my heart. I must
be allowed to " fill my mouth with arguments," and
make every appeal to God to move in my cause which
its urgent and clamant case suggests. And all the
while, believing that His counsel is formed from everlasting—that His counsel shall stand, and He shall do
all His pleasure—that He is of one mind, and none can
turn Him—believing this, and adoring, I am not to
concern myself about how this can consist with my
weakness which cannot rise beyond finite forms of expression, and desire, and address, and expectation.
Rather I must in this matter lay aside things too great
for me, and seek to have my heart as a weaned child.

For it lies at the foundation of all intercourse between
God and man that God should Himself address us,
and permit us to address Him, in expressions suited
to our weak capacities and conceptions, rather than
dictated by what were suitable to His infinite glory
and searchless being. Does it then follow that in thus
condescending unto the weakness of our nature, He does
injustice to His own,—or misrepresents it? That does
not follow. God can speak of Himself after the manner
of man, and what He thus speaks may yet be worthy
of God. And when the proof of this is sought, let it
be found in the glorious fact, that God made man in
His own image; and in the fact, still more glorious,
that One who was in the form of God, and thought
it not robbery to be equal with God, was found in

form and fashion as a man. Did Godhead and humanity in the one person of Emmanuel jostle, disagree, hamper or misrepresent each other? God forbid. The man Christ Jesus is the brightness of the Father's glory. His tears over Jerusalem, while as God He had eternally decreed and foreseen its destruction, were no misrepresentation of the very love wherewith the Godhead is affected in even handing over the impenitent to everlasting hell. The surprise, astonishment, and grief with which the man Christ Jesus listened to Peter denying Him,—and which He expressed in His ever-memorable "look,"—were no contradiction to the fact that the same one person, the eternal Son of God, knew from everlasting that Peter would deny Him. And so, if we would behold the endless and searchless glories that seem to withdraw the eternal Godhead for ever from our knowledge, or be convinced that, in ever-blessed perfect harmony with these, there are in the same Divine Being affections of grace, and tenderness, and condescension, admitting us more nearly and profoundly to His love and friendship, than the capacities of any human friend for love and intercourse ever could admit us, let us betake ourselves evermore to Him who is " God manifest "—God most manifest—" in the flesh." He "showeth us the Father, and it sufficeth us." O Thou that didst " command the light to shine out of darkness, shine in our hearts, and give us the light of the knowledge of the glory of God in the face of Jesus Christ " ! (2 Cor. iv. 6).

XX

NEW TESTAMENT COMMENTARIES: NO. II

THE PARALLEL

JONAH iii. 10

LUKE xi. 32.—" The men of Nineveh shall rise up in the judgment with this generation, and shall condemn it: for they repented at the preaching of Jonas; and, behold, a greater than Jonas is here."

> *"Thou art fairer than the children of men; grace is poured into thy lips."*
> —Ps. xlv. 2.

SUCH is the practical application which the Saviour Himself made of the singular incidents that have been engaging our attention. And it forms a striking instance of the duty of thoughtfully applying to our own case those things which were written of old, and which an apostle declares were " written for our admonition on whom the ends of the world are come " (1 Cor. x. 11). But it constitutes a still more imposing allusion to the great day of universal judgment, and reminds us how, not only all generations of men shall stand there face to face with God, but the character and doings of different generations, separated by wide gulfs in time, may have mutual bearings on each other, most intimate, and wonderful, and unexpected.

That the men of Nineveh, who had all disappeared from among the living more than eight hundred years before the day of Christ, should confront the very generation to whom the Saviour personally ministered in the days of His flesh, and should reflect light upon the character and destiny of that sinful generation, is surely a very extraordinary and solemnising thought; and a thought that is fitted to lead to many a train of singular and impressive meditation.   When we shall all stand in that most solemn assemblage;—when the whole race of man, from Adam to the youngest of the latest generation, shall appear in one vast body before the judgment-seat of Christ;—oh, what mutual relations will be found subsisting between individuals or communities that had never even seen each other in the flesh! Even among those who may have been contemporaneous, what strange bearings on each other's spiritual interests and eternal destinies will be disclosed!   How terrible a thought is it, for instance, that Christ's redeemed people may there meet with some on the left hand of the Judge to whose impenitence and consequent perdition, they may have been instrumental in ministering by their negligence, supineness, infirmities, or more easily besetting sins!   Alas! how many have been confirmed in their hatred to religion by the more obvious defects and blemishes in the character and conduct of religion's true friends!   And what child of

God can ever contemplate that judgment-seat without the agonising fear, that there may be present there, as heirs of wrath, some with whom he companied in the days of his ungodliness, and whom he contributed thereby in no small degree to harden,—and some whom, in the subsequent years of a true walk with God, he may have, even then also, done not a little by levity of intercourse or worldliness of spirit, or even by his falls or backsliding, to confirm in their dislike of Christianity. Oh, what disclosures must then be made as to the bearing of our lives and conduct upon the eternal interests and destinies of our fellow-men,—and of theirs on ours! If generations so far apart as those two of which the text speaks are seen on that day coming into a relation so singular, as that the " men of Nineveh shall rise up " with the men of Christ's day " and condemn them," how much more complicated, and amazing must many of those relations be in which individuals and communities much more closely interconnected shall stand one towards another! How glorious will the one entire process of the world's moral government and history then appear! How replete with evidence of God's glorious attributes! And if the brilliant shining of the sun at noon-day is a demonstration of our Creator's mighty power, how unspeakably more fully will that dispensation of judgment—that final disclosure and reckoning, that consummation of all things—bear on the face of it the vindication of the perfect rectitude, and profound wisdom, and magnificent unity with which the moral administration of this strange world's history had from first to last been conducted! It will be from the concurrence of over-whelming evidence that the saints will then enter into the exclamations of adoring wonder :—" Oh the depth of the riches both of the wisdom and knowledge of God! how unsearchable are his judgments, and his ways past finding out!" "And they sing the song of Moses the servant of God, and the song of the Lamb, saying, Great and marvellous are thy works, Lord God Almighty; just and true are thy ways, thou King of saints. Who shall not fear thee, O Lord, and glorify thy name? for thou only art holy: for all nations shall come and worship before thee; for thy judgments are made manifest" (Rom. xi. 33; Rev. xv. 3, 4).

But to return. On that great and awful day, amidst the irresistible. blaze of light that shall reveal the secrets of all hearts, among millions of amazing dis-closures, *this*, our Lord tells us, shall be a very patent and simple one :—" The men of Nineveh shall rise up in judgment with this generation, and shall condemn it : because they repented at the preaching of Jonas ; and behold, a greater than Jonas is here."

I. Jesus is greater than Jonah in the greatness of His *Person ;* and this consideration attaches a weight to His ministry incalculably greater than any belong-ing to that of Jonah.

The occasion which God took to call the men of Nineveh to repentance was one of those " sundry

times," and the singular commission given to Jonah,
one of "divers ways," in which "God spake" of
old to the ancient world "by the prophets." But He
"hath in these last days spoken unto us by His Son,
whom He hath appointed heir of all things, by whom
also He made the worlds" (Heb. i. 1). These are
the well remembered expressions with which Paul
commences that marvellous Epistle to the Hebrews, in
which the transition from the Old to the New Testament economy is so specially explained, authorised, and
vindicated ; and in which he lays the foundation of
his argument for the superiority and perfection of the
new economy, by referring to the fact that it was
initiated by the eternal Son of God in person, and
had thereby an honour conferred upon it incalculably
transcending all that had gone before. In the course
of his argument, and in his second chapter, he makes
special practical use in enforcing duty, of the fact that
these things "at the first began to be spoken of the
Lord;" and, in the third chapter, he expressly institutes
a comparison between Moses, the head, under God, of
the old dispensation, and Christ the eternal Son,—also
under God, who is all in all,—the head of the new. It
is precisely in substance and in spirit the argument of
our text. That argument implies, of course, that both
Jonah and Jesus were commissioned of God. Without
that, there could indeed be no comparison. It was in
both cases God's call that was delivered ; God's
message that was proclaimed ; the very preaching
which God commanded these respective preachers to

preach. They were both acting under authority ; and in
that respect the words uttered by Jonah were as much
Divine, and of Divine authority and infallibility, as the
words that were uttered by Jesus. But in the one case
the Godhead sent as its ambassador and envoy a mere
man ;—in the other, one of the three adorable, co-equal
persons of the Godhead. How glorious, therefore,
is the prophet of the new dispensation ! Hear how
His loyal and loving forerunner spake of Him : " He
must increase, but I must decrease ; He that cometh
from above is above all ; he that is of the earth is
earthly, and speaketh of the earth : He that cometh
from heaven is above all. And what He hath seen
and heard, that He testifieth " (John iii. 30, 31). Oh !
we shall never fathom the riches of love and glory,
implied in God giving His Son as His ambassador to
reveal His will, and call His strayed and alienated
children back to mercy and salvation. Most blessed
qualification for His office ! He is " the Only-begotten
which is in the bosom of the Father." Habakkuk would
get him to his post, his watch-tower, his high look-out ;
and wait for the message and the vision : " I will
stand upon my watch, and set me on my tower, and
will watch to see what He will say unto me." But
Christ's watch-tower,—Christ's post of observation for
learning the Father's will,—was the Father's very
bosom ! And what He hath seen and heard there,
that He testifieth. Yes ! the Father's bosom ! There
He hath ever dwelt without intermission. He was
in the bosom of the Father,—enjoying His un-

limited, absolutely unlimited confidence,—even while speaking with men upon the earth. Oh, how near Christ's hearers are to the bosom of the Father! How clearly open, in its infinite purity, and bliss, and love, the Father's bosom is, when the lips of Jesus speak! "Thou art fairer than the children of men; grace is poured into Thy lips,"—grace unalloyed, undeteriorated, straight from the Father's bosom;—" therefore God hath blessed thee for ever " (Ps. xlv. 2).

And when such a one speaks on earth personally by human lips, or by a written word, or by a preached gospel, not without the Holy Ghost sent down from heaven;—when such a one speaks on earth, —speaking forth from "the Father's bosom,"—and asks and entreats the long-alienated child to return and embrace the love, and joy, and protection, and purity of "the Father's bosom;" to leave behind, all that he cannot bring with him into "the Father's bosom,"—all the darkness which he cannot bring into the Father's light;—in a word, when such a one calls us to repentance, with what overwhelming urgency does the call come, and how great the guilt of rejecting it! If, at the preaching of a mere human being, the men of Nineveh repented, shall they not rise up in judgment against us, if we put away from us the preaching of Him who speaketh from "the Father's bosom?"

II. Christ is greater in *Office* than Jonah. The office, indeed, is in each case the same. But in the case of Jesus it is in the highest, the infinite degree.

All the prophets called unto repentance. It formed a leading portion of their duty. They denounced the anger of God upon the impenitent. In God's name they straitly commanded the people to repent; and they declared His readiness to forgive, as the greatest encouragement to repentance. But the commission which a prophet such as Jonah had, was but a very limited one. It was but a small number of his fellow-men that he could address, and a very much smaller number that he could expect to affect for good; it was but a small fragment of the truth of God he could be instrumental in disclosing; it was but a sectional, limited portion of the Church or world to which he could prophecy; and it was during but a very brief day that he could exercise his office. Christ, in *His* office, is the way, the truth, and the life; disclosing *all* the truth of God; officiating on behalf of the *whole* Church in *all* climes and ages, being from beginning to end the one *only* authoritative Teacher,—head of all other teachers, and source of all their illumination and knowledge. In Jonah, or in any mere human prophet, a *portion* of Divine wisdom and a *measure* of Divine words might dwell; but Jesus was *the* Wisdom of God and *the* Word of God. It was only on a very small portion of this world's ongoings that Jonah's preaching could directly exert any influence; but the whole history of the race, as affected by a revelation from heaven, is moulded by the prophetic office as wielded by Christ. Jonah and others, as servants in the house, brought now and then a fragmentary message from the Master and the Lord. Christ, as a Son over His own house, brought with Him the entire and exact transcript of all the Father's will. Yea, and He thus makes His people like Himself, not servants but sons, not servants but friends;—"Henceforth I call you not servants; for the servant knoweth not what his Lord doeth: but I have called you friends; for all things that I have heard of my Father I have made known unto you" (John xv. 15). In Him are hid all the treasures of wisdom and knowledge. With Him is the most perfect knowledge of the Father's affections, of every thought and purpose of the Father's heart. It is in rivulets of truth from His infinite intellect, as the very counterpart of the Father's intellect, that all communications to mere human prophets have flowed, as from an ocean full and overflowing as before. When He himself, therefore, deals with us; when, disdaining neither the nature nor the office of those by whom at sundry times and divers ways God spake unto the fathers, He comes forth Himself exercising the very original, the fulness, the transcendent perfection of the prophetic office;—surely the call which He delivers is infinitely urgent. And if the same call to repent has been delivered by a mere fellow-creature, and been respected and obeyed by the wicked community to whom it was addressed, shall not these men of Nineveh rise in the judgment against the men of gospel times, because they repented at the preaching of Jonah; and, behold, a greater than Jonah is among *us?*

III. But Christ is also greater than Jonah in respect of His *discharge* of the office. The Old Testament made men prophets which had infirmity; but the gospel age is inaugurated, and its ministrations carried forward by a Prophet who is infinitely perfect, infallible, unchangeable; in whom is light and no darkness at all; in whom is infinite store of truth and grace. For " the word was made flesh, and we beheld His glory; the glory as of the Only-begotten of the Father, full of grace and truth." Other prophets were liable to err, and did err. Elias was a man of like passions with ourselves. Behold of this Jonah; how grievously he erred! He fled from the presence of the Lord, refusing His commission to Nineveh. The "greater than Jonah " says, " Lo, I come : in the volume of the book it is written of me, I delight to do thy will, O my God." When the Lord spared Nineveh it displeased Jonah. Did ever any of the Father's doings displease Jesus? When the Father assigned to Him a houseless, homeless life ;—when for the birds of the air the Father appointed nests, and resting-places for the foxes; but appointed for His own Son that He should not have where to lay His head ;—did it displease Jesus? When His weary pilgrimage drew towards a close, and instead of His prospects clearing like the path of the just shining more and more unto the perfect day, they darkened more and more as the Just One suffered for the unjust, till, in the end, all accumulations of evil fell upon Him, saving and alone the one evil that never was but infinitely far from Him,—personal sin ;—when

His Father withdrew from Him the comfortable light
of His favour, and put on towards Him all the aspect
of an angry judge armed with Almighty wrath to
avenge the controversy which Jesus intervened to clear
away, and to exact the ransom which Jesus undertook
to pay, and uphold the offended justice which Jesus interposed to appease;—when He had to exclaim in amazement and anguish, "My God, why hast Thou forsaken
me?"—did this on His Father's part displease Jesus?
And oh! when His Father's mercy takes effect, and
threatened wrath is removed from any miserable soul;
when that soul, in its deep penitence,—the singular and
blissful element of heaven's sweetest joy being poured
into the cup of godly sorrow,—exclaims, "I will praise
thee, O Lord, for, though thou wast angry with me,
thine anger is turned away;"—is Jesus *then*, like
Jonah, displeased, disappointed, angry unto death?
What answer need we give? Oh! if even in the travail
of His soul and His exceeding sorrow He was not displeased; how when "He seeth of the travail of His soul
and is satisfied"? Displeased? Displeasure? Nay,
"the *pleasure* of the Lord doth prosper in His hand."

Were it not well that we sometimes meditated with
delight on the fact that Christ's discharge of office is
stained with no blemish; invalidated by no imperfection; incapable of any deduction from its infinite
excellence; standing alone in matchless, and incom-
parable, and unsullied glory? There is no want; there
is no excess; there is no defect; there is no spot, nor
wrinkle, nor any such thing in this "greater than Jonah,"

who now calls us to repentance.   And if we turn a deaf
ear to Him, how powerful must be the condemnation
which the men of Nineveh shall rise up to pronounce
upon us in the judgment!

IV. Jesus is greater than Jonah in that He has, in
one sense, a great *right* to call us to repentance.   There
is a sense in which the right of Jonah and of Jesus
were the same; grounded alike on the communications
given them respectively by the Lord to deliver.   But
personally, on His own account, Jesus has a claim upon
us, and a personal right to summon us peremptorily to
repent.   As representing the Godhead, Himself very
God, He may say unto us : "Against me, me only,
have ye sinned, and done evil in my sight, that I might
be just in judging and clear in speaking."   It is against
me that all your enmity and rebellion have been directed.
Against the Godhead, in my person, have ye lifted up
the hand.   As very God, and as God's ambassador,
alike in my own and in my Father's name, I charge
you with the guilt of rebellion : and I summon you
now to repent, and return, and surrender to God,—to
me, to my Father by me.   Jonah had no personal quarrel
with the Ninevites, and no personal claim upon them.
He might say of them as Paul said of his Galatian
converts : "Ye have not injured me at all."   But in
this respect a greater than Jonah is here ;—greater in the
relation in which He stands to us as entitled to all our
service, gratitude, love, and admiration; and entitled
to complain when these in any measure are withheld, or

given Him in less than absolute perfection; and to call
for satisfaction and redress. *His* has all the urgency
and force of a personal, a directly and intensely personal matter. He is Himself the representative of the
offended Godhead. He is Himself possessor of the
nature and substance of that offended Godhead. When
He calls to repentance, there cannot be a greater. With
infinite authority, and not as the scribes, must He
speak. We cannot adjourn the matter from Him, or
appeal it to another more closely implicated in it.
To Himself we are responsible; and the case cannot be
more accurately or more powerfully put to us than by
Him. If *His* call to repent is refused, our last prospect
or possibility is thrown away. It is amazing that Godhead should have delegated to none less than God, in
the person of the Son, the office of being a herald and
ambassador to proclaim peace, and thereon to insist
upon repentance. And it is altogether beyond eternal
admiration that when God in His absolute glory could
hold converse with no rebelling creature, and yet it was
desired to send to rebels an embassy of reconciliation
and a call to repent, Godhead should still have been
sent—the Only-begotten, dwelling in the bosom of the
Father—to press and secure the rights of His Father,
which in the unity of the Godhead are also His own.
There is no lowering, by transmission to a stranger, of
the authority with which the embassy and call are
clothed. There is no deteriorating of the majesty and
claims of the offended Sovereign by another party
foreign to the offence, and not affected by it, being

called in to fulfil the service of demanding or achieving
redress.   All men shall honour the Son even as they
honour the Father: I have set my King upon my holy
hill of Zion : kiss the Son, lest He be angry, and ye
perish from the way, when once His wrath is kindled
but a little.   With Him we have to do.   There is
none higher with whom we can have to do.   Assuredly,
in this respect, " a greater than Jonas is here ; "—in respect, namely, of His greater right to call to repentance.

V. While in His Godhead He is equal with the
Father, and therefore supreme in authority, He is, as
man, greater than Jonah, in that He has an *experience* of
His own with which to enforce His message, greater,
unspeakably, than Jonah had.   " As Jonah was three
days and three nights in the whale's belly, so was the
Son of man three days and three nights in the heart of
the earth."   Beyond question, Jonah informed the Ninevites of his own terrible experience of the anger of God.
In that experience,—in that altogether matchless history,—Jonah was a sign unto the Ninevites.   He could
enforce the certainty of judgment on transgression, by
quoting the things that had befallen himself; and the
greatness of that calamity, and the manifest evidence of
the immediate hand of God in it, could not fail to strike
terror into the hearts of the men of Nineveh, and convince them that the message of such a God would be
executed relentlessly and to the full.   They would, in
fact, argue that if these things were done to a prophet
of His own for one act of disobedience, what would

befall those who lived in perpetual and perfect rebellion? They would argue on the principle, "If these things be done in the green tree, what shall be done in the dry? If judgment begin at the house of God, what shall the end be of them that obey not God at all?" (Luke xxiii. 31; 1 Pet. iv. 17). Jonah, escaped from the deep and from the jaws of death, was to the men of Nineveh a sign of the certainty and terrors of the Lord's vengeance on sin.

Behold, a greater than Jonah is here! Jesus was three days and three nights in the heart of the earth. Jonah died and rose again in a figure, a metaphor; a figure carrying in it terrible reality, but stopping short of actual death. Jesus died and rose again. He suffered, the just for the unjust. In the room of transgressors He stood; in the name, and as bearing the persons, of transgressors He was judged, condemned, avenged upon in all the completeness and terrors of the wages of sin which is death, the wrath and curse of the Lord God Almighty. The arrows of Jehovah pierced Him: the curse of the Eternal Ruler's broken law descended on Him: He tasted the bitterness, yea, the sting, of death: His soul was exceeding sorrowful: He poured out His soul unto death. He "knoweth the power of God's wrath" unto the uttermost. And if the experience of Jonah was a sign and an enforcement conjoined with his message — oh, with what overwhelming urgency may Jesus refer to His experience! My reader, when Jesus counsels you to repent and flee from the wrath to come, the exhortation comes from

One—if we may reverently use, as we may with intense truth use, the saying—comes from One who knows what He is speaking of. Yes: He knoweth that wrath. The tears He sheds over lost souls are prompted, in part, by personal knowledge of the wrath whereinto they are plunging themselves. The melting calls, " Turn ye, turn ye, why will ye die "—oh! they come from One who knoweth what that cursed death is from which He labours to win and woo you to His own love and salvation. Greater in experience of the evils from which He desires to save you, there is none than this Saviour himself. Of all terrors and agonies, saving that alone of a self-accusing conscience, Jesus had, of all beings in the universe, the deepest and most dread experience. Great as was the anguish of Jonah,—as in the very " belly of hell," " cast out of God's sight "— behold, a greater than Jonah is here ;—greater in respect of the same endurances in infinitely higher degree, as pursued by the angry justice of God, avenged upon for God's quarrel with transgression. Study the psalms that open up to us the exercises of our Saviour's agonised soul in suffering for sins not His own. Bear in mind continually, it is this Sufferer that pleads with you to flee from the strokes of that sword of justice whose burning edge pierced keen to the dividing of His soul and spirit, and of the joints and marrow. It is He who bore the mighty load, that implores you not to rest an hour under the weight of your Creator's curse. It is He who drank the cup of trembling and of death to the dregs, that implores you to prefer the cup of blessing and salvation. Let your soul be quiet at His call. Let your ear incline at His voice; and sweetly and mournfully and most imploringly trembling through all its accents you shall hear an element of tenderest feeling, sighing after you lovingly and sorrowfully,—as of One who remembers the wormwood and the gall, the furnace and the sword, the clouded face of Jehovah, and the unspeakable sting of death, and fain would save you from them all, would you only give Him true belief, and turn even now that you may live.

VI. A greater than Jonah is here, in that He hath greater *power* than Jonah. Jonah may denounce wrath; but Jesus can *give* repentance. He hath the hearts of all in His keeping. He hath the fulness of the Spirit. He is exalted a Prince and a Saviour to give repentance to Israel and the remission of sins. Jonah may denounce the vengeance due to sin; but the Son of man hath power on earth to forgive sin. How unspeakably greater, then, is Jesus as a herald and ambassador to call men to repentance! How unspeakably more worthy of our believing and obedient reception! It may be a grace hard to flesh and blood, a grace altogether supernatural, to which He summons us, when He calls us to repent; to renounce our old nature, and put on another and a new one. But however difficult, however contrary to nature and above nature it may be, we are summoned to it by One greater than Jonah; by One so great by nature as to be able to give, and so great by office as to be commissioned and appointed to give, the very grace which He requires us to exercise. If you tell me merely that a Divine messenger summons me to lay aside all my old motives and principles of action, and aims and objects in life, and to begin and act truly and simply on the singular principles of really doing everything to promote the glory of God, and of consulting in everything the will of God, and framing my life not at all on my wishes but on God's will; you assign me a work perfectly hopeless, so far as any strength of mine for accomplishing it is concerned. I either do not see the greatness of this moral change —so great that greater could not be ;—or in seeing it, I at once despair of achieving it myself. " Who can bring a clean thing out of an unclean?" But tell me that "the Son," who summons me to be renewed in the spirit of my mind, " quickeneth whom He will; " hath the hearts of all in His keeping; and is only acting in His office when He giveth repentance and remission of sins ;—tell me that He is calling me to receive these very gifts from himself, and assuring me that if I only knew His nature and His love, I would not hesitate to ask, and asking would receive ; even as He said, " If thou knewest the gift of God, and who it is that saith unto thee, Give me to drink, thou wouldst have asked of Him, and He would have given thee living water ; "—tell me this ; and, combining the knowledge of my powerlessness with some insight into His power to work repentance in my heart, I am directed, urged, hemmed in, and shut up to Christ as my Royal Priest—effectually conferring on me the gracious and perfect forgiveness of sins, and the sin-hating, mourning, contrite, believing heart to receive all this mercy freely. Yes: a greater, verily, than Jonah is here. Paul may plant and Apollos may water; but God only giveth the increase. The treasure is in earthen vessels; but the excellency of the power is of God. And this " greater than Jonas " is " God—manifest in the flesh," and the Surety of an irrefragable covenant,—a covenant in which " grace reigns," and in which all that law demands is by grace supplied.

Had Nineveh rejected Jonah, they might still have said, It was merely a crier of danger that we put away from us. But he that rejecteth Jesus, rejecteth One that can *give* repentance and forgiveness of sins, and that can say :—" They shall look on me whom they have pierced, and shall mourn ; "—" Come unto me, all ye that labour and are heavy laden, and I will give you rest ; "—" If any man thirst, let him come unto me and drink: out of his belly shall flow rivers of living water."

Thou art the King of glory, O Christ! Grace is poured into Thy lips !

XXI

NEW TESTAMENT COMMENTARIES : NO. III

THE SIGN

JONAH i. 17 ; iii. 10

(MATT. xvi. 1-4 ; LUKE xi. 14-36 ; MATT. xii. 38-41)

LUKE xi. 29.—"This is an evil generation : they seek a sign ; and there shall no sign be given it, but the sign of Jonas the prophet."

LUKE ii. 12.—"And this shall be a sign unto you : Ye shall find the babe wrapped in swaddling-clothes, lying in a manger."

> "*What sign showest thou unto us, seeing that thou doest these things? Jesus answered and said unto them, Destroy this temple, and in three days I will raise it up.*"—JOHN ii. 18, 19.
>
> "*As Jonas was a sign unto the Ninevites, so shall the Son of man be to this generation.*"—LUKE xi. 30.
>
> "*For the Jews require a sign, and the Greeks seek after wisdom : but we preached Christ crucified . . . . the power of God, and the wisdom of God.*"—1 COR. i. 22, 24.

IN the days of His flesh, and in the course of His personal ministry, our Lord was pleased to make repeated comments on the history of Jonah. Nor is it unworthy of the King of Zion to assume towards the Church the position of a Commentator on Holy Scripture. He is but commenting on the record of His own earlier administration;—the *record* His own also, not less than the administration is. In virtue of the Plenary Inspiration of Scripture, it is—the Author, Commentator on Himself. *

In the present instance, with the Great Teacher himself for our Commentator, we find that the history of Jonah, when brought into juxtaposition with that of Jesus, affords a threefold topic. First, it presents for our consideration a type ; secondly, a parallel ; thirdly, a sign. And these three lines of thought exhaust our Lord's observations on the subject.

These three views of the same topic are apt to be indiscriminately massed up in one. The distinct ideas suggested by each are then lost sight of; the type, the parallel, the sign are all blended into one vague and indeterminate notion of some mere resemblance ; and even that resemblance is found to fade away into the shallow little element of the time being the same in both—the three days and the three nights. In order to avoid this, we have been careful to call attention in former chapters, *first*, to the consideration of the type, as set forth in the saying,—" As Jonas was three days and three nights in the whale's belly, so shall the Son of man be three days and three nights in the heart of the earth;" and, *secondly*, to the consideration of the parallel or comparison, turning as it does so unspeakably

* For an argument, in this line of thought, on behalf of Inspiration, I may be permitted to refer to "Christ's Presence in the Gospel History," pp. 124–146.

in favour of Jesus,—" The men of Nineveh repented at the preaching of Jonas; and, behold, a greater than Jonas is here." To complete our examination of what Christ's commentary suggests, we have now, *in the third place,* to consider Jonah as a sign.

That these are three distinct ideas, fitly designated by the expressions we have used,—the type, the parallel, the sign,—will be evident from considering the specific differences among the three passages from the Gospels which embody these Divine commentaries. For, very singularly, one of them presents the relation between Jonah and Jesus solely with reference to the sign; another presents it with reference to the sign and the parallel; the third brings into view all the three aspects—first the sign, then the parallel, and then the type.

1. Thus, to take them in the order indicated. In the sixteenth chapter of Matthew, at the beginning, we have the subject set before us in its briefest form. To the hypocritical demand for a sign, Jesus has nothing to say except in this curt, and, by itself alone, somewhat oracular and mysterious answer—" A wicked and adulterous generation seeketh after a sign; and there shall no sign be given to it, but the sign of the prophet Jonas. And He left them and departed."

Here Jesus draws no parallel between Jonah and Himself. He gives no hint that Jonah was a type of Himself. He confines Himself rigorously to the solitary thought of Jonah as a sign; and that without even indicating how this sign would be repeated, or how He

Himself would resemble Jonah sufficiently to be to them a repetition of the sign. Nay; He institutes, so far as this discourse goes;—and it must be held to have an intelligible and complete meaning by itself;—He really institutes no resemblance at all between Himself and Jonah; neither the more general resemblance of parallelism, nor the more specific and peculiar resemblance of type. He holds out no resemblance whatever. It is simply and solely the idea of the sign, whatever that may be, which in this passage the Saviour fastens on and confines Himself to. "There shall no sign be given to it, but the sign of the prophet Jonas." This is the whole statement; and having made it, "He left them and departed."

2. The passage in Luke is more full and explicit. Starting with the idea of the sign, as they all do,—for all Christ's allusions to Jonah are in reference to the demand for a sign,—it introduces the parallel also;— "And when the people were gathered thick together, He began to say, This is an evil generation: they seek a sign; and there shall no sign be given it, but the sign of Jonas the prophet. For as Jonas was a sign unto the Ninevites, so shall also the Son of man be to this generation. . . . The men of Nineveh shall rise up in the judgment with this generation, and shall condemn it: for they repented at the preaching of Jonas; and, behold, a greater than Jonas is here." Manifestly this gives a fuller insight into Christ's views of His relation to Jonah. We have here one or two particulars in addition to those afforded by the former passage.

For, first of all, we have it distinctly stated that the sign of the prophet Jonah which was to be given to that generation was a repetition in the person of Jesus of what had been given to the Ninevites in the person of Jonah. Suppose the only utterance Christ had ever made on this subject were the brief, mysterious one in the sixteenth chapter of Matthew,—"There shall no sign be given them, but the sign of the prophet Jonas;"—we must have been left comparatively in the dark as to what that sign, in the case of the Jews, could mean, or how it could be given to them. In this second passage, however, by introducing the parallel, Jesus explains the mystery. He tells us that He himself will be to that generation precisely such a sign as Jonas was to the Ninevites; that there shall be between Himself and this prophet of the olden dispensation such a resemblance or analogy, that in Him, and in His relation to that generation, the sign of Jonah shall be substantially transacted over again,—with this difference, that the repetition shall be something far more complete and wonderful than the old original, insomuch that "the men of Nineveh shall rise up in the judgment with this generation, and shall condemn it: for they repented at the preaching of Jonas; and, behold, a greater than Jonas is here."

3. But we have the most complete view of the matter in the twelfth chapter of Matthew, from the 38th verse. Here, as in the former passages, the idea of the SIGN is prominent:—Verse 39th: "An evil and adulterous generation seeketh after a sign; and there shall no

sign be given to it, but the sign of the prophet Jonas."
In verse 41st the PARALLEL is introduced as before:—
" The men of Nineveh shall rise in judgment with this
generation, and shall condemn it : because they repented
at the preaching of Jonas ; and, behold, a greater than
Jonas is here." But in verse 40th, the particular line
of parallelism, in respect of which Jonah was a TYPE of
Jesus, is specified : " For as Jonas was three days and
three nights in the whale's belly : so shall the Son of
man be three days and three nights in the heart of the
earth." Hence the three are bound together in the
singular relation which is expressed in the following
proposition : The prophet Jonah is a *sign*, in virtue of
that particular element in the *parallel* which constitutes
the *type*.

There is a parallel; there is a type; there is a
sign. A certain particular in the parallel is more than
a parallel : it is a type. And in virtue of that particular, Jonah is a sign. So closely are the three
connected.

Yet they are distinct. A type is something more
specific than a parallel. Many circumstances in the
life of every believer are parallel to corresponding circumstances in the life of every other believer; yet the
one series are not types of the other. A type is an
event or ordinance in one sphere, analogous to a corresponding event or ordinance in a higher sphere; as, for
instance, the ordinance of the brazen serpent,—an instrument or institution of healing in the lower sphere of
bodily disease, typical of Christ crucified, God's ordi-

nance in the sphere of the spiritual and eternal for healing the disease of sin. Thus the consignment of Jonah to death, and his subsequent deliverance, constitute a type of atonement by death and of justification in risen life; a type, in short, of Christ's death and resurrection. It is not a mere parallel or resemblance that is pointed out between two facts in history; it is a type,—a typical illustration and confirming seal of certain divine truths and doctrines,—when it is said, " As Jonas was three days and three nights in the whale's belly, so shall the Son of man be three days and three nights in the heart of the earth." A type is far more than a parallel.

A sign, again, is distinct from both.

Part First

THE SIGN ;—THE GENERAL PRINCIPLE

" What sign showest thou unto us, seeing thou doest these things? Jesus answered and said unto them, Destroy this temple, and in three days I will raise it up." —JOHN ii. 18, 19.

A SIGN is an evidence. It is a reason, or call, or ground for faith,—for believing. Thus the Apostle says ;—"Tongues are for a sign, not to them that believe, but to them that believe not." As a sign, they are unnecessary and superfluous to those who believe already: it is to unbelievers that they are capable of being a sign ; warranting them to believe ; requiring them to believe.

There are two frames of mind in which a sign may be demanded or desiderated. It may be demanded as a reason for believing; or the demand may be made as a pretext to avoid belief. You may ask for a sign, as a help to faith. You may ask a sign, to get an excuse for unbelief.

The two frames of mind thus indicated are wide as the poles asunder; and they might be contrasted very sharply on many other points than the one of asking a sign. But let us confine our attention to this one.

The Scribes and Pharisees pressed on Jesus to give them a sign. That they did not wish to believe on Him, but to plead that they were excusable in not believing, is evident. They had seen signs enough already to have constrained them, in the humble spirit of Nicodemus, to say;—"Rabbi, we know that thou art a teacher come from God: for no man can do these miracles that thou doest, except God were with him." But, disliking the righteousness of His character, and the holy, reformatory power of His doctrine and ministry, their desire was, not to acknowledge, but to stave off the conviction and acknowledgment of His Messiahship. Hence, they pretended to suspend their faith on evidences which they still desiderated and craved; and they made demands which, had they been granted, they would have treated precisely as they had treated those they had got already; while, on the other hand, the refusal of them they were pre-resolved to point to, as justifying their continued unbelief. Now God can, with infinitely perfect accuracy and righteousness, deal with this perverse frame of mind; and in doing so He can illustrate that solemn two-edged word of the Spirit;—" With an upright man thou wilt show thyself upright; with the froward, thou wilt show thyself froward." He can bring to bear upon men's minds a style of dispensation which, on the supposition of their uprightness of purpose, shall carry in it nothing but what is beneficial and comfortable, but which, on the supposition of their obliquity and dishonesty, shall at once unmask and punish them. So did Jesus deal with the deceitful demand for a sign.

Consider, for instance, how this comes out on the earliest occasion on which the demand was made (John ii. 14). As one having authority Jesus had dealt with the Temple as His Father's house; asserted His right to reform and purify it; driven out the money-changers, and overthrown their tables. Immediately the Jews demanded a proof of His right—an evidence of His having this authority. "Then answered the Jews and said unto him, What sign showest thou unto us, seeing that thou doest these things?" Mark our Lord's singular answer. "Jesus answered and said unto them, Destroy this temple, and in three days I will raise it up." We know that He spake of the temple of His body;—that body in which, being His own body, the fulness of the Godhead dwelt personally; —that body of which the tabernacle or the temple was a symbol or type;—that body which the Holy Ghost, speaking expressly, hath called " a greater and more perfect tabernacle not made with hands " (Heb. ix. 2).

We know also that the temple on Mount Moriah and the temple of our Lord's body stood so related to each other—the type and antitype, the sign and thing signified—that the Jews could not destroy the one without destroying the other also; that when they destroyed,—that is, put to death,—the temple of His body, they in point of fact signed the warrant for the destruction of their own temple and all its associated polity. For in rending the veil of the one temple, that is to say His flesh, they tore the veil of their own temple from top to bottom; and, because of their iniquity in crucifying the Lord of glory, the time came swiftly when not one stone of that building was left upon another. Farther: we know that the temple of Christ's body was raised up again in three days; and we also know that, by another bond between type and antitype in this matter,—namely, that subsisting between the temple of old and the spiritual Church of God, which is the temple of the Spirit,—the resurrection of Christ's body was the resurrection virtually in New Testament form of that very temple, spiritually and typically considered, whose doom the death of Christ's body sealed. All giving most singular depth of meaning to His utterance: "Destroy this temple, and in three days I will raise it up." For, as it refers necessarily, by reason of the typical bond, to the literal temple of Jerusalem, virtually informing the Jews, if they were able to hear it, that their destroying of His body would overthrow their own temple and the whole ritual and polity which had their seat and centre there;

so, by another typical bond, it equally informed them that by His resurrection their temple and polity would be raised from the dead,—" I will raise up again the tabernacle of David which is fallen down,"—though it would rise anew in more glorious form, in more spiritual aspect, in fact, in the superior grandeur of resurrection : for here one may almost apply the principle, " There is a natural body, and there is a spiritual body," the resurrection body, namely ; so there is a natural temple, and there is a spiritual temple and Gospel Church— even a resurrection one, the tabernacle of David, fallen down when David's Lord was slain, but raised in resurrection-spirituality when David's Son rose from the dead. All this, at least, is embraced in our Lord's most wonderful and enigmatic, but not misleading, answer to the demand for a sign. And all this depth and variety of meaning in it tended to make it ulti- mately, to the upright and pure-hearted disciples, an evidence most largely instructive—a sign most power- fully confirmatory.

But mark how it acted on the froward, and unmasked their frowardness,—how it brought to light their hypo- crisy and hollowness. They had asked a sign—a con- vincing token and proof of the Divine authority of this great Reformer. They of course desiderated a miracu- lous one,—one transcending man's power to give, and thereby proving God's presence when given. Such a feature must be an essential in the kind of sign which they have professed their anxiety to obtain. What- ever other features may belong to it, this at least must

not be wanting. This is the one indispensable characteristic of what they have expressed their desire to be
furnished with, and which they have thereby declared
themselves prepared to welcome. Could their utter
falseness be made more glaring, if this be found to be
the first, and indeed the only, feature in the proffered sign
which, instead of welcoming, they quarrel with? Yet
even to this extent they are snared in the meshes of
their own hypocrisy. "Then said they, Forty and six
years was this temple in building, and wilt thou rear it
up in three days?" This is what they take offence at
in the sign proposed: 'Wilt thou rear up, in three
days, what took forty and six years to build?' Had
He professed nothing more than power to raise it up
again in forty and six years, as at the first, the point
of their scoffing answer is gone—their objection taken
away. But then where were the value of such a *sign?*
The very force of the sign—even in their own view of
it—consisted in the brevity of the time; in the element
of miracle; in the in-bringing of the Divine hand;—the
very thing which they professed to desire; the solitary
thing also they object to, when they get it. So remorselessly, by Christ's wise dealing with them, are they
compelled to disclose their frowardness!

They acted in the same spirit, and were dealt with in
the same manner, when, on repeating their demand at
subsequent periods of His ministry, Jesus uniformly re-
mitted them to substantially the self-same sign—"the
sign of the prophet Jonah."

Part Second

THE SIGN—OF THE PROPHET JONAH

"As Jonas was a sign unto the Ninevites, so shall also the Son of man be to this generation."—LUKE xi. 30.

WHAT may " the sign of the prophet Jonah " import?

I. Let us take it, first of all, as set forth in its most enigmatical form in the discourse recorded in the sixteenth chapter of Matthew. Here Jesus draws no *parallel* between Himself and Jonah; and makes no allusion to the *type* of the burial and resurrection. Isolated, therefore, from all parallelism and from all typical idea, the sign must have in it meaning and force considered as by itself alone. We are bound to investigate its import, in the first instance, apart from the light thrown upon it by subsequent and additional illustration. Resigning, then, in the meantime, the aid of Christ's fuller explanations; what design and force may we perceive, in His thus nakedly propounding on this occasion the sign of the prophet Jonah?

We may see that it rebukes the spirit in which a sign was demanded.

Ye seek a proof of my claims. But ye do so, not in order that ye may intelligently, honestly yield to them, but that ye may, if possible, escape from doing so. Ye seek a sign, ye crave an evidence; not in the spirit of true humility; not even in the spirit of honourable science; not on the footstool of lowly inquiry; not even on the seat of manly wisdom;—but as sitting proudly, and sneering, on the judge's bench. Ye bring my claims before you,—to your bar; as if they must be greatly dependent on your decision; as if they and I were humble suitors for your valuable esteem, your indispensable support. And, while seated thus on the bench of judgment, you demand a sign. I give you—

(1.) A sign that drives you from the judgment-bench; that strips you of the affected dignity of judges, and panels you as miserable criminals at the bar. I give you " the sign of the prophet Jonah,"—the strict and terrible denunciator, the unwilling but enforced denunciator, of the wrath of God. I give you the sign of him who cried,—" Forty days, and Nineveh shall be destroyed; "—and besides this he cried nothing more. Ye forget that the wrath of God is revealed from heaven against all unrighteousness of men; and that ye are yourselves perishing in your iniquities beneath the anger of the Most High. Ye dally and tamper with my claims and protestations as a Saviour, as if ye yourselves did not need to be saved; as if ye were not lost souls yourselves, but sitting with as much ease as if ye were in heaven, while sneering with as much scorn as if ye were from hell. Ye deal with my pretensions as conceited critics, not as criminals condemned; and ye ask a sign. Be it so. I give you the sign of the one only minister of God into whose mouth was put nothing but the language of wrath; and I do so if by any means I may startle you into a better spirit,—the only spirit in which you could be capable of understanding the salvation of heaven. I give you,—ye proud, ye self-righteous hypocrites,—I give you a sign that may well scatter your lofty thoughts of yourselves, and bring down your high looks. I give you the sign of him whose preaching clothed proud Nineveh in sackcloth, and brought its high-minded king from his throne to the dust. And I tell you that no sign but this is suitable for you. Nay, more;—

(2.) It is more suitable to you than it was to them. "Ye are an evil and adulterous generation;" —an evil generation, as Nineveh was; but an adulterous, as Nineveh could not be. Ye were a people to your God,—bound to Him in a marriage covenant, and the God of Israel, your Maker, was your Husband. Ye have violated the marriage bond—the covenant of your God. Ye have gone and served your Husband's foes, and thwarted your Husband's will. Yet ye have greatly vaunted your union with Him. Ye have claimed it, when it served your purpose; and renounced it, when that pleased your pleasure. Ye have proudly claimed the name of Israel, and proudly scorned the heathen. But alike in that proud claim and in that proud scorn, ye have proved that ye are not Israelites indeed; nay, that ye are an adulterous people ; that ye are aliens from the true commonwealth of Israel— aliens, outcasts, enemies, heathen in your hearts.   I give you a sign at your demand; but I give you the sign of the only prophet to the aliens, the outcasts, the uncircumcised whom ye hate. It is *that* that makes it so intensely suitable to you. I give you the sign of the prophet Jonah,—God's ambassador to heathendom; for yours, even in Immanuel's land, is the spirit of heathendom; yea, a spirit worse than that of the uncircumcised and the unclean. And,—

(3.) Say not,—you dare not say,—that in this I am "your enemy, because I tell you the truth." In vain will you charge me herein with hatred to my own countrymen,—with malice or malignity towards you. It is a small thing that I be judged of your judgment; and my heart ye are incapable of reading. But what I thus do, in giving you the sign of Jonah—the denunciator of wrath to the heathen,—can pain you, can cut you to the quick, can injure you, *only* if ye are the proud, the evil and adulterous generation that I say. And then, rigorous and relentless as my word,—my sign,—to you in that case must be, it will, for that very reason, in that same proportion, be righteous and brightly unobjectionable, as in a flood of resistless light.

But is there one soul among you startled by the sign of the prophet Jonah; startled as Nineveh was; humbled; descending from the throne to the dust,—from the proud seat of judge or critic on the bench to the bar of self-condemnation, and of the criminal confessed? O heavy laden one! I give to thee the sign of the prophet Jonah; the sign of him under whose ministry—NO SOUL IN REPENTING NINEVEH PERISHED: NEITHER ASSUREDLY SHALL THINE! "HIM THAT COMETH TO ME I WILL IN NO WISE CAST OUT."

So gloriously triumphant in its righteousness, throned high above all objection; yea, so gloriously triumphant in its graciousness, when rightly read, is the sign given by Jesus : merciful unto the merciful; froward, only to the froward.

II. Taking now the passage in Luke xi. 29, we have the same general statement :—" There shall no sign be given them, but the sign of the prophet Jonas." But an explanation is now added :—" For as Jonas was a sign unto the Ninevites, so shall the Son of man be to this generation." What additional light does this throw on the theme in hand, on the import of the sign of the prophet Jonah? Doubtless, when we draw for greater information on our third, and final, and fullest passage, we shall see that it is chiefly in respect of His being three days and three nights in the heart of the earth, that the Son of man resembles the son of Amittai in being a sign. That particular consideration, however, is not introduced here.   And it is again to be observed that the statement as given in Luke must be intelligible by itself,—capable of being interpreted and expounded without drawing on information afforded by another evangelist.   What meaning would the readers of this one gospel—those who had no access to that of Matthew—attach, and be warranted in attaching, to the simple statement, " As Jonas was a sign unto the Ninevites, so shall the Son of man be to this generation " ?

The answer is not difficult.   They would, at least, regard it as affirming that the Son of man *Himself* is the sign spoken of: not something He might do ; some miracle He might work ; some isolated part of His

ministry or labours;—but *Himself;* His person. You
seek a sign; the Son of man shall be a sign unto this
generation. I am myself the sign. Ye shall have no
other from me,—none beyond and besides myself.

There is a great and precious truth here. You seek
a proof and evidence of Christianity? You desiderate
convincing demonstration for the truth of the Christian
religion? The great leading sign or proof of Christianity is CHRIST. To the demand for a sign, a sign of the
gospel and glad tidings which are to all people, we give
the angelic song in reply: " This shall be the sign:
you shall find the babe in swaddling bands, and lying
in a manger."

Surely Christ's own person may be taken as the
strongest proof of His pretensions. His sinlessness,
His absolute faultlessness,—enemies being judges: His
whole bearing, so lofty and majestic, yet so meek and
mild: His companionableness with men, so intense; yet
His distinctness from all men, and His separation, so
complete: His righteousness so rigorous, yet never
verging on the ascetic: His loving-kindness so wonderful, yet never tinged with weakness or facility: His
entire uniqueness: His divine singularity: His authority and power of command; in calm supremacy throned
high over all men, while yet He mingled with all; the
servant of all; not ministered unto but come to minister:—Oh! can this generation avoid feeling that a
greater than Jonah is here? If ye want higher proof
than He himself constitutes, must ye not be blind? It
is not light you need, but eyes; not a new medium of

proof, but vision; not an outward sign, but inward spiritual perception. " An evil generation " verily it must be, that in the presence of the Son of man, " seeketh a sign." They proclaim thereby that they are evil. They prove thereby that they are blind.

Ye Scribes and Pharisees, hypocrites,—demanding a sign! Ye be blind leaders of the blind. The Son of man Himself is the clearest of signs; the brightest of lights: and yet ye perceive it not. I am come a light into the world, and he that followeth me shall not walk in darkness, but have the light of life: yet ye seek an evidence; a sign; a light, whereby you may perceive me! When darkness hath covered the earth and gross darkness the people, I am come, the Bright and Morning Star,—yea, the Sun of Righteousness, with healing in His wings;—and ye seek the kindling of a taper whereby ye may perceive me! It is not evidence you need; but vision:—not a sign to prove the light; but eyes to see it. Know, therefore, that for judgment am I come into this world; that they which see not might see, and they which see might be made blind. True, you may sneer still, and reply, " Are we blind also?" My answer is, "If ye were blind, ye should have no sin; but now ye say, We see; therefore your sin remaineth."

Thus again " to the froward He shows Himself froward." Yet herein He is " upright unto the upright; pure unto the pure." This sign is a judgment on the evil generation: but is it not mercy, and love unbounded, to the humble? Your God will give you no

meaner sign and proof of your salvation than the Son
of His love, your own Divine Saviour himself. He
sends the Son of man to be a light unto you : and He
thereby gives you a light so great, so good, so brilliant,
so suitable to your capacity and so sufficient for your
need, that light greater or better, a sign more convincing and irresistible, it is impossible to bestow. He
giveth you a Prophet in whom are hid all the treasures
of wisdom and knowledge; Himself, in His own person, the light of lights; the sign of signs ; the miracle
of miracles ; the pledge of love and the fulness of blessings; the eternal Son of the Father of Lights, the
brightness of the Father's glory. No lesser sign does
He give you : the true light that lighteth all dark
places of the universe; the proof of all that is true ; the
sign of all that is good; the way, and the truth, and
the life. Shall not He himself be to you the best attestation of His own and His Father's grace and glory?
And when unbelievers seek a sign, will ye not answer
them and say :—This has been the sign; we have found
the babe in swaddling bands, and lying in a manger?
Will ye not welcome, as love and blessing boundless to
you, what through their own frowardness alone could
be a judgment to the froward,—the Saviour's own declaration that the Son of man shall be a sign to this
generation ?

That we have correctly indicated our Lord's own
special idea in the discourse as given by Luke, is rendered very strikingly plain by the train of thought
with which he closes the theme. It is profoundly

applicable as a continuation and conclusion of the subject, though at first sight it appears to be alien from it. The preceding remarks will show the continuity of idea; for Jesus now substantially tells them that they need, not more light, but a better eye: "No man, when he hath lighted a candle, putteth it in a secret place, neither under a bushel, but on a candlestick, that they which come in may see the light. The light of the body is the eye: therefore when thine eye is single, thy whole body also is full of light; but when thine eye is evil, thy whole body also is full of darkness. Take heed, therefore, that the light which is in thee be not darkness " (verses 33–35).

III. We now pass to the discourse in Matt. xii. 38–40, where Jesus completes the theme of " the sign of the prophet Jonah" by introducing the crowning idea of the death and resurrection. We have interpreted the former passages, each in a manner consistent with itself, without drawing for information on the others. The closing and completing idea is now to be found here:— " As Jonas was three days and three nights in the whale's belly, so shall the Son of man be three days and three nights in the heart of the earth." And therein shall he be a sign to this generation: therein shall they receive, in its completeness, the full sign of the prophet Jonah.

We may remark, in passing, that this is identically the sign which Jesus gave from the beginning; identically the same which He gave in answer to the very

first of this long series of tempting, dishonest demands,
—a reference of His questioners for satisfaction to His
own death and resurrection,—"Destroy this temple,
and in three days I will raise it up."

The question, then, is; How was Jonah a sign unto
the Ninevites in respect of his having been three days
and three nights in the whale's belly? How did that
render him a sign? And, correspondingly, How is
the Son of man a sign in respect of His death and
resurrection?

Evidently, as we have already seen, Jonah's terrible
experience was a sign, a testimony, a confirmation of
his message, in that it witnessed by a fact in his own
history—his own immediate history as the commissioned messenger from God—both to the certainty of
God's wrath and the riches of His grace. Jonah could
point to his own experience in connexion with his very
mission to Nineveh, and tell that God is not slack concerning judgment, as some men count slackness; not
prone merely to lift His hand in threatening, and too
facile and tender ever to bring it down in vengeance.
His very messenger of wrath had himself been in " the
belly of hell." And yet even from thence there was
salvation. Who, then, can tell but God may turn and
repent even concerning Nineveh?

Similarly, Christ's death and resurrection are a con-
joint sign and seal of His mission from the Father. It
is, indeed, in this respect that the Son of man becomes
truly that overpowering sign which either blinds and
dooms the unbelieving, or finally convinces and illumi-

nates the humble in heart. His person, even after all, would not, without His work—His work of atoning death and justifying resurrection—be such a sign as we have affirmed. His person truly is the sign; but it is so, and that conclusively, because the Son of man was three days and three nights in the heart of the earth. It was, even from the first, in the view of His sufferings and victory, that any light shone in the promised Deliverer. Save for this,—save for the light thrown forward from His coming cross and resurrection-Sabbath,—even the divineness of His person and the stainlessness of His character would have been no real light in a world covered with gross darkness; no light into God's purpose of mercy towards it, God's special moral administration in it. It is in the cross and empty grave that we truly, and for the first time, see light. It is there we see light into our state and case as the sinful subjects of a holy God, the guilty criminals before a righteous Judge, the trembling anticipants of death and eternity. It is there we see light into the malignity and odiousness of sin ; into what it deserves at God's hand, aad what He is resolved to inflict. It is there we see light into the infinite saving love of God, and into the greatest, deepest problem of eternal ages—how He can really and righteously forgive the guilty, and reclaim and renew His enemies. It is there we see heaven opened and a fathomless eternity waiting for us, bright with a loving welcome, and lighted up with a joy that is full of glory. Yes; it is in this respect—in that He was three days and three nights in the heart of the earth; it is in respect that the Son of man was dead, and is alive again; that He has become the clearest of all signs, the sweetest and brightest of lights.

No miracle so great as this; no sign so convincing; no evidence so conclusive; no light in earth or heaven so clear.

When the man of science desires to entrance his audience, he takes a portion of the humblest of substances, the base and blackened charcoal, a splinter of a brand from the burning; and manipulating with his tiny wires the force which roars in the thunder and flashes in the lightning, he makes to play on that valueless, unsightly substance two streams of influence from opposing poles of the hidden power; till soon a silvery gleam gathers on its humble surface, and gradually the brightest light that philosophy and art can generate shines out with dazzling splendour, paling the ineffectual fires of the lamps that until now had irradiated the assembly. You would not ask the aid of one of those depreciated and paler lamps to show you that the more brilliant light was there!

When the living God, in a dark world rushing on to outer darkness, resolved to give a "bright and a morning star,"—a "Sun of Righteousness,"—the strongest and the sweetest light that men or angels could see, He took the base, dishonourable tree of Calvary; and on the humbled person of His Beloved, there made sin for us, He caused to meet two mighty streams of influence unseen;—two streams of influence wide as the poles

asunder;—the one, of avenging Justice as it slew the
sacrifice;—the other, of redeeming Love providing it.
And as they met and blended into one, there blazed
forth on that dishonourable wood " the light of the
knowledge of the glory of God," while the sun in the
heavens grew pale, and the angels veiled their faces
with their wings.   For three days and three nights the
eyes of men were holden that they could not see it.
But the resurrection morn tore away all veils for ever,
and the dis-eclipsed sign of the prophet Jonah shone
out resistless—outshining all other signs and lights;
the very presence-chamber of the King Eternal affording now no glory more brilliant; " FOR THE LAMB IS
THE LIGHT THEREOF."

Therefore, while the Jews require a sign, and the
Greeks seek after wisdom, we preach—Christ crucified
and risen, the power of God, and the wisdom of God.

Part Third

THE SIGN :—CHRIST, THE POWER AND WISDOM OF GOD

" For the Jews require a sign, and the Greeks seek after wisdom ; but we preach
  Christ crucified . . .   the power of God, and the wisdom of God."—1 COR. i.
  22-24.

IT is with reference to the combined objections of Jew
and Greek—of a false ecclesiasticism and a false
philosophy—that Christ is here styled the Power of

God and the Wisdom of God. Otherwise, it would be somewhat remarkable that *these*, the natural, rather than the moral attributes of Godhead, should be specified.

Usually the Cross is spoken of as illustrating, displaying, and giving scope for the moral attributes of God; especially His Justice and Mercy. The wonderful harmony in which the apparently opposing claims of justice, rigorous and stern, and of mercy, gentle and compassionate, are reconciled in a substituted, suffering Saviour, fills the spiritually-enlightened mind with wonder, confidence, and praise; and is apt to attract our contemplation almost engrossingly. Glorious to the awakened and enlightened sinner is the cross or death of the great High Priest; as at once, on the one hand, satisfying Divine justice and declaring God's perfect rectitude as the Judge of all the earth; and, on the other hand, securing the forgiveness of iniquity, transgression, and sin: and, for one who trembled to see the Divine character truly, lest the sight should banish hope for ever; for such an one to see the Love of God finding a satisfaction for His offended Justice, and the Son of His love, who is the gift of love, making justice glorious in justifying the sinner who believeth—how blessed a surprise! how perfect a relief! how admirable an object and occasion of adoring joy! Never can we cease to preach Christ crucified, the righteousness of God and the love of God unto salvation, to every one that believeth; and never can we exhaust the fulness of the revelation thus given of the moral attributes of Deity.

Yet it is well to see arrayed in this same Cross of

Christ, and in the revelation it gives of God, the evidence and the forth-putting of His natural attributes too; His Power and Wisdom, as well as His Justice and His Love. A loyal subject will take delight in contemplating his monarch's glory as reflected in the stern rectitude of his character and the tender amiability of his disposition; and a finer combination cannot be conceived than the righteousness which shuns all wrong except to avenge and rectify it, and the mercy which seeks out misery to relieve it. And as the sovereign should stand before his subject, the embodiment of justice unswerving and compassion unwearying; combining the "righteousness" for which "scarcely one would die," but on the strength of which a nation can live and rest secure, with the "goodness" for which "some would even dare to die"—righteous and gracious alike—that sovereign must command warm, cordial, loyal admiration. It is the *moral* that thus enforces your esteem and love; and, in point of principle, it matters not though that monarch sway the weakest sceptre in the world, and have little either of prowess or of skill to support or to adorn the throne.

But while the moral is glorious irrespective of the natural, while justice and mercy form the essence of all that we must admire in character and action—how joyful if justice and mercy can command power and wisdom in their service.

Let the same monarch stand forth to view, surrounded by myriads in arms, pledging their *power* in the field; and by an inner circle of a nation's hierarchy of talent in counsel, pledging their *wisdom* in the cabinet : the spectacle becomes still more attractive; and the moral glory of a just and gracious throne is seen to be established by power and adorned with wisdom.

Seen in the light of God, such a throne is the Cross of Christ; where mercy and truth meet together, righteousness and peace embrace each other;—it is the power of God and the wisdom of God unto salvation ;—with *this* difference, that Christ alone is All.

Yet we shall see in the cross neither Power nor Wisdom, if we look away from Grace and Righteousness. It is in effecting the alliance of righteousness and grace that the wisdom of God conspicuously appears, and His power is put forth unto salvation. Listen, for instance, to an Apostle in a parallel passage in Romans i. 16 :— " I am not ashamed of the gospel of Christ, for it is the *power* of God unto salvation to every one that believeth." But why is the preaching of Christ crucified the power of God ? " For therein is the righteousness of God revealed from faith to faith "—the perfect, justice-satisfying righteousness imputed unto faith is therein revealed ; for that reason the gospel of the cross is the power of God. And it is grace that reveals that righteousness : for the wrath of God is revealed from heaven against all unrighteousness of men—and grace, compassion, mercy, love is the counterpart of wrath. Grace, therefore, in the gospel reveals righteousness, and righteousness gives holy scope for grace ; therefore this gospel is the power of God unto salvation. Moreover, also, it is the wisdom of God.

And how precious is this combination ! Power alone, apart from wisdom, is mere force ; and wisdom, without power, is in danger of becoming mere subtlety and policy. Power, not guided by wisdom, is blind force ; and wisdom, destitute of power to achieve its purpose, is apt to degenerate into deception or manœuvre. Power without wisdom seeks to compel ; Wisdom without power is apt to deceive and overreach. Satan, in Paradise, had no *power* over holy Eve ; his *wisdom* was, therefore, all exerted in trick, " subtlety," sneaking deception. The powerful world, persecuting the Church, is far from wise ; its power, therefore, is brutish force. The persecutor is at once a tyrant and a fool.

But wisdom combined with equal power is not subtle stratagem : it is intelligent will. Power combined with equal wisdom is not blind immeasurable force, but quiet efficiency. There is a combination of wisdom and of power in the starry heavens ; and the wisdom is that of most marvellous simplicity ; the power is that of quiet and noiseless energy. Powerful wisdom is not full of strange devices ; but straightforward and grand in its simplicity. Wise power is not distinguished by noise and crash ; but by the planet-like silence of its sure accomplishments. Even so the Power of the Cross " cometh not with observation ; " and the Wisdom of the Cross is " the simplicity which is in Christ."

So very simple is this wisdom, and so noiseless is this power, that the one has been counted " foolishness," and the other " of none effect." Not but that men are fond of power, and fond of wisdom too, could they

only get them to their mind. " For the Jews require a
sign, and the Greeks seek after wisdom." The whole
world, Jewish and Gentile, are in quest of these very
things.

The Jew stipulates for a "sign;" some astounding
manifestation; something wonderful, miraculous, faith-
compelling; something that shall *force* his belief; that
shall make it impossible for him to disbelieve any longer.
It is just *power* that he demands. But it is power
apart from Christ; power prior to Christ; power greater
than Christ. Ah! little does he know that a sign
better than Christ there is none; a power higher than
Christ there is none. Christ himself is the sign; the
miracle of miracles; the power of God unto salvation.
True; that power of God which Christ crucified is, is a
quiet, unobtrusive power. He does not " come down
from the cross " and scatter His crucifiers as by the
whirlwind. When the Jews in seeking a sign exclaim:
" Let him come down from the cross and we will believe him;" He quietly refuses their demand. He
continues to suffer in apparent weakness. But " the
weakness of God is stronger than men "! In this very
weakness He is the POWER of God.

The Greek, in like manner, seeks after "wisdom."
The Jew demands a miracle, the Greek an argument,
to compel their faith. Both unite in this, that they
would have their faith forced, their unbelief made impossible any more. The Jew seeks this by some forth-
putting of power; the Greek by reasoning or logic.
The Greeks delighted in speculation. They would be

lighted along by the path of argument, their faith constrained by wisdom.   But the cross! A murdered man! An executed felon! A professed Saviour of others, himself in shame and death, the prey of others! Does that stand to reason? Is that philosophy? " Foolishness "!—stupidity!—exclaims the Greek, as the Jew had complained of a " stumbling-block."

Nevertheless, Christ is at once the Power and the Wisdom of God.   If any one join with the Jews and seek " a sign," or powerful, faith-engaging evidence, Christ himself is the infinite power; the best of signs; the very Omnipotence of God.   If any one fall in with the Greeks and seek " wisdom," truth, infallible knowledge and certainty, Christ himself is the truth infallible; the infinite wisdom; the very Omniscience of God.   Almighty power operates in Him : infinite light shines in Him.   The heavens and the earth were powerfully made; but Christ is *the power* of God.   In wisdom did the Lord make them all; but Christ is *the wisdom* of God.   Created nature is a limited result of Divine power and wisdom.   Christ unlimitedly is all God's power and wisdom unto salvation.

It is by seeing Christ to be both the Wisdom and the Power of God that we really see Him to be either.   It is Wisdom that redeems from apparent weakness, and it is Power that redeems from apparent folly.

I. It is Wisdom that redeems the Cross from apparent weakness.

Contemplate the cross of Christ; contemplate Christ crucified. And view Him, simply in the light of sense and human history and reason. In vain do you search for any evidence of omnipotence. On the contrary, you can find nothing but humiliating tokens of weakness. He is oppressed; He is afflicted; He is stricken, smitten of God, and afflicted. He is bruised, and grieved, and apparently fainting through thirst. Stripes are laid upon Him, and He resents it not. His soul is being poured out unto death. He is " crucified in weakness." And nothing but weakness can the eye of sense or intellect discover. In vain you search thus for the Power of God.

But bring unto view the Wisdom. Let the light of God's Word and God's Spirit show you the wise scheme in hand; the wondrous plan in progress. Be it yours to see what intellect and history cannot show you in the Cross of Christ; what the revealed will and wisdom of God alone can show. Be it yours to get, reverently speaking, behind the scenes; away from the shallow, superficial, garish world, with its love for the external, the hollow, the transient, the deceiving. Get out by faith into the unseen realm of which this dying malefactor is the Prince and Lord; and there learn the exceeding sinfulness of sin; its terrible, righteous, inevitable doom in the wrath and curse of the great Judge of all; and the loving substitution of this Saviour, bearing sin and the wrath due to sin, in our room and stead. Contemplate the power of God inflicting righteous wrath; and think of the power unseen by mortal eye—eye of flesh or eye of reason—that must be silently engaged in bearing it.   Contemplate the power of sin, of Satan, of death, and hell, all bearing down on this suffering Saviour.   And think of the greater power of this Saviour himself, not borne down and swept away by the flood-tide of hell's utmost effort, but maintaining His ground, abiding by His cross, drinking His Father's cup of wrath, and baffling His enemies' attempts to vanquish Him.   See the Cross as Wisdom shows it: and you see a Power that silently, noiselessly, unobtrusively, yet with secret and resistless efficiency, is quelling all other power; breaking the power of Jew and Gentile, Church and State, priest and potentate of earth; breaking the power of Satan and his hosts of hell; breaking the power of death and sin; exhausting all the power even in God's most awesome malediction!   Ah! be it that He is "crucified in weakness;" yet this "weakness of God is stronger than men"!   It is the very power of God.   It is omnipotence unto salvation.   Because of the Wisdom of God, Christ crucified is the Power of God.

II. Conversely; to see again how intimately the two are blended:—It is Power that redeems the Cross from apparent folly.

Contemplate again the cross of Christ, the dying Saviour.   And, whereas formerly you sought to see the power, you are looking now for the wisdom.   You are in search of traces of profound wisdom in this asserted scheme or plan of salvation.   Where do you find

them ? Again it becomes plain that the eye of sense
or natural reason cannot find them. Nay; the more
you see of what is going on beneath the eye of sense,
and the more you examine it in the light of human
intellect unaided, the more apparently hopeless is this
strange arrangement; the more foolish this miserable
failure. For, is it not an utter failure? A Saviour of
others, who cannot save himself! A Saviour of sinners; and sinners slaying *him!* A peculiar Son of
God; and God forsaking him! A Deliverer from death;
and death carrying him away as his prey! How can
these things be? Where is there *wisdom* here?

And you cannot see it, till you bring into view the
power. Consider the mighty forces that are in action;
the grand and august agencies at 'work. *Then* you see
the wisdom that encountered them in this peculiar
manner; the wisdom that baffled all their subtlety;
that drew them out in all their might and in all their
scheming; in all their force and all their fraud; that
compelled them to stake and peril in the combat all
their resources; and then eternally defeated them.
You see that—with powers like these in operation, and
victory gained over them all exterminatingly, even in
Christ's hour of utmost woe and weakness—this is the
arrangement of " prudence and of understanding, finding out wonderful inventions : " and admitting that the
idea of a Saviour of others who cannot save himself
is " foolishness ";—it is a " foolishness of God that is
wiser than men "! and Christ crucified is the Wisdom
of God unto salvation.

Thus it is the Power that redeems from apparent folly, as it is the Wisdom that redeems from apparent weakness. The Cross would have been foolishness but for the noiseless, unobtrusive, secret power. The Cross would have been weakness but for the hidden wisdom of God. Combine these; and Christ crucified is the Power of God and the Wisdom of God.

Let it be observed very specially that it is " Christ crucified " that is the Power and the Wisdom of God. It is Christ in the fundamental act of His priesthood; offering Himself a sacrifice to satisfy Divine justice and reconcile us to God. This is indeed remarkable. Would we not have thought that when Christ was to be called the Wisdom of God, we would have been asked to contemplate His Prophetic office? and when Christ was to be called the Power of God, to contemplate His Kingly office?   As a teacher, He might have been called God's Wisdom; and as a prince, God's Power.   But not so.   He is a wise teacher; and He is a powerful prince.   But it is as a priest on His Cross that He is the Power of God and the Wisdom of God.

As a Teacher, He might have taught us many truths; but there could have been no *power* in them but for the Cross.   Gospel morality might have been very beautiful —but weak.   It might have been very acceptable to the Greeks in their search for wisdom.   But oh ! the folly of being followers of a dead, a murdered Teacher ! Yes; and that folly is undeniable, if the sufferer be not a Priest.

And so, as a King, He might have done many great
and powerful things; but there could have been no
wisdom in them; no adaptation for the cancelling of
guilt; for reconciling men to God; for giving peace of
conscience and power over Satan and death:—none but
for the Cross. The astounding signs and wonders
might have been very acceptable to Jews. Gladly
would they have accepted Him as king; taken Him
by force and made Him a king. But oh! the shameful
Cross! The King of the Jews crucified! Write not,
"the King of the Jews,"—but only that he said it. Our
king crucified! They stumbled at that stumbling-stone.
A king should be with great power and observation.

Yet not in the kingly office are we to look for
all the power of God; and not in the prophetic for all
His wisdom. It is the priest,—the sacrifice,—the
Lamb of God,—Christ crucified,—who is the power of
God, and the wisdom of God unto salvation. If He is
not a priest, the Greek may rightly reject Him as a
teacher, and call the whole exhibition folly; and the
Jew reject Him as a king, and call it weakness and
unprofitableness unto the uttermost. The Greek inevitably falls into *his* error, and the Jew into *his*,
because they both are blind to the priestly nature and
glory of His death. The Greek seeks a wise teacher—
and the Jew a powerful king. A crucified king and
teacher seems absurdity and imbecility. And it really
is so, except upon the ground that Christ crucified is
an atoning priest for ever after the order of Melchi-
zedec. As a prophet, there is wisdom in His instruc-

tive voice. As a king, there is might in His majestic arm. His Cross may cast a cloud over His wisdom; and cast more than a doubt upon His power; yet, rightly seen, the Cross, as the altar of eternal propitiation, proves that He was not merely powerful and wise, but the Power of God and the Wisdom of God.

It may illustrate more fully the unison and reciprocal action of these attributes in the person of Christ crucified, if we consider the import of His mournful cry in the garden as it appealed to His Father's wisdom and power both, and even seemed to question them:—"Father, if it be possible, let this cup pass from me."

1. Take it as an appeal to His Father's *wisdom*. O my Father,—Father of lights,—can all thy penetrating insight into all possible conditions and contingencies descry nothing for me but this coming cross, this present cup of woe? Can Omniscience discover no alternative,—no open door of escape from this dire necessity? Can no Divine and all-wise device render this agony and woe unnecessary?

And none is forthcoming. Is Wisdom, therefore, at fault? Yes, if Wisdom has not found in this the grandest scope and exhibition for Power. But Omnipotence acts, and glorifies Omniscience. Omnipotence is to have opportunity now as it never had before, and never will again. The Almighty "will" of God is coming into play; and its almightiness is to be specially illustrated. "Father, not my will, but thine be done": Thy will; Thy will omnipotent. "I come to do Thy will"—not to suffer Satan's. "I come to do Thy will"—not to do mine own. Let me be borne through in doing Thy will. "I delight to do Thy will." Save me not from dying; but save me from death. Strengthen me to vanquish death by dying; and to destroy him that hath the power of death. For this, O Father, is Thy will omnipotent; "by the which will my people shall be sanctified through the offering of my body once for all." And now in the Power of this "will" of God on the Cross, Wisdom is seen to be not at all at fault; under no eclipse; but shining in its fullest splendours;—a calm and steady light; able to wait its vindication,—its judgment brought forth as the noonday. And just by its apparent failure, when no device was forthcoming to open for the sufferer a door of escape from suffering—no plan devised for causing the cup to pass from Him; just by its apparent "foolishness," the Cross shines out as the Wisdom of God.

2. But the appeal may be regarded still more simply and directly as an appeal to the *power* of God. "Father, if it be *possible?*" Art Thou not able? Is it not within the compass of Thy power to make this cup pass from me? Is not Thy power almighty; and is anything too hard for Thee?

It is for Wisdom to reply: and how? The appeal to Wisdom is answered by Power:—Thy will—Thy mighty, Thine Almighty will—be done. Even so the appeal to Power is answered by Wisdom; and Wisdom can show that *finite* power might carry the cup aside, but Omnipotence—the power of God—shall be displayed in drinking it. Yes : twelve legions of angels might have borne Christ away from His Cross. But they would have borne Him away from the opportunity of showing that the power of God is Almighty. A flashing sign from heaven in the cohorts of seraphim carrying the Sufferer aloft upon their wings, would have pleased the sign-seeking Jew. But it would have been limited, created, finite strength displayed. Grappling with hell, and the curse, and the wrath of God, and the power of sin, and the sting of death ;—drinking His Father's cup ;—Jesus, in apparent " weakness," was the infinite Power of God.

We rejoice to " preach " this. " We preach Christ crucified, the Power of God, and the Wisdom of God." When we preach Christ, we keep this in our own view, —we set this in your view ;—namely, that the Christ whom we preach, whom we press on your acceptance, is the infinite Power, the omniscient Wisdom of God. In Him there is not merely perfect righteousness to justify you from all sin, and infinite love and grace to make that righteousness freely over to you, "sinner," "enemy" (Rom. v. 8, 10), though you be : but this very Christ is the power of God, the wisdom of God.

Can you fail to see how very thoroughly this meets your case, and shuts you up to an immediate reception of the Saviour?

You tell us you are not merely guilty. In the moral attributes of God, as they meet in Christ crucified ;—in Divine Justice, satisfied, and owning the righteousness brought in,—in Divine Love, willing that that righteousness be immediately yours;—in mercy and truth meeting together, righteousness and peace embracing each other;—you see a satisfactory provision for the removal of your guilt and condemnation. But alas! you are utterly ignorant of how to embrace it, and utterly powerless, though you knew the way. You stand upon your want of wisdom, and your want of strength. You know not how to believe to the saving of your soul. You have no power to come unto Him that you may have life.

But is not all this most unsuitable, out of place, in a word, impertinent, if Christ crucified is the power of God and the wisdom of God? You cannot see through this difficulty, and that other mystery, in the scheme of salvation! But what barrier is that to be allowed to place in the way of your receiving Christ? He is " the Wisdom of God;" and to tarry, and hesitate, and scruple, and hang back from receiving Him, till your difficulties are all removed, is just to say that you will not receive Him who can, and alone can, remove them all. And then your weakness! You cannot come till you are drawn. You are overwhelmed in moral inability and spiritual death! But what of that? It implies your want of power. Shall that be a barrier in the way of your receiving Him who is "the Power of God"? If inability is your disease; if want of power is your danger; is not Christ your very remedy, seeing He is " the Power of God"?

Oh, that " stumbling " Cross!—Omnipotence is in

it;—not indeed to save you *in* your unbelief. Omnipotence was not in it to save Christ from His cup of woe; it would have needed far less than omnipotence to save Him from that. But omnipotence was there to save Him from being overwhelmed in His dying hour;—to give Him the victory by dying. And so omnipotence is in it,—not to save you *in* unbelief, but *from* unbelief; —to save you in dying to all hope but Christ;—to save you in dying unto all hope without Christ, and all hope except Christ; and in believing into all hope in Him who is able to save unto the uttermost.

Indeed, there is no omnipotence in Christ's cross to save you, if you become not one by faith with Him as your living Head; even as there was no omnipotence— and because there was no omnipotence—put forth to save Him from becoming one with you, His death-doomed members; or from the death to which His oneness with you then doomed Him. It would not have needed omnipotence to save Christ from becoming one with you, and standing at the bar of an angry God in your room. That would have given no display of God's power. Something infinitely less than almightiness could have done it. "Twelve legions of angels" might have done it. It did not need God's uttermost of power to save Christ from dying. It *did*, to save Him *in* dying, and to make Him conqueror of death and Satan when the curse of God due to sin was on the side of death and him that had the power of death: and now, therefore, He is able to save unto the uttermost them that come unto God by Him, identifying themselves by faith with Him. The omnipotence of God in the Cross contemplated Christ as one with you, and gave Him victory over all that His oneness with you brought down upon Him. And now it contemplates making you one with Him, in opposition to all that would prevent that oneness; and therefore saving you unto the very uttermost,—"mighty to save"!

There is a drawing power in the Cross, utterly unbounded; able to bring and to save the chief of sinners. Give yourself up unto it; it will bring you into the love of God, into your Father's bosom. There is power in the planetary system, and in the pathless spaces of the stellar heavens. But the power there is limited: God's power could go greatly farther in its efforts than the heavens and the earth give proof of. It cannot go farther than it goes in the Cross. *There*, there is not merely a display of power, leaving infinite efforts and effects for God's power to achieve behind and after all; there is all God's very power itself—the Power of God, His Omnipotence unto salvation.

There are obstacles in the way of your salvation; your forgiveness, your holiness; your coming unto Jesus, your believing on His name, your walking worthy of His love;—obstacles manifold and strong. Are they almighty? One need scarcely seek an answer. Earth and hell and all creation may join their power to destroy you; but their allied forces do not make Omnipotence. Finite powers at the uttermost, they fall infinitely short of Almightiness. And can Almightiness not cope with them? Yea, verily. But where does almighty power emanate, to overthrow them? In what direction—what line—may I so place myself, as to find Omnipotence coming forth to draw me to the Lord? In the line of the Cross. In your looking unto Jesus. "I, when I am lifted up, will draw all men unto me." Through the blood of the dying Surety, almighty Power comes forth on all them that believe.

Yea: and the splendours of omniscient Wisdom break around your enlightened spirit also.

If it were not so; if God should lay aside His Wisdom; and make a mere diplomatic stroke of policy in saving sinners,—a subtle compromise with the claims of law,—a mere trickful appearance and illusion of justice,—an exhibition of indulgence without remission of sin, or of proffered remission without shedding of blood,—a gift of general, uncovenanted, unmediatorial mercy;—there could be no power needed, and no power put forth, in such a scheme of saving you. But God maintains His Wisdom, and glorifies it to the uttermost in the Cross. All shall be wisely done. "My servant shall deal prudently." There shall be nothing to regret afterwards. There shall be no real, no rightful interest injured, either in the meantime or in the long run; no, not in all the eternal issues. All shall be rightly, fairly, justly done. All shall be candidly explained. All shall be fitly and righteously transacted. This "judgment shall rest for a light unto the people:"— clear as "light" itself: conclusive as a final "rest:"— no claim of justice set aside; no voice of truth silenced; and no gift of grace, but righteousness shall sanction it;

and no entrance into glory, but holiness itself shall smile approval. Such shall this salvation be. Ah! then, it must be a wisely-planned salvation; devising for the eternal best; a "wisdom ordained before the world was for your glory,"—for God's glory also in the highest,—and for making great the glory of Him who is the Mediator between God and man. Very specially, and very graciously, it is a wisdom ordained for your glory; for your true holy dignity and honour; for making you a king and a priest; for admitting you to see and to share the glory of the Son of God; for making you altogether like Him when you shall see Him as He is. It is no blind, sheer force that carries you from the darkness of guilt and of the shadow of death, through many a paroxysm of conflict with Satan and with sin, to the presence of the Lamb. It is infinitely wise Power. And it is not mere scheming which brings you off, as by a stroke of policy. It is infinitely powerful Wisdom, making you more than conqueror. Christ is to you both the Power of God and the Wisdom of God, when He saves you. "The Lord is your *light* and your salvation. He also is the *strength* of your life."

Yes: Strength and Light are thine, O Zion; for Christ the Power of God and the Wisdom of God, is thine. "Arise; shine: for thy LIGHT is come." "Awake; awake: put on thy STRENGTH, O Zion."

XXII

CONCLUSION

JONAH'S ANGER,—AND THE GOURD

JONAH iv. 1–11

" But it displeased Jonah exceedingly, and he was very angry. And
he prayed unto the Lord, and said, I pray thee, O Lord, was not
this my saying when I was yet in my country? therefore I fled
before unto Tarshish : for I knew that thou art a gracious God,
and merciful, slow to anger, and of great kindness, and repentest
thee of the evil. Therefore now, O Lord, take, I beseech thee, my
life from me : for it is better for me to die than to live. Then
said the Lord, Doest thou well to be angry?" &c., &c.

" Why art thou wroth? and why is thy
countenance fallen?"—GEN. iv. 6.
" Although the fig-tree shall not blossom."—
HABAK. iii. 17.

THIS chapter describes the effect produced on Jonah's
mind by the Lord's mercy to penitent Nineveh,
and the method taken by the Lord to rebuke and correct him.

When God saw the works of the Ninevites that they
turned from their evil ways, and when He repented of

the evil that He had said that He would do unto them, and He did it not; this "displeased Jonah exceedingly, and he was very angry." A marvellous state of mind in a man of God contemplating a splendid instance of the Lord's long-suffering—His mercy to them that repent, and His grace in blessing and prospering the preaching of His servant! It is, indeed, difficult to enter into Jonah's state of mind sufficiently to do him justice as well as to condemn his error. But while his sin is here exposed for condemnation, let us do him, at least, this justice,—to bear in remembrance that it is exposed by himself. It is he himself who has put on record the story of his inexcusable frame of spirit. He has ingenuously recorded for all generations the feelings with which, at this painful crisis, he was exercised, concealing nothing, and nothing extenuating. He softens not the expressions which he felt were necessary to indicate the violence of his emotion. The prophet, with his own pen, narrates that he was "displeased,"—nay, "displeased exceedingly,"—nay, farther, that "he was very angry."

Let us not forget, therefore, that he has with much simplicity and frankness owned all his sin in this matter. He has "acknowledged his transgression: and his iniquity he has not hid." All his heart he has laid bare and open. He was afraid lest he should be regarded as a false prophet; and while, by the Ninevites in their softened and subdued frame of mind, this was not likely to occur, yet among the Israelites, in their wild and perverse rebelliousness, it was highly probable.

The treatment which they were ever ready to mete out to their prophets, is too clearly implied in Christ's up-braiding question, "Which of the prophets have not your fathers killed?" They would lie on the watch for anything that might be perverted into a handle against them and their commission; and Jonah, no doubt, anticipated with perfect agony the laughter and ridicule with which he should be received on his return, as having gone on a fool's errand; threatening the greatest city in the world with destruction in a specified time, and returning without a hair of their heads being injured! He foresaw the utter weakening of his hands, —the destruction of his usefulness,—among his country-men. The overthrow of Nineveh by Divine judg-ments, according to his proclamation, would most mightily have strengthened him on his return to his countrymen, enforcing the repentance which he should preach to them also; and although he could not, save most inhumanly, have rejoiced in the perdition of the great city, yet the favourable reaction that might have ensued among Israel, he had apparently begun to cal-culate upon. He expected to return with a terrible instance to quote of the truth implied in the psalmist's question to the peculiar people, "He that chastiseth the heathen, shall not he correct" *you?* But when this was taken out of his hands; and not only so, but the issue turned against him,—in the sense of being manifestly capable of being wrested by Israel to their own destruc-tion, and to the painful questioning of his Divine com-mission as a prophet; Jonah's heart despaired of his

country; and the event—so infinitely blessed to Nineveh—he saw would be turned to the spiritual and eternal
damage of his "kinsmen according to the flesh." It was
not his own honour merely, nor chiefly, nor indeed at
all, that Jonah cared for. Anything so grovelling is
not for a moment to be imagined in the case of a servant
of God, so exercised, so true, so loyal, so ingenuous, and
truthful as Jonah was. But the contempt likely to fall
on himself as a prophet, he saw would fall on the honour
of the Lord who had sent him; and the people who were
dear to him as his own countrymen, he saw would be
confirmed in their mockings and perverseness; and so
would ultimately incur the very destruction from which
Nineveh had by timeous repentance delivered herself,
and from which Israel, alarmed by Nineveh's destruction, might have delivered herself, had the original
denunciation taken effect. All his official influence in
and over Israel, which the destruction of Nineveh might
have greatly confirmed, he beholds suddenly scattered
and destroyed. His fond hopes for his country he
suddenly sees blighted. He was afraid, indeed, from
the first, that it might be so. It was for this reason
that he attempted from the first to evade the commission
to Nineveh. Was not this his saying when he was yet
in his country? Therefore he fled before unto Tarshish
(ver. 2).

And mark here, and in confirmation of this explanation of his displeasure and anger,—mark with what
emphasis he speaks of his country. "Was not this my
saying while I was yet in my country?" "*My*

country!" *My own country!* He is not merely pointing out the locality where he said this originally. He
is indicating that his heart is full of thoughts about
his " country ;" about the bearing of this matter on his
"country;" his "kinsmen according to the flesh, for whom
his heart's desire and prayer to God is, that they might
be saved." He is viewing it intensely in the light of
its bearing upon his country; it is for his country's
sake that he is keenly agitated ; it is in love to his
own people that his emotions are stirred even beyond
control. There is nothing selfish, worldly, mean, in
this painful aberration of a godly man's heart. It
were easy to pour forth condemnations on him; but it
is more difficult to emulate the strong love to God's
honour, and cause, and kingdom, and people, without
which he could not have exhibited this unparalleled
manifestation of character and temper. Assuredly he
erred : he erred most grievously. Let no attempt be
made to cover over the guilt of his procedure. Charity
rejoiceth not in iniquity, but rejoiceth in the truth.
Still let no gross, and easy, and short-hand, and indis-
criminating denunciation be pronounced. It was manifestly in the ill-regulated and unbalanced force of
principles and desires far from blameworthy, that
Jonah was hurried into his present sinful extremes of
feeling. He erred not in lamenting the probable perversion of God's mercy by the Israelites. It was no sin
in Jonah to regret with his whole soul their probable
wresting to their own destruction of this blessed event ;
their acceptance of it as a proof that Jonah had never

been sent of God, that his pretensions now were proven false, and that his denunciations were only such as might safely be laughed to scorn. But he did err in not pouring his regrets and griefs in this matter into the bosom of God submissively. He did err greatly in not acquiescing in the Divine arrangement as righteous, and wise, and holy, and good, and best. He did err in not bringing all his own wisdom into subjection to the appointment of God, and placing his desires, with their relative hopes on the one hand, or their fears on the other, under the control and rein of the word and work of the Lord. Ought he not to have poured out his patriotic longings and spiritual love for Israel into the ear of the God of Israel? Ought he not to have bowed in repentance, and said, "Not my will, but Thine be done"? Ought he not to have rejoiced in the meantime in the deliverance of so very great a multitude of fellow-creatures, and trusted that the same God who had so unexpectedly given them repentance and salvation, could make even this event work, in its influence on Israel, in a very different direction from what the prophet feared—seeing that "with God all things are possible"? And instead of indulging in gloomy anticipations, ought he not joyfully to have celebrated the Divine power and mercy in crowning his ministry to the heathen city with such success, and implored, in quickened faith, a like blessing on his future labours in Israel? To grieve; to be "displeased;" was very inexcusable. But to be "exceedingly displeased;" to be "very angry;" angry with God; was lamentable sin!

Still this was the infirmity of a friend of God, and not the malice of an enemy. And that it was so, is very evident from the fact, that the prophet carried the whole matter to God in prayer. "And he prayed unto the Lord, and said, I pray thee, O Lord, was not this my saying when I was yet in my country? Therefore I fled before unto Tarshish: for I knew that thou art a gracious God, and merciful, and slow to anger, and of great kindness, and repentest thee of the evil."

Here Jonah seems to palliate, or rather justify, his flight, and to undo the repentance to which he had been already brought. He seems also to expostulate and remonstrate with God for sparing Nineveh. These are amazing instances of what the corruption of a believer may attain to, in its opposition to the will and work of God. But still the evidence that this is the corruption of a *believer* is conclusive, from the fact that Jonah carried the whole matter to God in the exercise of prayer. "He prayed unto the Lord, and said." When his sorrow was stirred; while he mused painfully; while the fire of anxiety burned within him; he wisely resolved against "keeping silence." He went with all his burden to the Lord; he opened up to Him all his grief. Even the wild tumultuous lustings of the flesh against the spirit,—he made the Lord cognisant of them all. He made God his counsellor; honestly and unreservedly he unbosomed himself to God; his whole case and his whole heart he laid open, even as they were, to Him. He had no secret from God. Even the injustice which his wild feelings did to God,—even *that* he did not conceal. Even those sinful emotions over which he had not yet obtained the mastery, he explains before the Lord. His very "infirmity" he spreads out before Him; even though he seems to be forgetting "the years of the right hand of the Most High."

Here is Jonah's integrity; and here is Jonah's safety.

1. Here is his *integrity*. He is no enemy of God;— he is a friend and child of God, notwithstanding the perplexity into which his feelings have fallen. He cannot rest in a state of distance from God. Wretched as he is, through the predominance of his own fears, and the complainings against God to which these fears lead him, he would be more wretched still were he to restrain prayer before God, shut up his soul from Him, and determinedly and consciously depart from Him by an evil heart of unbelief. Sick at heart, and overwhelmed with bitter despondency, he pours out his complaint unto the Lord; even though, through the temporary predominance of the flesh, it is a complaint against the Lord himself. In every prayer of God's children there is some mixture of sin. The mixture *here* is very conspicuous and very alarming. There is, however, a secret element of grace, a secret seed of faith and submission,—proved to be present by the confidence in God implied in making Him the referee and counsellor. When prayer is suppressed, duplicity is begun to reign. Iniquity is regarded in the heart; conscious sin is cherished and clung to; presumptuous iniquity has obtained dominion; and the soul is not upright; when God

is shunned, and a cloak or mask of concealment drawn over the soul in His presence.   But so long as all can yet be declared unto the Lord, even though it be your infirmity, *there* integrity still reigns.   And the Lord in infinite condescension will acknowledge it.

2. For, secondly, here was Jonah's *safety*, as well as his integrity.   But for this, he would, mentally and spiritually, have been fleeing again from the Lord, even as formerly he attempted to flee to Tarshish.   His danger formerly was in fleeing from the Lord.   Agitated and alarmed, he fled *from* the Lord.   Agitated and alarmed now again, he flees *to* the Lord.   This is the safety of his position now.   He does not seek a refuge from God. He makes God his refuge.   He tells Him the grounds of his alarm and agitation.   He expostulates with God.   He seeks to clear his case with God.   And though there is excess, and violence, and inexcusable haste and passion, still the Lord condescends to his prayer, stained though it is by such grievous infirmity.

He thus bore testimony to the reality of faith and grace that was in His servant;—and God is the best witness of His people's estate.   It was Jonah's safety to call upon the Lord; for the Lord "hath not despised the prayer of the afflicted, nor hid His face when he hath cried:" nor is He ready to cast off or to reject our supplications because of their impurities and sins, provided we truly wait upon Him, and make Him the witness of all our desires,—the counsellor, and referee, and confidant in all that concerneth us.

Jonah had anticipated the sparing of Nineveh, provided they should repent. And he grounded this expectation on his knowledge of the character of God. " I knew that thou art a gracious God, and merciful, slow to anger, and of great kindness, and repentest thee of the evil."

This is the uniform character assigned to God in the law, and the psalms, and the prophets. It is the memorial of God to all generations. It is the name, or the exhibition of character, by which He revealed Himself to Moses, and by which He desires in all ages to be known. "I knew that Thou art a gracious God;"— gratuitously benevolent; having a disposition of goodness; Fountain of actual mercy. Hence Thou art "slow to anger"; not speedily provoked, but longsuffering; being not willing that any should perish. Hence, also, Thou art " of great kindness," abundant in goodness, and " repentest Thee of the evil." Let it be carefully observed that all actual patience, kindness, mercy, and forgiveness are here traced up solely to the graciousness of God's nature. It is in Himself alone that He finds reason for saving sinners. It is in His own nature exclusively that He finds ground and motive for bringing salvation. " Not for your sakes do I this, be it known unto you, O house of Israel, but for mine own name's sake." In myself alone, I find the reason why I should ask you to return, and promise you a good reception when you do. And for this cause we ought in all our prayers to carry our appeal to the gracious disposition of God, as the only source and fountain of all our hopes. " God so loved the world that he gave his only-begotten Son, that whosoever believeth on him may not perish but have everlasting life." " Of His own will begat He us by the word of His truth, that we might be a kind of first fruits from among His creatures." " By grace are we saved ": " being justified freely by His grace." Let us in prayer resign, therefore, the aid of everything save the grace of God. Let us ground our hopes alone on that, and on the righteousness of Christ which God in His grace has provided for us. Let us take all our encouragement in prayer from God only. Let His memorial and name be graven on our hearts for ever.

It was in accordance with this name, or memorial, or nature, or character, that God acted when He spared Nineveh; and however much His doing so might appear to Jonah adverse to the prospects of Israel, adverse to the prophet's own usefulness, adverse to the promotion of God's own glory, yet we may here learn that to exercise His mercy towards the truly penitent, God will—reverently speaking—run all hazards. Israel may blaspheme; and Israel may ridicule Jonah as a false prophet, and harden themselves against His denunciations, reminding him of the little harm that came on Nineveh, though he predicted a total and swift destruction. But God will not alter His memorial, nor resile from His gracious designs to the penitent, on that account. His name will be more honoured in the end; and in the meantime, if men will have it so, they may take occasion to wrest His procedure to their own destruction; but the responsibility and the peril are their own. The legitimate use of God's doings is very different; and it is hard for them to kick against the pricks. "The ways of the Lord are right, and the just shall walk in them: but the transgressors shall fall therein."

Thus, in general, the doctrine of free grace is frequently said to encourage men in sin; but we are not to modify the freeness of God's offered mercy on pretence of taking care of the glory of God, and the maintenance of His law. This was substantially Jonah's sin;—the sin of pretending to be more careful of God's glory, and more qualified to advance it, than God himself. It is a glorious fact that His thoughts are not as our thoughts; and we reduce them to a measure that would render them useless to ourselves, when we constrain them within the limits of our own judgment or capacity. God is able to vindicate His own procedure and all its principles; and He will do so without the aid of man's wisdom. "The weakness of God is stronger than men; and the foolishness of God is wiser than men."

But what sort of reasoning is this? "*Therefore*, now, O Lord, take, I beseech thee, my life from me: for it is better for me to die than to live" (ver. 3). Most miserable inference; most painful exclamation! It is the exclamation of a believer, a saint, a man of God. But it is the cry of a soul far aside from its duty. Unable to guide either his mind or his ministry amidst the perplexity which the apparent vacillation or change of purpose on the part of God occasioned, Jonah prefers death to life. He prefers death to the apprehended dishonour of God and the destruction of His own usefulness as God's prophet. Excessive though His grief is—uncontrolled though his feelings are—they are evidently the feelings and the grief of a godly man. An earthly-minded man were incapable of such emotions. Yet are they altogether indefensible and inexcusable. Our life is in the hands of God; and He can threaten the removal of it in a thousand ways, every one of them sufficient to cause a displeased prophet repent of his rash desire. He had but escaped from a species of living death that had filled him with anguish, and extorted from him the most agonising cries for the Lord's pity and deliverance: and how can he forget that God might again plunge him into the jaws of destruction, and "answer his prayer by terrible things in righteousness"!

Very different was the decision of Paul on the question of death, or life continued. He had "a desire to depart and be with Christ." He felt that *that* was "far better." Nevertheless, he saw that it was for the good of the Church that he should abide in the flesh. He was willing, therefore, to die or to live at the pleasure of the Lord. He lost and merged his own will in God's; living or dying he was the Lord's. All the days of his appointed time would he wait patiently till his change came. Unquestionably the chief element of Paul's devotedness was in Jonah, though acting erroneously under a pressure which he could not bear—under a perplexity of feeling which he could not unravel. He fancied that it could not be serviceable for the Church that he should abide in the flesh. He saw, or thought he saw, all his usefulness destroyed. He judged according to his own wisdom, that to minister in the prophetic office in Israel, after the sparing of Nineveh, would henceforth be altogether unavailing; and the same consideration which reconciled Paul to live, induced Jonah, under a perverted imagination, to desire to die. But he erred in judging according to reason, to human prospects and probabilities. He ought to have left all issues and results in the hand of God himself. His whole life, and all its serviceableness in the kingdom of the Lord, were in the Lord's own disposal. And if circumstances in providence rendered his future prosecution of the duties of his office more difficult, more fruitless of good, more destitute of seeming results, ought he not still to have said : "Lord, what wilt thou have me to do? Make a plain path before me, because of mine enemies. Lord, here am I : send me"?

But instead of this, he assumed the right of judging that the salvation of Nineveh would eclipse the honour of God, destroy the credit of his ministry, and harden the hearts of his countrymen. And rather than live to see such issues he would cry to be removed from the evil to come. "It is better for me to die than to live."

The Lord reproves him in a twofold manner. First, by a verbal, and, secondly, by a symbolical rebuke.

I. First:—" Then said the Lord, Doest thou well to

be angry?" How gracious! How condescending! How considerate! Feeling for the sad though sinful perplexity of His servant, the Lord does not break forth in punishment of his irritability, his petulance, his "anger," and "exceeding great displeasure." He does not upbraid him for making his own narrow capacity the measure by which to judge of the Divine will and the Divine procedure, in sparing that great city. He simply calls him to reflection. He points out to him his state of mind; "Doest thou well to be angry?" Thou art "angry"; thou art morose; harsh in thy feelings, and uncontrolled in the expression of them; murmuring, complaining, angry at the good hand of God. Is this justifiable? "Doest thou well?" Hast thou ground for it? Thy grounds for joy and gladness are real;—a spared city; angels rejoicing over their repentance; thy God proved to be gracious, and merciful, and slow to anger, and of great kindness, repenting Him of the evil; thine own ministry eminently, marvellously, matchlessly successful. These are grounds for joy and gladness, thanksgiving and the voice of melody. These grounds of gratitude are plain and patent and present, immediate and sure and great. Thy grounds for displeasure,—are they not distant, future, imaginary, of thine own portending, at the best but doubtful, and such as events may negative and disappoint. Doest thou well, then, to be angry? Angry! angry at the good hand and good pleasure of the Lord!

II. Secondly:—The Lord resumes and continues this

expostulation, aided by a very significant and symbolical mode of tuition. He means to show to Jonah that the Lord's heart was greatly set on Nineveh, penitent and reforming Nineveh, wicked and provoking as it had been. He means to lead Jonah into sympathy with Himself concerning Nineveh. He means to show him how the Divine affections are twined around the human race as God's own workmanship, capable of sharing His mercy, and tasting and knowing that He is gracious. And for this purpose He rears right suddenly, and soon removes, a little object for the prophet's own affections to twine around.

And it happened thus. "So Jonah went out of the city, and sat on the east side of the city, and there made him a booth, and sat under it in the shadow, till he might see what would become of the city" (ver. 5).

There he sits! engrossed with the one solitary thought, *what shall become of the city.* Not an imagination of the thoughts of his heart can be spared from considering and contemplating *to see what shall become of the city.* He takes time, indeed, to put a few rude branches together, forming a rural, rugged booth—a little arbour, rapidly extemporised; and he takes time for that, solely because it serves his purpose, and shelters him from the burning eastern sun, while he watches *to see what shall become of the city.* But the Lord is to bring into play some object on which the prophet's tender affections may strongly rest. It must not be such as would thwart the stream of all his thoughts, and turn them aside from considering *what shall become of the city*. Anything so introduced to his notice now would prove offensive and unwelcome; and would counteract the very purpose of the Lord in bringing it forward. Let it be something serviceable to him, while he sits and still watches *to see what shall become of the city*. Let a large-leafed, spreading plant ascend, and cover all his rustic and unsightly bower, leaving no crevice for the burning rays to pierce and beat upon the watcher's weary frame. Let the palmchrist, ivy-like, thatch with sudden beauty and impervious foliage, and thereby altogether perfect, the prophet's little booth. It is precisely what his strangely troubled heart will dearly welcome in its present engrossing exercise.

"And the Lord prepared a gourd,* and made it to come up over Jonah, that it might be a shadow over his head, to deliver him from his grief." And it wrought precisely as the Lord expected and designed. "So Jonah was exceeding glad of the gourd" (ver. 6).

Ah! so had the living God, the God of love, been "exceeding glad" over Nineveh's repentance; the same God who, in the form of man, sat afterwards over a city that would not repent, and was "exceeding sorrowful," shedding tears of matchless and unfathomable grief. By this beautiful device of the gourd, and Jonah's exceeding gladness, the Lord is preparing Jonah, if not

---

* See "Biblical Natural Science," vol. ii., p. 540, and "Science and Christian Thought," pp. 169-171, by JOHN DUNS, D.D., Professor of Natural Science in the New College, Edinburgh.

to be glad in Nineveh's salvation, at least to understand the Lord's own gladness.

"But God prepared a worm, when the morning rose the next day, and it smote the gourd that it withered. And it came to pass, when the sun did arise, that God prepared a vehement east wind; and the sun beat upon the head of Jonah, that he fainted, and wished in himself to die, and said, It is better for me to die than to live. And God said to Jonah, Doest thou well to be angry for the gourd? And he said, I do well to be angry, even unto death" (verses 7-9).

So highly had he begun to value the gourd! So ill could he bear the want of it! So uncontrollable were his feelings when it withered! So deeply had his affections twined around it!

Who but must admire the Divine wisdom in turning off in this direction all the keen intensity of the prophet's excited, morbid, powerful affections? The very emotions of anguish and anger with which his perplexed soul was formerly contemplating the deliverance of Nineveh, are now turned towards lamenting the destruction of his welcome, beloved, brief-lived gourd. And now the Lord argues with him;—If thine affections were twined around the gourd, because it pleased thy fancy and served thy wish,—wilt thou not allow mine to repose with satisfaction on the teeming multitudes, the workmanship of my hands, which throng the alarmed, the humbled, the obedient, the saved city? "Thou hast had pity on the gourd, for the which thou hast not laboured, neither madest it grow; which came up in a night, and perished in a night;"—this little shrub; in no sense thine own; neither planted, nor watered, nor cared for, nor pruned by thee; brief-lived, too—passing hastily away in a night from the place that only for a day hath known it. And "should not I spare" immortal men; the workmanship of my hands; cultivated and cared for, and fed, and clothed, and dealt with variously in patience and in pity, because I am not willing that any should perish, but rather that they should come to repentance :—" Should not I spare Nineveh, that great city, wherein are more than six score thousand persons that cannot discern between their right hand and their left hand; and also much cattle ?"

Is there anything in which I am, like Jonah, unreconciled to the will of God—His will in His Word; His procedure in providence? And when He expostulates kindly with me,—" Doest thou well to be angry ?"—do I allow His condescending remonstrance to pass away unimproved? Let me beware. God's purpose, though unwelcome to me, is very dear to Him : it is after the counsel of His own will ; it is according to the good pleasure of His will; and I must, if I am a child of God, be constrained to feel that it is so, and constrained to sympathise with Him, and acquiesce.

And He may teach me practically, as He taught Jonah. He may send me a welcome gift—a lovely, serviceable ivy plant—a sudden, acceptable, gladsome gourd.

I become exceeding glad of my gourd. My heart entwines around it. This pleasing prospect; this budding hope; this successful movement; this dawn of charming friendship with the bright-hearted and the noble; this light of sunshine falling most unlooked for on my vexed and weary heart; this welcome visitant, the golden-haired little one within my earthly home, crowing in my arms, searching my eye for the kindling glance of joy and love, and dancing gleefully on finding it;—ah! in many a form my gourd may grow; and I am exceeding glad of my gourd. Even when I quarrel with God, I may be all the more glad of my gourd.

For what end may it have been planted? For what end may it have grown? To the end, perhaps, that it may wither, and droop, and die; and that my heart untractable may at last, by losing it, be taught to feel, that if the object which my poor foolish love fastens on be hard to part with, how infinitely wrong in me to desire God to abandon those purposes which His infinitely wise will hath cherished from eternity, and which He hath bound in with and wrapt around my destiny, at once to bless and train me—exercising my faith and patience, stripping me of all creature confidence that He may fill me with uncreated good, and rendering me one trophy more among the many thousands of the poor and needy whom angels have seen sitting *not* desolate even with every idol shattered, and whom angels have heard, through grace, exclaiming;—Though my flesh

and my heart fail; though my house be not so with
God; though the fig-tree shall not blossom; yet will
I rejoice in the Lord; for " He hath made with me an
everlasting covenant, ordered in all things, and sure:
this is all my salvation, and all my desire."